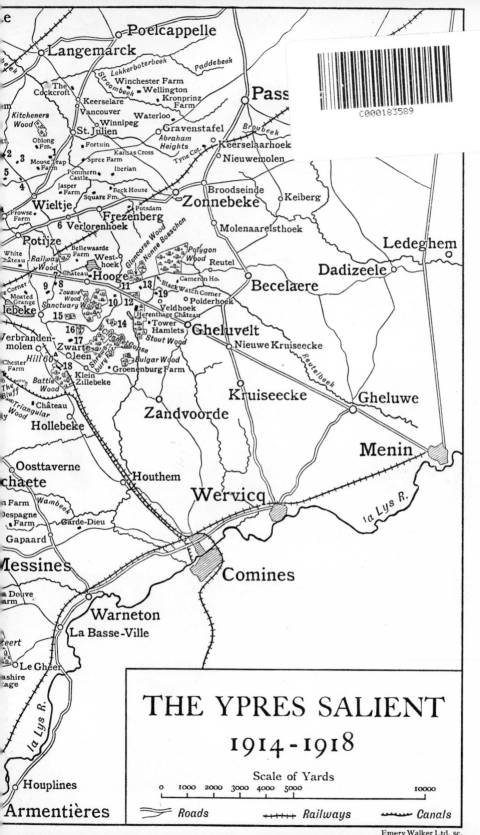

THE YPRES SALIENT
1914-1918

Scale of Yards

0   1000   2000   3000   4000   5000   10000

~~~ Roads   +++++ Railways   ~~~ Canals

Emery Walker Ltd. sc.

THE BATTLE BOOK OF YPRES

THE SALIENT.
"Hold!"
From a drawing by Captain Ernest H. Shepard, M.C.

[*Frontispiece*

THE
BATTLE BOOK OF YPRES

COMPILED BY BEATRIX BRICE

WITH THE ASSISTANCE OF
LIEUT.-GENERAL SIR WILLIAM PULTENEY, K.C.B., ETC.

AND WITH A FOREWORD BY
FIELD-MARSHAL THE LORD PLUMER OF MESSINES, G.C.B., ETC.

SPA BOOKS in association with
TOM DONOVAN MILITARY BOOKS

ISBN: 0–907590–17–9

Publishing History: This work was first issued in 1927 and has been out of print for many years. This edition reproduces the original text complete and unabridged except for the substitution of a new, annotated bibliography and the inclusion of some previously unpublished contemporary photographs.

Published by SPA BOOKS LTD in association with
TOM DONOVAN PUBLISHING LTD
PO Box 47
STEVENAGE
Herts   SG2 8UH

Printed in Great Britain at The Bath Press, Avon

FOREWORD

By Field-Marshal The Lord Plumer of Messines, G.C.B., etc.

The inception of this book was the desire to publish a memorial book of Ypres in furtherance of the aims of the Ypres League ; " To perpetuate the tradition of the four years' defence of the Salient as an ideal, and a source of inspiration for all time."

A letter was addressed to every Regiment in the British Army, signed by the late Field-Marshal the Earl of Ypres, General Sir Charles Harington, and myself, in which we asked for an account of some outstanding achievement that the Regiment would specially wish commemorated in the Ypres Salient. We said that we wished in this way to make a very distinctive book ; one that should be " a memorial both in the Regiments and in the families of the soldiers, and that it would give expression to our thought that ' Ypres ' does not stand for a ruined town, but for a very high ideal built up by the lives of men." Miss Beatrix Brice was asked to undertake the work of compilation, as she has devoted her writings to soldier themes since her poem " The Vanguard '14 " led to the first general recognition by the people of what their country owes to the " First Seven Divisions."

An enthusiastic response was received from the regiments, most of whom sent us contributions, but unfortunately these proved to be somewhat similar in character—descriptions of fine engagements, seen from a purely military view. A collection of these would only have repeated the work of regimental and divisional historians. It was therefore decided to include the gist of these accounts, and also to gather together narratives of outstanding deeds from authoritative sources.

The welcome extended to *The Immortal Salient*, the historical guide to Ypres, pointed clearly to the most acceptable form for the new book, i.e. a sequel that would fill every sector of the Salient with the fuller story of the great events that took place there.

We wish to stress the fact that no attempt is made to choose the finest deeds that were performed at each place, nor to extol the achievement of one unit more than another. The narratives given are of a variety of episodes and conditions, chosen as representative, so as to create a vivid picture of what was meant by battle fighting in the awful and immortal Salient of Ypres.

Our thanks are due to the Regiments who have contributed incidents and impressions to this book.

To Members of the Historical Section (Military Branch) who most kindly advised and checked the historical Foreword. This has enabled the author to give a condensed history of the Battles of Ypres—an accurate and graphic summary that will enable readers to follow the course of the great epic.

To the Curator and Staff of the Imperial War Museum who gave access to their books and the use of a room, while the library was in the throes of being housed.

To Lieut.-General Sir Herbert Uniacke for help in compiling the narratives of Hill 60 and of Kortekeer, and some narratives of the Royal Artillery. To Captain E. H. Shepard, M.C., for the drawing made expressly for this book that is so vivid a representation of the tenacity and doggedness that defended Ypres. To Lieut.-Colonel John Murray, D.S.O., for advice and help in editing the book.

AUTHOR'S PREFACE

IT has been difficult to make this book, searching between the dry dust of technical accounts and the deep waters of good yarns. And just because it has been so difficult it seems to be worth the writing. With the comprehensive store of books of the Imperial War Museum open before me, I have found no condensed and authentic collection of the heroic narratives of Ypres. Correspondence during a long time direct with regiments has yielded a rather meagre harvest, chiefly because of that very British quality that accepts duty as duty, and deprecates any comment beyond the bare recognition of work well done. Such histories as I have gleaned vary enormously in their scope and in the manner of the telling, so that I must emphasise the fact that no story is given here as chosen for supreme virtue, but each one represents a number of very similar deeds. It is in the repetition again and again of supreme heroism, the endurance again and again of supreme trial, the sacrifice again and again in supreme agony, that the wonder lies. If we read that a unit claims to have saved the day, we must remember that to many units came the ordeal and the honour of holding a critical point at a critical hour. The afflicting phrase " practically annihilated " occurs so constantly that it has been absurdly difficult to avoid it. The wildest deeds of conspicuous bravery are repeated word for word in the Gazette of the Victoria Cross —and for each one, how many exploits are only known to God ?

So I have gathered what stories I could collect and I have written them in plain words, it being as it is a tale of plain men, and fearing lest rhetoric or chosen language should carry the romantic story into the regions of pure romance, and cynics doubt its truth. Stark and unembroidered as the telling is the truth. But I feel that it should be read to the rhythm and stir of music, with minds attune that men hear the beat and roll of drums, the urgent call of bugles, the triumphant song of trumpets. So that, in whatever book it may be told, the story, freed from the poverty of words, shall take its place in drama, among the epics of the world.

CONTENTS

LIST OF ILLUSTRATIONS

THE BATTLE BOOK OF YPRES

PROLOGUE

THE German Army, in the fullness of its chosen hour, had struck and missed the blow. That Army, overwhelming in numbers, prepared and organised through forty years to the last bayonet, bullet, and button, had been staggered by the British at Mons and Le Cateau, turned back by French and British from Paris, defeated in the open battle of the Marne, and now lay across France from Switzerland to the Aisne entrenched in previously prepared positions.

From the Aisne, Allies and Germans raced to the north, each trying to outflank the other, and the fall of Antwerp gave the whip-hand to the Germans. That event also relieved them of the Belgian menace in the west and set another German force, 90,000 strong, free to attack. Britain had sent the 7th Division out to Antwerp, but arriving too late, it fell back with the remnant of the Belgians, and turned at bay near the old capital of Flanders—Ypres. By this time the French had made good the line as far north as La Bassée, but between this point and Ypres lay twenty-five miles open to the enemy, the gateway to Calais and all Channel Ports, and an easy line to Paris.

At this juncture Field-Marshal Sir John French, drawing out his little army from its hard-won position on the Aisne, rushed it northward and threw it into that ominous gap, giving to Britons the task of protecting the Channel Ports from which Germany hoped to threaten England. This movement also had the merit of shortening his lines of communication. The way this army was withdrawn, and replaced by the French in the face of the enemy, was a feat of great strategic skill.

The II Corps arrived first and came into action on 11th October. The struggle that then opened was to continue without pause or rest until the middle of November, and that Homeric contest centring in and about the Flemish capital is known as the " First Ypres " or " Battles of Ypres 1914."

To put it in the plainest language, the vast German Army had concentrated on passing through this twenty-five-mile gap from Ypres to La Bassée, and some troops had already penetrated to the west.

The II and III British Army Corps arrived from the south and, together forming a line from east to west, the right flank resting on La Bassée, wheeled on this pivot, swinging north and east, drove the Germans back and back, and formed a line from south to north barring the dangerous gap. North of them the

7th Division strung out to the utmost, and with some French Territorials kept touch with the Belgians on the coast. The Cavalry Corps linked across the final gap between the III Corps and the 7th Division, and so was the battle fought.

The I Corps arrived at St. Omer when the II Corps, after the two weeks of desperate fighting that had battered the enemy to the east of the chosen line, were greatly exhausted, and Sir John French had to decide whether to reinforce that desperate resistance or to throw the I Corps into the weak place where, in the north, the 7th Division reached out to the Belgians. He decided for the latter course, and the II Corps continued to " do the impossible " while the I Corps went into action at Ypres. The wisdom of this move was shortly proved when it became apparent that the Kaiser had set his heart on the capture of that city. The Lahore Division from India joined the southern part of the line later, when units of the II Corps moved nearer the city.

The whole part played by the II Corps, that had already borne the brunt of battle at Mons and Le Cateau under that great General Sir Horace Smith-Dorrien, and the one division of the III Corps south of Armentières, cannot be dealt with in this book which treats only of the Ypres Salient. But the repulse of Germany and the forming of our impregnable battle-line depended on the stand of the whole British Expeditionary Force.

TO THE VANGUARD

Oh, little mighty Force that stood for England !
That, with your bodies for a living shield,
Guarded her slow awaking, that defied
The sudden challenge of tremendous odds
And fought the rushing legions to a stand—
Then stark in grim endurance held the line.
O little Force that in your agony
Stood fast while England girt her armour on,
Held high our honour in your wounded hands,
Carried our honour safe with bleeding feet—
We have no glory great enough for you,
The very soul of Britain keeps your day !
Procession ?—Marches forth a Race in Arms ;
And, for the thunder of the crowd's applause,
Crash upon crash the voice of monstrous guns
Fed by the sweat, served by the life of England,
Shouting your battle-cry across the world.

Oh, little mighty Force, your way is ours,
This land inviolate your monument.

HISTORICAL FOREWORD

"FIRST YPRES," BATTLES OF YPRES, 1914

THE first Battle of Ypres, lasting for three weeks, was a terrific and prolonged struggle from day to day in which a hundred minor battles were fought. The British Expeditionary Force came to this trial with every disadvantage and difficulty on their side. The Germans outnumbered them enormously, and were fully equipped with every modern weapon and every material of war, crowned by an artillery of tremendous guns. The British had not numbers sufficient to man the line, every form of material was short or entirely unobtainable, from ammunition downward. Trenches were very shallow, and in short lengths separated by wide gaps, that extended in places to a width as great as 400 yards. Throughout the battle the fighting never ceased night or day, and the groups of men holding the inadequate trenches, rushed from place to menaced place—withdrawn to be flung forward in smashing counter-attacks—were men physically at their weakest from exhaustion and want of sleep.

A steadily flowing torrent of men, equipped with overwhelming and enormous artillery, rolled day after day against that thin-drawn line, that skeleton army. On the one hand, successive Army Corps, fresh men ; on the other, the shattered remnant of seven Divisions, a single line without support or reinforcements. So thin the line that a break anywhere meant flanks left in the air, and again and again a little body of men was cut off, and left fighting back to back to the finish. Battalions reduced in a day or two to companies—100 men and a couple of officers . . . these held back the might of Germany, and held fast the barrier across the road to the Channel seas.

We learn the standard of their quality from the reports of the enemy, who failed to overcome them because they were unable to believe the simple truth of the situation. They could not believe so few men could defy them, and imagined a strong reserve. They could not believe such rapid speed of rifle fire could possibly be attained, and imagined a vast number of machine guns. They could not believe that field guns could stay in action and repulse them with a dole of ammunition.

3

They failed to realise the quality of the Race that opposed
them, and being convinced of huge material forces, they dared
not press their challenge beyond the mystery of the unbroken
line.

To make the progress of the battle quite clear, it is imperative
to treat its history in sectors. Any other method of describing
what took place creates a confused idea, jumping from north to
south of the Salient as each attack and counter-attack came
about. The Battle Nomenclature Report gives us the following
battles :

Battle of Armentières   .   . 13th October to 2nd November.
Battle of Messines   .   . 12th October to 2nd November.
Battles of Gheluvelt, 1914 :
    Langemarck .   .   .   . 21st to 24th October.
    Gheluvelt   .   .   .   . 29th to 31st October.
    Nonne Bosschen .   .   . 11th November.

But to picture the Salient during this great battle it will be
best to think first of the map in broad bands—as all fighting
was east and west—these bands enclosing the attack and defence
of each sector.

NORTH SECTOR

The first Battle of Ypres may be said to have begun on the
15th October 1914, when the 7th Division, falling back through
Ghent, reached that picturesque and historical Flemish town.
At one time this division had been in a somewhat precarious
position, being practically in the heart of the enemy's area of
operation without any supports nearer than the coast. German
troops were north, south, and east of them ; an attack from the
direction of Courtrai or Roulers might well have forced them
back on the sea-board and, if pressed heavily, with the overwhelming forces available, would in all probability have driven
the division into the sea or over the Dutch frontier.

On reaching Ypres, the 7th Division took up a position some
five to six miles east of the town, occupying the line Houthem—
Gheluvelt—St. Julien, where on the 16th they were in touch
with German outposts ; the 3rd Cavalry Division covered their
left flank from Zonnebeke to Westroosebeke ; while French
troops, mainly, however, of the " second line," were collecting
on the Yser. Both divisions, after what they had already under-
gone, were sadly in need of rest and refit. During the afternoon
of the 17th arrangements were completed for an advance to be

made next day towards Menin with the object of seizing the
bridges over the River Lys, and thus impeding the further
advance of strong German reinforcements which it was known
were being steadily railed up from the direction of Lille. This
advance started on the 18th, but the rapidly increasing power
and weight of the enemy's forces now beginning to threaten our
left flank, and the opposition met with, made the carrying out
of the task so perilous an undertaking that it had to be countermanded. It was a race as to which army could concentrate
with the greater rapidity, and the Germans—having by far the
easier task and by far the shorter road to travel—got in first.

So the curtain rose on the great contest and, in the words of
Sir John French, " The stakes for which we were playing at the
great Battle of Ypres (1914) were nothing less than the safety,
indeed, the very existence, of the British Empire."

On the 19th, 20th, and 21st October 1914 fierce and bitter
fighting raged round Zonnebeke, where the Germans had made
continuous and desperate efforts to break through the left of
the 7th Division and force their way into Ypres. The 22nd
Infantry Brigade (2nd Queens, 1st Royal Welch Fusiliers, 2nd
Royal Warwickshire, and 1st South Staffordshire), weary and
depleted by three days of incessant fighting, had succeeded in
keeping back the invading flood of the enemy by a display of
those astonishing fighting powers which made the first seven
divisions famous. The retirement of the French from Houthulst
Forest exposed the flank of the 3rd Cavalry Division. By the
evening of the 21st things began to look black indeed, and it
seemed hardly conceivable that the enemy's advance round our
left could be checked by the cavalry for another 24 hours ; two
fresh and hitherto unsuspected German army corps had suddenly
appeared from the direction of Courtrai, the pressure from the
north-west became very great, and while our defence, suffering
continuous losses and worn to the last stage of mental and
physical exhaustion by sleeplessness and by unceasing digging
and fighting, was getting weaker and weaker, the German attacking force was being perpetually augmented by fresh troops. All
at once, with dramatic suddenness, the situation changed—the
I Corps under Sir Douglas Haig was, by the momentous decision
of the Commander-in-Chief, Sir John French, thrown into the
fight, and took over the whole of our line from Zonnebeke to
Bixschoote. A critical struggle followed north of the Boesinghe
—Langemarck Road, where the fight, centring around the Kortekeer Cabaret, prevented the German attempt to break through
on the north-east of Ypres. From these events, thus lightly

touched on but of infinite consequence, when at times the destiny of our country hung in the balance, was born the Ypres Salient.

CENTRE SECTOR, ON THE MENIN ROAD

The Menin Road first comes into notice when the 7th Division, after fighting to Ghent, back along the forty miles of retirement, and withstanding the first attacks upon Ypres, initiated an offensive against very superior numbers, and on the 19th October had reached a position within two miles of Menin.   This attacking movement was countermanded on information being received of the advance of hitherto unsuspected enemy forces, threatening our left flank in great strength, and the division took up a line astride the road at Kruiseecke in order to meet this new menace. Here they fought, sore pressed, but holding fast until, on the 24th October, Polygon Wood was menaced by successful enemy assaults.   The I Corps, that had been fighting furiously on the northern face of the Salient, had been relieved by the French ; and as the position of the 7th Division became desperate, the 2nd Division were ordered to join the left flank, moving up along the Menin Road.   The troops fell upon the enemy, and in furious hand-to-hand fighting drove him out of Polygon Wood, and by evening the whole line held by the 7th Division was still intact, and on the left an advance of over 1,000 yards had been made by the 6th Brigade.   An effort was made to attack Reutel, and our troops, fighting for every yard of ground, got across the Becelaere—Passchendaele Road.   The line now formed an acute salient at Kruiseecke, and on the 26th the Germans succeeded by means of a ruse, giving an order to retire to one of our battalions, in piercing the sides of this out-thrust point and annihilated the troops in the village.   Further loss of ground was checked by our counter-attacks and the line re-formed on a blunter curve.   The pressure of the enemy increased daily, being relieved temporarily by brilliant counter-attacks of the two divisions ; as the position, however, became more and more dangerous the 1st Division was ordered up in support.   The French troops, now on our north, made small progress, but the British flank fought their way forward for over 1,000 yards, reaching the valley between Passchendaele Ridge and Keiberg Spur.   On the 27th October Sir Douglas Haig moved the 7th Division south of the road to hold the line to Zandwoorde, the 1st Division reaching from their left to Reutel Village and the 2nd carrying along to Zonnebeke, where they touched the French. On the 27th October enemy wireless messages were intercepted during the day ordering a mass assault by the Germans on the Kruiseecke—Gheluvelt position. An advance to forestall this was attempted by the 2nd Division with the 1st in support, and the 7th still holding on south of the road. The enemy's attack opened on the morning of the 29th in dense fog, and German troops attacking in mass from all sides succeeded in penetrating unseen and caused very heavy casualties ; they only succeeded, however, in gaining some 500 yards of the cross-roads at the cost of very heavy losses to themselves. Unknown to our command, the enemy was massing weighty reinforcements in front of the thinly held line throughout the 30th. Our wearied men, without material, could do little to strengthen the position, beyond digging some new fire trenches where urgently needed. The line, so called, was more in the nature of an outpost system, consisting of isolated groups, and the quite inadequate reserve could only be thrust in at any threatened point to stop a gap, or, as was then said, " to putty-up " the Front.

The climax of the battle was reached on the 31st October. The enemy surged forward in overwhelming strength between the scattered posts, penetrated behind isolated companies and succeeded in entering Gheluvelt. Here, by one of the grandest charges of the grand defence, a counter-attack was launched from the north-west, the Germans were hurled back and Gheluvelt recaptured.[1] Later our front was found to hold so sharp a salient that when the enemy attacks had died down, our troops were withdrawn west of Gheluvelt and the line re-formed. But the possibility of holding it without further help seemed remote. Our troops, reduced to a quarter of their strength, exhausted with ceaseless fighting, lacking sleep and rest, lacking ammunition, reached their blackest hour, and hope of saving the Channel Ports, of saving England, became a fearful doubt. So short had ammunition become that half of the Field Artillery were withdrawn from the line, as they were useless and helpless without shells. The 7th Division was now so depleted and exhausted that on the 5th November it was withdrawn from the Line and its place taken by ten shrunken battalions from the II Corps.

It would appear that the Kaiser, who had been waiting at Courtrai ready to head his victorious troops after the assault of the 31st October but had returned disappointed to his normal headquarters on the 2nd November, now reached the limit of exasperation, and ordered his picked and most famous regiments to smash their way through this contemptible foe. The final

1 P. 138.

and great attack came on the 11th November. Twelve and a half divisions attacked on a nine-mile front, and of these the flower of the German Army, the Prussian Guard, the Pomeranians, and West Prussians, fell upon this centre sector of the Menin Road, heralded by the most overwhelming shell fire that had yet been launched. Seventeen thousand five hundred men opposed by the little, weary, battle-worn force, seven thousand eight hundred and fifty in all.

This tremendous onslaught [1] smashed into the front-line defence, found some positions from which they could enfilade our disconnected trenches, and penetrated at last at one point, reaching the woods north of the road. The British met them hand to hand, fought them to a standstill, flung them back from the guns at point-blank range, and drove them back with the bayonet.

This was the crowning effort of Germany in the pride of her military eminence when war opened, and it failed.

CENTRE SECTOR, SOUTH OF THE MENIN ROAD

On the 22nd October the interception of an enemy order warned the troops south of the Menin Road to expect a vigorous attack south of the Becelaere—Zandwoorde position, a sector which was held by part of the 7th Division and the 3rd Cavalry Division ; but although heavily shelled, the position was not attacked until the 26th, when the loss of Kruiseecke (the apex of an acute salient) on their north threatened a grave disaster. To assist in covering the retirement of the 20th Infantry Brigade at the position to the north the Royal Horse Guards—in reserve in the Klein Zillebeke Wood—were called upon to make a demonstration. They effected their purpose by galloping eastward over Zandwoorde Ridge and threatening the enemy's flank. The Germans turned to meet them and the attack on the 7th Division was consequently checked. As evening fell, the squadrons were able to withdraw. Next day the 7th Division moved over and took the line from the Menin Road down to Zandwoorde, a front of 3,000 yards. On the night of the 26th the 3rd Cavalry Division had dug in by Zandwoorde. This line, the northern end of the Cavalry Corps, was so thinly held that the men were scattered in such small parties as to be almost invisible, and in view of the risky outlook, General Allenby collected a small corps reserve from each brigade of the 2nd Cavalry Division and 1st Battery R.H.A. at Klein Zillebeke. The German attack broke upon this line on the 30th October, and during the battle that followed the odds against us here were 6 to 1 in rifles and

[1] P. 147.

horse and field artillery. The first day they made no impression at all on the British south of the road, but in front of Zandwoorde the fire of a number of heavy guns was concentrated on the trenches of the 1st and 2nd Life Guards in the early morning, blasting them to pieces. The cavalrymen stuck it out, until at 8 a.m. an order came to withdraw. The Germans reached the Zandwoorde Ridge by 10 o'clock and were then in a position to enfilade the Infantry Brigade from the north, overwhelming the nearest battalion, but reinforcements were hastily thrust forward and a fresh line formed west of Zandwoorde, covering the gap. During the afternoon the attack died away, and in spite of the apparently irresistible advance of the early hours, the enemy between Gheluvelt and Zandwoorde had been brought to a standstill. Farther south the German guns were moved near during the morning of this day, and concentrated upon a sector of the I Cavalry Brigade around Hollebeke Village. Many of the trenches were blown in, and the cavalry wheeled back into the open, clear of the village, but holding the Canal Bridge. The regiments of the 2nd Cavalry Division gradually withdrew to the prepared position along Ypres Ridge, the I Cavalry Brigade being along the Canal to the Bridge, and the line south-east of Ypres was stabilised by the end of the day. Still, so great was the enemy's preponderance of force that this line was in deadly peril, and orders were issued that it must be held from Hollebeke to Gheluvelt at all costs. It was so weak opposite Zandwoorde that some shrunken battalions which formed the reserve of the 2nd Division were sent down from behind Polygon Wood and dug in as a support line about a mile east of Klein Zillebeke.

The 31st October brought the critical attacks when Gheluvelt was lost and recaptured, and an unsuccessful attempt to counter-attack, aided by three battalions of French, was made at 6 a.m. against Hollebeke and Zandwoorde. The tremendous bombardment by the enemy began at 8 o'clock, and at midday they attacked in great strength and got into Shrewsbury Forest, but were driven out by a magnificent counter-attack.[1] The losses of the day had been terrible, but still the line held.

Determined attacks were made against it the following days, and on the 2nd November French reinforcements arrived, and took over some five miles of front from a point near Zwarteleen southward. On the north they touched the right of the 7th Division where the composite reinforcement was brigaded under Lord Cavan. Fierce fighting continued from day to day, but the splendid fire discipline of the dogged battalions always re-

<hr />

[1] P. 140.

pulsed the enemy, though by this time the roll of the 7th Division
was a fifth of its original strength. On the 5th November, as
one diary puts it, the Germans seemed to realise it was Guy
Fawkes Day and brought up an immense number of guns and
extra ammunition from which our troops suffered heavy casualties, at the same time that an order was issued to our own artillery
limiting ammunition to 20 rounds per 18-pounder and 10 rounds
per 4·5 howitzer. This day is notable as marking the relief of
the 7th Division. It was now a skeleton of its original form.
It had been fighting with no rest since the 14th October. For
part of this time it had held a front of seven miles, and though
this was shortened, the depleted ranks could supply fewer and
fewer men per yard as each day of destruction passed and each
assault was flung back. It was decided that what remained of
the division must be withdrawn, and the fragments of ten
battalions from the 5th replaced them. This reinforcement
consisted of troops that had been in action since August, borne
the brunt of the Battles of Mons and Le Cateau, had fought
through the great Retreat, and now, being pulled out of the line
south of Ypres, had had but two days' rest.
A German success against the French on the 6th November
in thick fog brought the defending line at one point to within
only two miles of Ypres. The enemy penetrated the gap thus
formed, and thrust through nearly to Verbrandenmolen. The
7th Cavalry Brigade charged with some of the French under
General Moussy, recaptured Zwarteleen while all guns were
turned on the danger-point, and such reinforcements as could
be collected were flung forward to save the flanks uncovered by
the retirement of troops not under British command. On the
7th Lord Cavan's Brigade, realising the urgency of the danger,
charged the enemy, fighting with great élan, while the French
came up again and refilled the gap. Our line, bent back to join
theirs, had now formed yet another salient, and on the 11th
November, the day of the great final attack by the Prussian
Guard, the position was most critical, the Germans attacked
with tremendous shelling and weight of men, but they were
repulsed yet again by fine artillery work and counter-attacks,
and Lord Cavan's detachment did not lose a trench. The central
thrust of the spear-head that day broke on the Menin Road and
the result of the first Battle of Ypres was definitely decided.

MESSINES SECTOR

On the eve of the first Battle of Ypres the sector from the
River Douve to the Comines Canal, between the 4th and 7th

Divisions, was held by the Cavalry Corps (the 1st and 2nd Cavalry Divisions). They had reached this position after severe fighting for the command of the ridges, and on the 21st October their orders were to entrench and hold on at all costs.

Splendid among the splendid deeds of the old Army in 1914 was the part played by the cavalry. These mobile troops, whose essence was speed and movement, took their part in a *stand*—the incongruous word holds the gist of their achievement. Deprived of their horses, of the excitement and élan of their calling, they joined in the locked grapple of the defence with so stiff, so grim a resolution, that though the enemy flung some of his heaviest forces against the front they held—held with a line of only some thousand men to each mile—the assault was made in vain.

By the 20th October they had stabilised the Douve—Comines Line, and were holding the front from Messines—Oosttaverne— Hollebeke. So constant were the enemy attacks that the defending troops could never relax the strain of continual fighting. On the 22nd October the Lahore Division, straight from India, came up in support, and against the small forces at this point the enemy threw six Cavalry Divisions, supported by four Jäger and two Cyclist Battalions. They utterly failed to break the line, and it is asserted that it was impossible for them to get within 1,000 yards of the rifles and machine guns firing with such deadly accuracy. So incessant was the firing that in the 2nd Cavalry Division four guns out of the eighteen of their artillery had their recoil springs broken.

On the 26th October the two Cavalry Divisions launched an attack, and captured the enemy front-line trenches, gaining about a quarter of a mile of ground ; but the new position was not in any way so good as the old one, and the troops were ordered to return to their own trenches.

The fighting grew in fury, until on the 31st October a tremendous thrust was made by the Germans at Messines, but in spite of odds of 6 to 1 against them, the cavalrymen held on and the enemy attacks failed.[1]

The Germans attacked in the dark of the early morning and reached the village, but the squadrons, manning the barricade, drove them back with the bayonet ; our artillery turned upon them, and they fell back suffering heavy loss. Another attempt to break through the line north of the village failed. As the morning mist cleared, heavy German guns and trench mortars were concentrated on the village. The flanking trenches soon

[1] P. 165.

became untenable, though the men in those facing the enemy still held fast, but the position was an acute salient. The twelve squadrons supported by only one battery of horse artillery bade fair to be annihilated, and it was resolved to straighten the line to a position running through the town of Messines. Terrible had been the cost, one regiment having lost three-quarters of its officers and over a third of its men. Two battalions from the II Corps were sent up to reinforce the line, and a battalion of Territorials, the first Territorial battalion to go into action. The battle raged in the streets of Messines, a death-trap of machine-gun fire and houses in flames.

During these days the attack developed with equal force against the 2nd Cavalry Division farther north at Wytschaete, but though five times the number of the defenders, the enemy failed to make any advance, and the right of the British division even stretched over to help repel the attack on Messines. At the end of this day of enormous pressure the whole line from the Douve to the Canal was intact, except where the little salient had been flattened out in front of Messines. Through the night of the 1st November Wytschaete was held by the composite Household Regiment—415 fighting strength, and the Germans assailed them with nine battalions, making a balance of 12 to 1. The line was held in a series of detached groups, and the tide of the enemy flooded through, attacking from flank and rear. In hand-to-hand contest Wytschaete was lost, and wonderfully re-captured.[1] At length the crushing weight of the enemy's superior numbers was realised and the order came to make a deliberate retirement of the still unbroken line. The 1st Cavalry Division withdrew unpursued to Wulverghem Ridge. The main position south of Wytschaete was still intact, and time had been gained to allow of French reinforcements to come up, and take over the sector northward to Zwarteleen. On the 2nd November, attacked by double their numbers, the French were driven out of Wytschaete Village, and their left flank with the left of the British I Cavalry Brigade fell back a short distance, but the British line was swiftly restored, and the enemy mastered. Gallant as was the advance of the French, they were driven back, and the British line, swinging round to touch them, made an acute angle. This line was held until the final great effort of the enemy on the 10th November, but now the assailing troops seemed to have lost the spirit and energy to come again with a whole-hearted attack ; they seemed to be worn down by so stubborn a resistance, and only freshly arrived

[1] P. 234.

battalions made any really dangerous assault. The effort
spent itself in vain along the unbreakable line, and the
Battle of Messines died out as the enemy gave up the attempt
to break through.

SOUTH SECTOR

The German forces, bludgeoning their way towards the Channel
Sea, thrust against the whole strung-out line of British troops,
and nowhere was this line more pitifully slender than where the
4th Division clung tenaciously to its position in the south of
the Salient.

When the III Corps, commanded by Major-General Sir William
Pulteney, and Cavalry Corps, under Lieut.-General E. E. H.
Allenby, arrived from the Aisne in the first week of October
they found the enemy on the hills that lie from the Mont des
Cats to Kemmel. From this position he was driven back across
the upper Lys, the 4th Division entering Armentières and extending northward to Le Gheer in front of Ploegsteert Wood.

The line was trenched, machine-gun posts built, and Divisional
H.Q. established at Nieppe. The 6th Division—the other half
of the III Corps—fought south of Armentières and their doings
do not come within the boundaries of the Salient, although
naturally their movements influenced and were influenced by
fighting to the north.

As the battle developed, the III Corps held a twelve-mile
front, of which the 4th Division held eight, and the fighting here
between the 21st October and the 2nd November is part of
what is known as the Battle of Armentières.

The orders for the corps were to entrench and hold on, and
this they most valiantly did. Attacked by forces of more than
double their own strength, of which one corps working as " shock
troops " searched along their front prying for a vulnerable
point, they withstood every onslaught.

Heavy shelling and increasing pressure developed on the
21st October into a strong attack along the front of the 12th
Infantry Brigade near Le Gheer. The enemy penetrated into
the village and were able to enfilade the battalions to the south
and outflank the cavalry to the north. A counter-attack with
mixed companies from the 11th and 12th Brigades, backed by
the Divisional Artillery on Hill 63, and two squadrons of the
9th Lancers on the left, drove the enemy back with great loss.
By evening the ground was recaptured and the whole line consolidated, and, in spite of the great length and weakness of their

front, the hazardous position of the Cavalry Corps to their
north demanded a further straining of the 4th Division.   They
sent two companies of infantry and an R.E. field company up
to Messines, and extended their own front line up to the River
Douve north of Ploegsteert Wood, the only reinforcement they
received being two battalions—much under strength—from the
II Corps.   Two or three days of comparative quiet followed.
There was lull enough to enable the line of defence to be
improved during the hours of darkness, though there was no
cessation of shelling and sniping, and the enemy made a number
of attacks, which, failing entirely, are only noted as minor affairs.
A notable feature of this sector was the effective action of the
artillery, so arranged that it was possible to switch nearly all
the guns in any threatened direction.

On the 29th October, during the days that marked the enemy's
desperate essay on the Menin Road, all reserves of the 4th
Division had been collected ready to help at Messines in the
north of the line.   At this moment the Germans struck out at
the point where in the south one battalion was holding from the
Douve to Le Gheer, 2,000 yards of intermittent trenches.

So long was the front that every man of the battalion was in
the firing line and for ten minutes the Germans were actually
in among them ; but a fierce counter-attack by the brigade
reserves drove the enemy out, although in one trench a platoon
was found, every man dead at his post.

Next day the enemy attacked this point again ; they reached
the trenches, but were repulsed by rifle fire and retreated without
the necessity of a counter-attack.

During the remaining days that the fighting lasted, the division
held fast with indomitable tenacity in face of continuous attacks,
of constant shelling and sniping.   The Battle of Ypres ended on
the 11th November, when the fiercely tried men had forced the
enemy to submit before a spirit that was their master and to
realise the barrier was impregnable.

When the end came, the 4th Division had lost no ground,
Ploegsteert Wood had never passed into enemy hands, and was
held intact by the division throughout the winter.   So rigid was
the line, so contained the battleground, that the wire here bore
its ghastly burden of the dead, and of the waste of war, mercilessly
exposed until the year's end.

.   .   .   .   .   .

The Old Army of England, wounded to the death, held its
dying arms outstretched across the way, and against the nobility
of that last stand nothing could prevail.

EPILOGUE, 1914

A scanty line—an outpost line,
  But that line a ring of fire!
Impregnable their flaming guard
  Who made our shield their pyre.

We staked an Empire on their hold,
  Our world to win or lose.
The few that held that line held all. . . .
  We had no right to choose.

Flame of the Spirit was their guard
  Oh grim, heroic bluff!
God only knew how few they were—
  He knew they were enough.

BATTLES OF YPRES, 1915

THE British Army lay in the marshes and mud of Flanders after the great and exhausting battles of 1914. It had established a record for indomitable fighting against overwhelming odds and endured the monotonous misery of the first winter in the trenches unrelieved by any important engagement in the Salient, although south of Armentières the II Corps had fought a notable battle at Neuve Chapelle.

In April 1915 there blazed out again a great feat of heroism and endurance which remains one of the outstanding exploits of the War ; the capture and defence of Hill 60 are described in full hereafter in the story of The Roads. The tremendous struggle that followed shortly in the north of the Salient altogether dwarfed the importance of the achievement, but it cannot shadow the glory of the regiments involved. As Sir John French said, addressing the troops after the battle : " Nothing ever required greater tenacity and courage."

ST. GEORGE'S EVE—YPRES, 1915

St. George for England—Stand !
The blood-red cross upheld in thy strong hand,
Appeal to God.
The way of suffering after Him you trod.
Now Britain lead
This hour of fearful need.

St. George for England—Hold !
All battle-anguish here endured the bold.
From Hell to-day,
The fumes evoked that suffocate and slay,
No stroke can meet,
No warrior defeat.

St. George for England—Praise !
The Race that trod the ages in thy ways
Still guards our lands.
Amid the dead, a little remnant stands—
The foe repelled,
The blood-bought Salient held.

16

"SECOND YPRES"[1]

THE heroic defence that established the Salient line in October and November 1914 set an aureole around Ypres, and the city assumed a significance in the War beyond any military value. Germany, determined on a spectacular triumph, employed every device to capture the town, but only added to the glory of the name, and by making the Salient the testing-ground of the first asphyxiating gas called out a display of sacrifice and courage that crowned " Ypres " afresh and immortally.

As in 1914, the British in 1915 fought in a position of disadvantage and intense difficulty. In the beginning of February they had taken over five more miles of front from the French at the request of General Joffre, so carrying the line north of the Menin Road and reaching the Ypres—Poelcappelle Road. The front trenches that were taken over required a great deal of work ; many were very inadequate and all built rather above than below ground, mere breastworks sited at intervals, not bullet-proof and lacking communication trenches. They had been planned with a view to defence by the " Soixante-Quinze " which the French had in numbers and well supplied with ammunition. In places things were made worse by the nauseating smell from numerous long-unburied bodies.

Behind the line lay a second, known to us as " G.H.Q. 2nd Line." This, built by the French, was a well-prepared system for defence, well sited and protected by a six-yard-wide belt of wire broken only by openings where required for passage. The ground was too waterlogged to allow of deep dugouts, and there were no bomb-proof shelters.

On the 22nd April the British V Corps, commanded by Lieut.-General Sir Herbert Plumer, was holding two-thirds of the Ypres Front, facing east and south : an arc of ten miles curving from Hill 60 out to Polygon Wood, touching Broodseinde Village, and round to a point half a mile south of Poelcappelle on the road from that town to Ypres. The belt of ground south of Polygon Wood was held by the 27th Division, north of it the 28th Division faced due east, and between the 28th Division and the French right lay the Canadian Division. The stalwart Belgian defence commenced at Steenstraate, and the stretch of country between them and the British left was manned by two French divisions of second quality, the 45th (Algerian) and 87th (Territorials), and a detachment of cavalry.

[1] Second Ypres is so very difficult a battle to follow that, in order to do justice to the troops involved, it has been found necessary to give a more detailed description of the fighting and of the units engaged, in this battle foreword, than in the others.

On April 14th a prisoner taken by the French disclosed the preparation of a gas attack, but his story was disbelieved, partly because he was so glib that the French General considered he had been primed, and partly because the use of asphyxiating gas was prohibited by the accepted laws of warfare.

BATTLE OF GRAFENSTAFEL RIDGE

The 22nd April was a day of unusual spring beauty, and drew to a calm evening disturbed by no abnormal enemy attack. At 5 p.m. the calm was shattered by an appalling outburst of heavy howitzer fire. The town and the villages north-east of Ypres—still inhabited by Belgian civilians and hitherto hardly touched—were bombarded furiously by a concentration of heavy shell. Then from the front of the German line beyond Langemarck there emerged an uncanny vision : two strange yellow wraiths of fog crept forward, spread, drew together, took on the blue-white tint of water-mists, and drifted before a gentle wind, down upon the rather puzzled but unsuspecting lines. Presently unofficered coloured men were seen falling back, then French Territorials in hurried retreat ; teams and wagons of the French artillery retiring, though the 75's still fired ; men pointing to their throats, coughing, suffocating, terrified ; a retreat growing into a rout : then suddenly at 7 p.m. the French guns fell silent. The treacherous attack had very thoroughly succeeded, and as the gas cloud rolled forward a great gap swiftly widened in its wake, into which pressed the German infantry.

Directly the attack started, Brig.-General Turner, V.C. (G.O.C. 3rd Canadian Brigade), whose 15th and 13th Battalions were the last troops of the British left, looked round for means to meet it. He drew up his reserves, the 14th Battalion, and moved two and a half companies out to cover the village of St. Julien. General Alderson, commanding the Canadian Division, at the same time ordered his divisional artillery to help the French. Immediately on the Canadian left the 1/1 Tirailleurs and the 1/2 bis Zouaves in support held their ground, being unaffected by the gas ; but beyond them nearly all the Territorials and Algerians had joined the rout, and the Germans, unopposed, were pushing on near to the Poelcappelle Road and to Mouse-trap Farm,[1] Brig.-General Turner's H.Q. Two platoons of the 13th Canadian Battalion here blocked their way, fighting till every man was killed, and a company of the 14th held the enemy at Hampshire Farm. Two guns of the 10th Canadian Battery

---

[1] Also known as " Shell-trap " Farm.

in action north of St. Julien brought the enemy advance to a
halt, but there was no one now beyond the flank, and a wide
road lay open clear to Ypres.

General Alderson sent up the 16th (Canadian Scottish) to Brig.-
General Turner, and directed the other reserve battalion, the
10th Canadians, to report as a working party ; but being held up
by the stream of fugitives, this battalion turned into G.H.Q.
line east and south-east of Wieltje. The 3rd Canadian Brigade
and the 2nd immediately on its right were urged to hold on to
their position at the edge of the gap, and the 7th Battalion moved
up behind them in reserve. By 8.25 p.m. all these manœuvres
had secured the flank east and north of Mouse-trap Farm.

In the meanwhile the news had reached General Smith-Dorrien
that a gap of over 3,000 yards—though indeed it proved to be
8,000—had suddenly been forced open on the north of the Second
Army, menacing not only the town of Ypres but all the troops
and guns in the rear. He immediately sent up the 1st Canadian
Brigade and the 2/East Yorkshires to reinforce the line. On
the right of the Canadians Generals Snow and Bulfin had grasped
the fact that though the Canadians were holding their flank there
was nothing beyond them, and without waiting for orders these
two Divisional Commanders had already sent some of the reserves
of the 27th and 28th Divisions towards St. Jean and Potijze
to meet the menace on the British left, the 4/Rifle Brigade, the
2/K.S.L.I., the 2/Buffs, and 3/Middlesex. These four battalions
were at midnight put under the command of Colonel A. D. Geddes,
of the Buffs, the senior officer, and under the name of " Geddes'
Detachment " fought at the disposal of the Canadian Division.
Half of the 3/Middlesex was detached to guard the Brielen
Bridge over the Canal. The 2/Cheshire and 1/Monmouths—
last battalion of General Bulfin's Divisional Reserve—took up a
position under Frezenberg Ridge as a local reserve.

As the reinforcements arrived, they came upon a situation
of extraordinary danger. The left flank of the whole British
Expeditionary Force ended abruptly just west of St. Julien and
Mouse-trap Farm. Beyond the original Canadian line four and a
half miles had been left undefended nearly due west to Brielen :
in the whole of this distance only three points were held : a
short flank thrown back by the 3rd Canadian Brigade and part
of the 1/1 Tirailleurs on the extreme right ; two and a half
companies in front of St. Julien ; four companies of Zouaves
and the 3rd Canadian Brigade Reserves at Shell-trap Farm.
The French were now west of the Canal, and the Germans,
pouring across the country thus cleared for their passage, were

driving down upon this gap from north and east. At about 9 o'clock they attacked the Tirailleurs near the Poelcappelle Road, but six companies of the 13th Canadians in the new throw-back, with 200 of the Tirailleurs (the rest gave way), brought the enemy to a halt. Brig.-General Turner then called for Colonel Geddes (still so far only in command of the Buffs) for help. He sent up from St. Julien all he could spare—one company under Captain F. W. Tomlinson. This company with two platoons of the 13th Canadians arrived in the nick of time, finding the left company of the Canadians falling back at daybreak towards the St. Julien—Poelcappelle Road. The original line was swiftly reoccupied, the Buffs securing the apex of the salient, before the Germans had seen the temporary withdrawal. The Canadian artillery about this time were compelled by exposure of their position to move from the neighbourhood of St. Julien back to St. Jean and La Brique. The 2nd London Battery was in Kitchener's Wood, and with only seven rifles among the detachment, with-drew, taking with them the sights and breech-blocks of the guns.

The battle lulled during the night, the Germans apparently halting to dig in, and so the British gained invaluable time to push their few, their very few available troops into the breach.

This then was the situation. The enemy onslaught had rent the allied defence wide open north of the British, had passed behind her guard and attacked her unarmoured side. Troops, rushed up at upmost speed during the night hours, too few in numbers to man more than a series of outposts, were called upon to fight where there was no prepared position whatever, neither trenches nor wire. Moreover, the menace that turned the British defence right back upon itself so narrowed the Salient that the defenders of the northern line had their backs but four miles from their comrades in the south. The Germans employed a method of attack that is the most difficult of any for troops short of artillery and ammunition, and dependent almost entirely on the human factor, to meet. They made use of an enormous concentration of artillery that bombarded a sector until the trenches were shattered and the defenders all killed or wounded. The infantry then advanced in a short rush to occupy the devas-tated zone; the bombardment moved forward, and the process was repeated. To meet this strategy by attack and counter-attack is hopeless without adequate artillery, yet these were the tactics ordered by General Foch. His troops were not able to carry them out; and the British endured appalling losses in delivering infantry attacks against an enemy in position backed by powerful heavy artillery, in the attempt loyally to support their allies.

The story that follows is clearer if we bear these conditions in mind.

To return to the opening hours, the enemy lull was broken by an attack on the eastern face of the Salient which, though it failed completely, prevented the diverting of all reserves from this front to the danger zone in the north.

Before midnight General Smith-Dorrien, Commander of the Second Army, informed General Foch of the formation of his protective flank, and in consequence of an agreement by the French to counter-attack in co-operation with the British, a very fine and successful charge was made at 12 o'clock by two battalions of the 10th and 16th Canadians (from Divisional Reserve), who drove valiantly through Kitchener's Wood and dug in on the north-east border.   The French, however, did not move, and under heavy fire the two Canadian battalions were reduced to some 400 men, while a company from the 1st Brigade sent up at dawn was nearly wiped out.   It was impossible to hold the dearly gained ground, and the line was withdrawn to the southern edge of the wood and prolonged towards St. Julien by half of the 3rd Battalion of the 1st Brigade.

After consultation between General Plumer and General Alderson, Colonel Geddes pushed his detachment up on the Canadian left, and sought to find the right of the French ; the remaining two battalions of the 1st Canadian Brigade were sent up to hold the Canal north of Ypres to ensure the safety of the British flank.   By dawn of the 23rd the great gap was strung across by isolated posts of the strength of some ten battalions under Brig.-General Turner and Colonel Geddes, with three and a half battalions from the 27th Divisional Reserve in second line, supported by half the artillery of one division.   Some of these troops were able to accomplish a little digging and wiring, but some had only had time to reach their positions and lie down. This thinly held line was attacked by forty-two German battalions with a superiority of five to one divisional guns, backed by tremendous weight of heavy artillery.

.   .   .   .   .   .

St. George's Day opened with another lovely dawn.   At 4 o'clock Colonel Geddes's detachment (less the company of the 2/Buffs still with the Canadians) advanced across the open, the Buffs under furious fire gaining a position between Hampshire and Mouse-trap Farms.   Two companies of the 3rd Middlesex joined the 1st and 4th Canadian Battalions in an effort to link up with the French on the left.   Although the French did not start, the British troops under very heavy fire pressed forward

over the western end of Hill-top Ridge, and gained a position
within 700 yards of the enemy before violent enfilade fire stopped
further progress. Here throughout the morning they were
assailed by such a stream of gas shells that every man was
affected, though in most cases only for the time being. The
establishment of this very sketchy and precarious line, and the
stubborn resistance of its defenders, stayed the German infantry
advance from the north, and throughout the day the Boche
was seen strengthening the positions he had gained. But the
tremendous bombardment of Ypres continued unabated, sweeping
the whole front of the V Corps and especially the apex at the
north-east, which was plastered with shell fire and gas, and
enfiladed by machine guns from the trenches vacated by the
French troops near by. Here the 15th and 13th Canadians, with
the parts of those battalions that formed the new flank, held
on heroically though short of food, water, and ammunition, as
supplies could not be got through to them. The French now
again declared themselves ready to act, and called upon the
British for co-operation, and a general attack was ordered from
between Kitchener's Wood and the Canal towards Pilckem.
The 13th Brigade of the 5th Division, fresh from the devastating
ordeal of Hill 60, had by now been sent up. The troops already
on the spot waited for its arrival, when, weary from the march,
it went straight up into the attack: Brig.-General Wanless
O'Gowan being given command of the operation. It was a
wonderful effort, but one that had no hope of success. Without
any preliminary bombardment, over very open country in broad
daylight, Geddes', O'Gowan's, and Tuson's men went up into
the face of the devastating fire of a hidden enemy, gained within
a distance of between 30 and 200 yards of his position, and
could get no farther, an example of sheer courage and discipline
of the grandest order. The French offensive was limited to the
advance and withdrawal of some 400 Zouaves.

When dark, the British made a new line behind the further
point of advance 600 yards from the enemy, from Hampshire
Farm westwards. Here the troops dug in, and this remained
the forward line for the next five days. General Joffre's request
had been honoured, the German advance stopped, but little
ground was gained. The losses had been grievous, and in the
13th Brigade hardly an officer was left who had been through
the great II Corps battles of 1914. At the north-eastern apex
the 13th Canadians with the company of the Buffs held on till
night, though their position, holding an angle of 60°, was fired
into from front and rear. At evening it was decided to withdraw

from the tip and form a rounded line behind it ; this was done without disturbance by the enemy. By night of St. George's Day the new front facing north and east had been manned ; but to patch the rents in the allied line every battalion in Divisional and Corps Reserve, as well as two from the Second Army Reserves, had been pressed into service. The French were now standing, though behind the Canal, and in touch with the Belgians on their left. The enemy had established seven bridges across the Canal, and, being checked in his onrush by the new British flank, attempted a breach between the French and Belgians. In view of this fresh menace at the side of his army, General Smith-Dorrien sent the 1st Cavalry Division to reinforce Sir H. Plumer. The enemy succeeded in capturing Lizerne, but this proved the limit of his advance ; the Belgians, bravely extending their flank west of Lizerne, regained touch with the French.

BATTLE OF ST. JULIEN

The 24th opened with violent bombardment in the early hours of the morning, and this was followed by a cloud of gas that swept across a thousand yards of front : across the northern side of the Salient on the Canadian line, but behind and parallel with the new north-western front. Four six-battalioned brigades of the enemy followed the gas waves, attacking from near Gravenstafel Road by St. Julien to Kitchener's Wood, and assaulting our line, now held by the equivalent of eight battalions, with nothing left in reserve but three whole and two half companies. A wall of poison fog 15 feet high rolled down upon the defenders. With no more protection than that afforded by any rag dipped in any obtainable liquid tied across their mouths, the 8th Canadian Battalion and part of the 15th manned the parapets and drove the enemy back. Every officer of the 15th was killed or captured, and after fighting desperately they gave way and fell back westward ; but two platoons stuck fast alongside the Buffs at the extreme apex. On the right the 8th Battalion held on heroically in spite of a hail of bombs from the captured trenches on their flank. The fire of the Canadians and the Buffs checked the Germans, who had expected the gas to clear their way.

The next attack was made upon the north-west front. For a considerable time this attack was held by the fire of the 122nd Heavy Battery and of Canadians and Buffs, but numbers of the enemy pushed through the gap left by the 15th on the right, and threatened the rear of the line. A retirement was deemed necessary to shorten and bridge the gap, and the Canadians withdrew, losing heavily under tremendous fire of every sort.

Unfortunately Captain Tomlinson's company did not receive
the order to retire, and these men of the Buffs, who had so
magnificently stiffened the defence at the apex, fought on with
the two platoons of the 15th until, with ammunition done, and
nearly every man killed or wounded, they were surrounded and
taken.   The result after these hours was a breach of 1,500 yards
in the front of the 3rd Brigade, and to meet this fresh danger
the 4/East Yorkshire and 4/Green Howards were sent from the
Canal bank to the G.H.Q. line in front of Wieltje and Fortuin.
The German infantry had also suffered very severe losses, and
there followed a lull in their attack, but before noon another
annihilating bombardment opened, and the Germans advanced
upon either side of the second Canadian position.   A retirement
from the exposed forward slope of Gravenstafel Ridge had
become necessary, and the Canadians fell back in small parties,
fighting for each step of the way, while every yard of ground
and approach was smashed by shells of enormous calibre.   Still
the enemy failed to push through the broken front of the 3rd
Canadian Brigade and were held back by the indomitable fire
of the artillery, in spite of the paltry allowance of ammunition.
The flanks either side of the gaps still held, and two battalions
of the 150th (York and Durham) Brigade came up under the
heavy shell fire and joined what was left of the 3rd Canadian
Brigade in front of St. Julien, while the 1/Royal Irish moved
up to stop the enemy at Fortuin.   That afternoon the Germans,
having advanced on either side of the extreme jut of the Salient
and entered trenches covering St. Julien, a retirement had become
inevitable, and the Canadians withdrew to man the G.H.Q.
line covering Wieltje from Fortuin to Mouse-trap Farm.   Two
companies of the 3rd Battalion received the order too late, and
were annihilated, after successfully holding back the Germans
west of St. Julien for some hours.   The mixed troops in the
village held out till 4 o'clock, when the Germans took St. Julien.
   A very gallant defence during these hours was made on the
right of the gap within the Canadian Front by the 5th (Western)
Cavalry and the 8th (Winnipeg Rifles) Battalion, that still clung
to the original front of the 2nd Canadian Brigade.
   St. Julien—Fortuin had now become the chief danger-point,
and the extreme step was taken of robbing the 28th Division
on the Zonnebeke front of its reserves, and the 1/Suffolks and
12/Northumberland Rangers were thrown into the defence at
Fortuin.   Every available man was called upon to stop the
German assault here at all costs.   In a grand counter-attack the
4/Green Howards and the 4/East Yorkshires drove the advancing

enemy back through St. Julien ; so successful was this check that no further attack was made in the area by the enemy that day. Towards evening the Canadians on the west side of the gap called on the 28th Division for help, and such detachments as could be spared—the 28th was hard pressed itself—were sent up between Gravenstafel and Fortuin. Reinforcements from various quarters were hurrying throughout the day to the Canadian Division, among them some fine Territorial troops, the 151st (Durham L.I.). Late in the afternoon orders from G.H.Q. were received that the situation at St. Julien must be restored, the French having now promised to attack in force. General Smith-Dorrien covered the juncture with the Allies by placing General Allenby's Cavalry Corps under the French command. A collection of fifteen battalions was made into a special force and placed under Brig.-General Hull (10th Brigade), and sent to launch an attack and drive the Germans from St. Julien and Kitchener's Wood north-eastward. This somewhat unwieldy command of infantry and artillery was without signal company or other details, and had only the staff of a brigade.

It was a wet, dark night, there was no time for reconnaissance, nor to rendezvous the commanders of the different units, and the whole situation was extremely obscure. The Germans were dug in north of St. Julien, our line here was very ragged and a gap of 2¾ miles divided the 3rd Canadian Brigade from where the 2nd—cumbered with gassed and wounded men—were still holding on. In this gap were only two detachments : a mixed force of Suffolks, Northumberland Fusiliers, Cheshires, Monmouths, and Canadians, holding 800 yards near Boetleer's Farm, while an isolated 1,200-yards-long section of the Gravenstafel Road was in charge of the London Rangers and Suffolks. North of Wieltje the G.H.Q. line was manned by the survivors of the 3rd Canadian Brigade and its various reinforcements, while Geddes' detachment lay beyond.

Brig.-General Hull attacked at dawn of the 28th. The 10th Brigade, fresh and at war strength, advanced at once to the attack. Its five battalions were watched going forward in perfect formation till they were within a hundred yards of St. Julien ; here they came into so frightful a tempest of machine-gun fire from the houses that they were mown down, leaving their dead in swathes across the field. Advance was impossible —few came back. When the supports came up, a new line was formed, curving right and left from the Vanheule Farm south of St. Julien to the Hannebeek and Mouse-trap Farms. The appalling losses of the 10th Brigade, 73 officers and 2,346 other ranks, trained men of the first quality, were not utterly in vain. The enemy was blocked at St. Julien, and this position was held until the 4th May, when the salient line was deliberately withdrawn.

During the 25th the 3rd Canadian Brigade was relieved, the flank of the 8th, that had been exposed in the gas attack that drove back the 15th Battalion, was by now reinforced, and at evening this battalion, exhausted after forty-eight hours of fighting, lacking food, and with many men wounded and gassed, was taken into reserve.

On this day the eastern face of the Salient was heavily attacked. Opening with bombardment of very high explosive and gas, the enemy charged the front of the 28th Division, but only at one point, where every officer had fallen, did he succeed in occupying a short sixty yards of breastwork.

In the sector to the north the Germans advanced through the gap on the right of Boetleer's Farm, where reinforcements were unable to come up under the terrific shelling. Brig.-General Currie, learning that the 151st Brigade were occupying a line along the Gravenstafel—Fortuin Road and would not be used to reinforce him, ordered the 2nd Canadian Brigade to retire to the right of this new position. The flank of the 85th Brigade was thus in the air, and throwing back its left it formed a short flank, which it held until the general retirement on 4th May.

That night the gap was strung across by isolated bodies of weary men not even under one command.

The 26th April was distinguished by the attack of the Lahore Division. This division came up from Outerdom and assembled between St. Jean and Wieltje, with the object of an advance in co-operation with the French. The division attacked at 2 o'clock. Two brigades advanced upon the enemy at Mauser Ridge and came under appalling fire. Their ranks were devastated, but they pushed forward, leaving their dead in great heaps, and the two British battalions, 1/Manchester and the Connaught Rangers, actually reached within 120 yards of the German line. Just as they came to the wire a cloud of gas was released, blowing across the advancing troops. The British battalion, with the 40 Pathans and 47/Sikhs, held on, though some of the Indians, all having no protection from gas, fell back. The French did not advance after the release of the poison cloud, and the Lahore Division consolidated the line to touch them at Turco Farm.

On this afternoon the 149th (Northumberland) Brigade received orders to advance and join the attack, but received them after the time set for the advance. Without hesitation the brigade went forward, loading up extra ammunition, and charged into the face of overwhelming machine-gun fire, obeying the call to attempt an impossible task, and in the attempt losing over two-thirds of its strength. These were the first Territorials to go into action as a brigade.

While the enemy was repulsing, chiefly by artillery fire, British attacks on the left, his efforts on the right were aimed by the most violent attack to drive the 85th and the 11th Brigades from Gravenstafel Ridge, even as he had driven the 3rd Canadian Brigade. But failing in his surprise assault, he continued to ravage the shoulder of the ridge with shell. His view-point on higher ground overlooked every yard of the position, and he directed fire from front enfilade and reverse, maintaining this devastating bombardment unceasingly throughout the sixteen hours of daylight during the following eight days. His repeated efforts to break in through the gaps in the line north of Berlin Wood failed, though at terrible cost to the units that held the way.

On the night of the 26th the V Corps were reinforced by the arrival of the 2nd Cavalry Division east of the Canal.

Throughout this phase of the defence, tactics inspired by General Foch had demanded of the troops that continuous attacks should be made though with no artillery support. These attacks were doomed to failure even before their inception ; and General Smith-Dorrien was of the opinion that unless the French could restore their front, a retirement to straighten the British line was the only possible course. However, a combined offensive, French and British, was ordered for the 27th. The Lahore Division once again attacked, and coming again under heavy fire pushed on to Canadian Farm and Colne Valley, whence it could get no farther. The French troops, bombarded during their assembly, did not advance. A fresh attack was launched at evening, supported by a composite brigade formed by the only units that could be scraped together, a total of 1,290 men under Colonel Tuson.

This started hopefully, but unfortunately the Turcos were met by gas shell and fled, and only some of the French held on. The Indian brigades were therefore brought back behind Hill-top Ridge covered by outposts from their battalions.

On this afternoon while fighting was in progress, a telegram from G.H.Q. transferred the command of all troops serving in the Salient to General Plumer, with Major-General G. F. Milne as Chief Staff Officer, and this command was known as " Plumer's Force." His orders were to prepare a line as had been advised by General Smith-Dorrien, but to continue the offensive if

required with the French.   This was followed by a reorganisation
of troops, battalions being returned to their own brigades.

The Salient had now become almost untenable.   The confines
of its narrowed shape enclosed a space in which troops must be
closely packed if sufficient in numbers to hold the long encircling
line.   The Canal at the back cramped the passage of transport
into an approach that had become a mere target.   Artillery west
of the Canal was out of effective reach.   Yet this impossible line
had been forced upon the British, and unless the French could
come forward again on the north, it must be held in this deadly
shape or else withdrawn.

During the next few days some attacks took place in con-
sonance with some, generally abortive, efforts of the French,
and a withdrawal was postponed by General Foch's reiterated
wish, in spite of the hazardous position of our troops, heavily
shelled in the narrow space, and unable to reply.

At last on the 1st May General Foch's views were overridden
by General Joffre, and the British command was free to com-
mence a withdrawal from the tip of the Salient.   This was
carried out by degrees during the following nights.   At noon
on the 2nd, the 4th Division on the north face was assailed by
violent bombardment and gas, but the enemy was met and
beaten back, and our artillery immediately opened fire on the
area behind the gas cloud, and checked the effort of the enemy
infantry to follow it up.   Further attacks were broken up, as
in 1914, by the wonderful rifle fire of the British.

The new line chosen by General Plumer was planned to run
from Hill 60, east of Hooge, round Frezenberg Ridge to Mouse-
trap Farm, thence continuing as before westward to the Canal.
This entailed giving up a depth of from $2\frac{1}{2}$ miles by Frezenberg
to 1 mile near Hooge, on a five-mile-base line, and to this line
the forces were withdrawn.   On the night of the 3rd-4th May the
infantry of the 27th, 28th, and 4th Divisions moved back from
the front line, first one half, then another quarter, and finally
in small bodies, slipping away unseen by the enemy.   The
success of this withdrawal was menaced by a concentration of
hostile shelling on Berlin Wood on the evening of the 3rd ; but
the Buffs, fighting till every man in the front line was killed or
wounded, and the 1st Rifle Brigade with only one man to every
12 yards of trench, held fast until reinforcements were rushed
up.   The Germans were stayed ; and the 3rd Division, although
their line was in places only a few feet from the enemy, drew
away unmolested, veiled by the usual Salient ground-mist.
The trenches were left in perfect order, that the entering Germans

might appreciate that the retirement was a voluntary one ; and so little were they aware of what was forward that they continued next morning to shell the abandoned trenches.

On this date ends the phase that is known by the battle name " St. Julien."

THE BATTLE OF FREZENBERG RIDGE

The comparatively quiet period of six days followed while the Germans moved forward into the evacuated zone, though some severe fighting took place about Mouse-trap Farm. After this lull the enemy seems to have taken heart of grace from the withdrawal of the line that had so fiercely opposed him, and on the 8th he massed three corps against the two divisions—27th and 28th—that lay from across the Menin Road to the Frezenberg Ridge, and there began so desperate a battle that the defence at times bade fair to be overwhelmed.

In the early hours of the 8th May the storm broke ; a tempest of enormous shell fire, high explosives being used by all guns, in the terrible effort made by the Germans to smash their way through. Parapets, trenches, were destroyed, and the men beating back the German infantry time and again were killed and buried as they fought. Again and again the storm broke upon the line, and only when the gallant battalions of the 83rd Brigade in the heart of the onslaught on the forward slope of Frezenberg Ridge had been nearly exterminated was the remnant drawn back to the support trench 400 yards behind. The right of the brigade, and the 80th Brigade beyond them, made a magnificent stand in the " perfect Inferno " of annihilating shell fire, and the line held—the 4th Royal Rifle Corps and Princess Patricia's calling up signallers, pioneers, and batmen. To their north the retirement of part of the 83rd Brigade had left open the flank of the 84th, which hung on with matchless tenacity ; the 12/London (Rangers), fighting their way up to reinforce, were killed almost to a man. But their action with an attack by the 2/East Yorkshires and 5/King's Own checked the enemy for a time. The Germans were now, however, pouring through the gap, and whilst still storming the front line, attacked from flank and rear. The brigade fought on desperately, magnificently, while unit by unit was surrounded and destroyed, and so few came back to tell the tale that but a confused idea of the course of the battle could be formed. Of the six battalions only 1,400 men mustered next day, but though there was now a two-mile gap pierced in the 28th Division's front, the line was still held. On the right the 80th Brigade formed a defensive flank, and on

the left the Northumberland Fusiliers stood steadfast. In the
gap the Germans entrenched their position, obviously preparing
for the accustomed speedy counter-stroke by the British. This
came in the form of a counter-attack by the 85th Brigade that
came up on the right, but meeting the shattering fire of the
tremendous artillery, the reinforcements were broken up before
they could gain a position from which to attack. The 10th
Brigade came in on the left soon afterwards, sweeping down
from Mouse-trap Farm, and this advance, following on the
attack of the 85th Brigade, had a most remarkable result. The
enemy in the position of advantage he had gained in the midst
of our line abandoned the ground and withdrew ; and not only
was he thrown on the defensive, but he made no further effort
here for the following five days.

The British troops were directed to re-form the front, and
retrench across the gap. This was done behind Verlorenhoek
Ridge three-quarters of a mile behind the position previously
held, but less exposed to the artillery fire in which the enemy
had so great a mastery.

This day, the 8th May, stands out in the annals of British
warfare. The battalions that had opposed mortal strength to
the overwhelming force of enormous shell fire had so held their
own that the enemy reports claimed no success that day. Their
claim of but 800 prisoners taken, where their guns crashed so
large a breach in the line, give the count, dolorous and proud, of
those who fought it out to the death.

During the following two days the enemy diverted their
attention to the front held by the 27th Division, proceeding
on the same plan of a sequence of violent bombardments ; but
though they swept the line systematically with every form of
shell, they failed, in the infantry attacks that followed, to meet
the rifle fire and close with the British line. Our losses were
again grievous in the 80th and 81st Brigades, but the enemy
did not break through. During the night of the 12th/13th May,
the 28th Division, that had resisted the storm on the 8th and
been shattered in the doing, was relieved by the 1st and 3rd
Cavalry Divisions. At this period the terrible shortage of
ammunition had become most critical. Yet in spite of the
weekly report to the War Office, showing the fatal lack in the
Second Army, now in the midst of a battle with back to the
wall, an order was received for the dispatch of ammunition
from this front to the Dardanelles.

The arrival of the cavalry force relieving the remnant of the
28th Division on the night of the 12th/13th was greeted by a

bombardment of heavy shell that never ceased throughout the
following day and is reported in the V Corps diary as the heaviest
yet endured. At one time over 150 shells per minute were
counted to fall on Mouse-trap Farm.

The cavalry force was disposed from Bellewaarde Lake to a
point where it linked to the 4th Division, 600 yards south-east
of Mouse-trap Farm : the 1st Cavalry Division on the left, the
2nd on the right. The trenches that had been improvised were
very inadequate, with no wire to speak of, and the enormous
bombardment coupled with heavy rain had made a quagmire
of the position. The enemy succeeded in breaking in where
part of the 7th Cavalry Brigade front was very lightly held,
and bombed out the cavalry men, who were without hand-
grenades to repulse the attack. Advance into the gap was
checked by rifle fire from the Leicester Yeomanry in support
trenches behind. The front-line trenches in the centre and on
the extreme left of the 1st Cavalry Division were also pulverised
and rendered untenable, but local commanders flung supports
into the gaps, recovering the positions almost at once, though at
the cost of heavy loss of life. The charge on foot of part of the
11th Hussars and 2nd Essex was one of the most gallant of these
counter-attacks. In the sector of the 2nd Cavalry Division where
the gap torn in the line was hidden by a pall of inky smoke from
shell fire, the 8th Cavalry Brigade were deployed to restore
the line. In a grand charge they reached and in places passed
the original front, but nothing could live in this fire zone, and
a line of shell holes a thousand yards in rear was consolidated.
The cavalry had suffered so fearfully that a part of their front
on either side was taken over by the 4th and 27th Divisions.
But for all their stupendous effort against troops so piteously
handicapped by lack of guns and ammunition, the German
success was limited to the taking of a thousand yards' depth of
ground between Hooge and Mouse-trap Farm, by shelling the
defenders of an untenable forward slope.

The German accounts, as in 1914, are the most flattering
comment on the tenacity and heroism of the British troops.
The enemy was fought to a standstill.

There followed another lull, and for ten days no further attack
took place. During this pause measures were taken to improve
the line of defence, and vermoral sprayers and some gas helmets
(flannel bags with eye-pieces) were issued to the troops. Changes
were made in organisation, and between the 17th and 19th May
the 27th Division, that for four weeks without relief had put up
a stone-wall defence, was relieved by the 1st Cavalry Division.

BATTLE OF BELLEWAARDE RIDGE

On Whit-Monday, the 24th May, the lull was roughly broken. With a herald of four red lights that shot into the sky, a new bombardment crashed out and from the closest enemy trenches a deadly hissing sound was heard. A vast cloud of gas drove down against the whole four and a half miles of the V Corps front, from south of Hooge to Turco Farm, and hanging in a light wind towered 40 feet above the trenches in a dense wall of darkness. So narrow was No Man's Land that although an attack was looked for, the trench garrison had hardly time to put on respirators, and many were overwhelmed while unprotected. The hostile infantry assault followed swiftly on the gas wave, but there was no panic flight before it. Like a living bastion the survivors of that army that blocked the way in 1914, stood again indomitable : inspiring the half-trained reinforcements with that great tradition. For five and a half hours the conflict lasted ; a battle waged in an unceasing storm of shell fire and miasma of poison gas, the gigantic struggle hidden in the black curtain of smoke. With all communications cut, it was difficult to record how the different battalions fared, and the most hard hit were naturally least able to give times and details of how the day went with them. The 85th Brigade stuck all day long invincible in its position on the western slope of Verlorenhoek Ridge, though companies of the Middlesex and East Surrey were slain to a man ; into the gap south of the ridge the enemy thrust their way, and here, when all officers were casualties, the few survivors of the killed, gassed, or wounded men manned the trench line behind Railway Wood, and there they clung for the rest of the day, flinging back every enemy assault. South again the Woods of Hooge were filled with the gas fumes, and the 2nd Cavalry Brigade was so vitally affected that its unyielding ranks had to be strengthened by reinforcement of three companies of infantry. The spear-point thrust of the enemy between Hooge and Bellewaarde was stopped by the invincible stand of the 9/Lancers south of the gap, the remaining reserves manned Zouave Wood, and the 3/Royal Fusiliers were strung along the railway, guarding the flank north of the German thrust. In the middle of the line the enemy were held, and could not overcome the wonderful accuracy of British musketry. But the left of the British line was gravely threatened by the capture of Mouse-trap Farm in the first wave of gas. This permitted a lodgment in the front and devastating machine-gun fire in enfilade. The main line was held by the 10th and 12th Brigades in face of never-ceasing bombardment and repeated attacks ;

but a second gap was torn round the point lost at Mouse-trap
Farm, and the angle where the Salient recoiled was overwhelmed
in an annihilating cloud of gas. Few were left of the Irish
regiments that so steadily fought it out.

While this was happening in the north, the 84th Brigade,
warned for attack, pushed forward without waiting for food, to
stem the advance of the enemy in the Bellewaarde gap ; and
under heavy fire pushed up through the wire of G.H.Q. line
and drove the enemy out of Witte Poort Farm, which he had
reached not far from Railway Farm. The 80th Brigade came up
that afternoon from Brandhoek deploying behind the 84th, and
at night the two brigades counter-attacked, gaining to within a
few yards of the German trenches ; but they were unable to
live in the hurricane of machine-gun and rifle fire, and, being
compelled to desist, remained holding the line east of Witte
Poort Farm, gaining touch with the cavalry towards Zouave
Wood and holding on, though no water or rations could reach
them, and their casualties were grievous.

The 84th Brigade had lost about 60 per cent. of their strength,
and the 80th over 500 officers and men.

This evening two companies of the 1/York and Lancaster
drove the enemy out of the houses on the Menin Road near
Zouave Wood, and during the night the situation became so
quiet that the 1st Cavalry Division—leaving the 4/Green Howards
and 4/East Yorkshire in the line—were relieved by the 2nd
Cavalry Division. Their losses during these four days had been
over 650 all ranks.

In the northern sector of the line the 4th Division awaited
the co-operation of three promised battalions of the French
before counter-attacking to regain the Mouse-trap Farm trenches ;
but on learning that the French—who seem to have considered
our attacks of greater magnificence than of military value—would
only be available in support, a decision was made to evacuate
the triangle of ground behind the farm, and to organise a fresh
line in the position still held by the Irish Fusiliers along the
western side of the road from Wieltje to Turco Farm.

With slackening bombardment the battle died down. And
now, if the aim of the mightily staged battle was a break-through
or the capture of Ypres, then indeed was victory for the British,
for both these aims had been defeated. After thirty-three days
of desperate ordeal, of a fight of man-power against gun-power,
of men unarmoured against a new and treacherous weapon, the
British still covered Ypres with a shield emblazoned " Thus
far . . ."

SOLDIERS OF YPRES [1]

All Souls', 1914—1917

SOLDIERS OF '14 :
" Who comes ? Who gives our password, with the right
To join our ranks ? "

SOLDIERS OF '17 :   " Soldiers of England——"

SOLDIERS OF '14 :
                                      " Nay,

Not these, we know our own.   No host like this
Bore arms for England."

SOLDIERS OF '17 :   " Yet we are her sons——"

SOLDIERS OF '14 :
" Whence come you ? "

SOLDIERS OF '17 :   " From your Calvary of Ypres,
That holy spot where valour reached a height,
And unsupported, held, and saved the world.
You came more nearly to the high ideal
Of One who died for men, than e'er you dreamed.
There, where for God and Right—naught else—you raised
The standard in the face of awful odds,
One watch-word only, ' duty,' on your lips ;
Your passion steadfastly endured, your faith,
Your unconsidered sacrifice, have drawn
A world of men aflame to serve the cause.
We are of those who follow where you led.
We hold aloft the standard you bequeathed,
We keep the gate to Britain that you barred.
So dare we fight, and when our task is done,
So dare we follow where you serve to-day."

SOLDIERS OF '14 :
" Now God be thanked, and be you welcome—friends ! "

[1] Written during the battle.

"THIRD YPRES," 1917

MESSINES—PASSCHENDAELE

THE drama of Ypres drew in 1917 to its most tragic period.
The fierce and magnificent days of 1914 had been one tense,
unparalleled struggle that established the line. The poison
horror of 1915 had been met and overcome. In three years
Britain had placed in the field an army more adequate in size
to the necessities of a Power at war, and Britain had produced
material to support her arms. Germany's thunderbolt had
not crashed through to speedy victory, and from the Channel
to the Alps deadlock had been reached. Great battles in one
sector or another—Verdun, the Somme—that failed from either
side to break through, proved that the wearing-down stage,
la période d'usure, had been reached. In the spring of 1916 the
French Army that had laboured during our time of preparation,
and achieved the triumph of Verdun, was paying for that achievement in exhaustion and strain. Britain lifted her burden on
the Somme ; and in 1917 at Arras loyally seconded France in a
scheme alien to the strategy of our command, and for the last
six months of that year attacked Germany alone. Russia had
collapsed, and Italy was at a standstill. Nivelle's debacle on
the Aisne had a disastrous repercussion on the French Army,
already bled white, and the offensive spirit was out of it.
Passchendaele, so criticised, so deplored, was the outcome of
this crisis. The British in the slow, stricken days, as the offensive
dragged through the sticky bog of the Salient, crept on and on
indomitably ; no suffering of war or nature crushed the sombre
menace of her slow advance. And so overwhelming was this
menace that the force of Germany on the Western Front throughout these months was pinned to that dismal battlefield. France
needed the time to recover her strength and *moral*. She was
given that time. In October 1917 the German strength before
Ypres was over five and a half men per yard of front, his maximum
elsewhere reaching two men per yard ; and all his free artillery
were massed against this sector. And not only was Germany
deprived of freedom of attack elsewhere, but—as we now may
read—Ludendorff dreaded that the splendid courage and *moral*
of his mighty war-engine was being slowly sapped and under-
mined in the ghastly ordeal of those autumn days.

.   .   .   .   .   .

35

In choosing the area for the required British offensive, an attack in Flanders offered the best result ; at the worst our position would be enormously improved by the capture of the ridges that dominated the Salient ; at the best a break-through to the Dutch frontier, 30 miles distant, would have cleared the Belgian coast, and threatened the main artery of enemy communication at Liège. Moreover, this offensive had been already envisaged and plotted for the early spring, when with the summer months before us the chance of swift advance had been more promising. This scheme had been put back in favour of the glowing expectations of Nivelle.

[1] The operations opened with the storming of the Messines— Wytschaete Ridge, the object being to deny the enemy observation from the southern heights, along the few depressions in the ground, that could be used in our attack on the ridges to the north-east. This battle was mounted with the greatest thoroughness, and monster mines, holding 470 tons of high explosive prepared by months of labour, were long since in readiness. A concentration of artillery, a preliminary discharge of 70 tons of gas, every preparation was welded together and rendered effective by the intensive training of the troops, working with a complete model which showed in perfect detail the position to be attacked.

The German line along the ridge was one of great natural strength, augmented in every way by the fortification of the villages of Messines and Wytschaete, while the many hamlets, farms, and copses had been turned into strong-points. The British troops allocated to the attack were nine divisions, with three in support. Along the battle-front lay in readiness from left to right the X Corps (41st, 47th, and 23rd Divisions with the 24th in support) ; the IX Corps (36th, 16th, and 19th Divisions with the 11th in support) ; the II Anzac Corps (Australian 32nd Division, New Zealand Division, and 25th Division with the Australian 4th Division in support).

The German position formed the shape of a bow, of which the cord was the final objective of the British attack, and careful timing was worked out to allow for the longer distance to be covered in the centre of advance.

At ten minutes past three in the morning of 7th June the first mine fired—a magnificent sheet of flame from the Ridge. There followed a half-minute of enormous convulsion, of towering fire, of awe-inspiring noise that has no parallel in any earth upheaval wrought by the hand of man.

The German front line was blasted away. As the shattering

[1] P. 170.

explosion burst up from beneath, an appalling bombardment broke out along the front, and very little resistance was shown when the British troops charged up the ridges to their first objective.   They moved on almost at once, in the strange murk that made vision difficult, the thin light of dawn being obscured by the high-flung dust of the great convulsion.   The 36th (Ulster Division) and the 16th (Irish) fighting side by side captured Wytschaete ; Messines—as planned—fell to the New Zealanders ; the 47th (London) pushed on stubbornly on the left where the trough of the Ypres—Comines Canal, cutting through high ground, was formidably defended.   So fast was the advance of the infantry that in many places the tanks were not up in time to support the attack on the second line of defence, and by the early afternoon the troops had seized and consolidated the whole of the Messines—Wytschaete Ridge, and held a line on the eastern slopes looking down—at last the positions were reversed —looking down upon the German positions.

Before nightfall the whole of the objectives were in British hands, in spite of some counter-attacks and the stalwart resistance of the enemy in many strong-points.   The casualties were light in proportion to the troops engaged in the capture of so strong and so strongly fortified a position.   The whole design and the fashion in which the battle was carried out was a masterpiece of soldier-craft.

This triumphant success was followed by a tantalising six weeks while preparations for the main attack across the Salient were being hastened forward by every means that energy and skill could devise.   In the irony of fate these were six weeks of fine campaigning weather that, had the battle started earlier, would have meant a very different battle-ground in Flanders. During this time the Germans sent over their first experiment with mustard gas.   During the night of 12th July a bombardment opened on the line between the railway and the Potijze Road, 3,000 to 4,000 gas shells burst against the battery positions, and with the first whiff the usual precautions were taken.   But a new horror developed ; men began to go blind.   Great blisters came up on their bodies.   Hundreds, chiefly artillery men, were affected.   It was found to prove not always fatal, the effect wearing off in about fourteen days ; but where it was inhaled in strength the organs of the victim were blistered throughout his body, and slow and agonising death followed.

It is not intended in this Foreword to give so close an account of these prolonged battles as of those which in 1914 and 1915 lasted for a comparatively short time and were of a more immedi-

ately critical nature. The following is a general outline of
events, and in the Stories of the Roads representative divisions
in each sector describe how the battles went on their fronts.
The general scheme was an attack by the 5th Army due east
from Ypres, gaining the first low ridges east and north-eastward
until the low ground of the Salient should be cleared and the
Passchendaele Ridge gained. French and Belgian troops were
to protect our left flank, and on the right the Second British
Army would drive forward to the Lys. The operations opened
on 22nd July with an enormous bombardment, and during the
ten days that led up in an appalling crescendo to the final crash
of the barrage when the infantry attacked, no less than 2,300
guns fired some 65,000 tons of ammunition. Reckoning the
main front of attack at 13,700 yards, the average is one gun
and over 28 tons of ammunition to every 6 yards of front. On
the 27th the enemy unexpectedly evacuated their front-line
system on nearly the whole of the Fifth Army front, greatly
facilitating thereby the crossing of the Yser Canal.

The battle opened on the 31st July. The II, XIX, XVIII,
and XIV Corps sprang forward between the Zillebeke—Zandwoorde Road and Boesinghe. The plan of attack was for a series
of short, swift rushes, strongly supported and protected by
artillery and kept well within the forward sweep of the barrage.
This system was elaborated to meet the new German defence in
depth. The consolidation of each short step gained being
covered, and any counter-attacks broken up by the exploding
shells, a deliberate and steady progress step by step would be
driven through the densely fortified area. This system—
tactically sound—demanded one condition, normally dry weather.
That condition was denied. The rain came down on the 31st July,
and the abnormal weather which followed must be insisted upon
even at the risk of labouring the point. Records over the whole
period for which weather conditions have been recorded in
Flanders show that this was the wettest August since 1878,
with the one exception of 1897, when the rainfall was equalled
but not surpassed. The figure is 189 mm. against an average
of 80 mm. over the whole of this period. It is with no exaggerated
attempt to absolve our Command from the responsibility of the
prolonged misery of the struggle, that this weather is pronounced
our greatest enemy.

On the first day the whole fifteen-mile front was moved to
its first objective. The Second Army, south of Ypres, fulfilled
its part, making a short advance planned to deceive the enemy
as to the extent of the line of attack. On the northern sector

the Fifth Army reached and even passed beyond the first objective. In the centre of the sector the objective was reached ; the one disappointment came in the important and difficult sector across the Menin Road. This, being at the junction of the two armies, was the weakest point, and the units of the Fifth Army here were allotted the more strenuous task. The 8th Division thrust out to the second objective and got in touch with the XIX Corps on its left ; and the 18th Division, leap-frogging the 30th, made some little progress beyond their first line. Northward the line bulged out, through the XIX Corps which had gained and been forced back from its final line of advance, round to the foremost line reached and now consolidated by the XVIII and XIV Corps.

In spite of the hold-up of the II Corps, the success of this first day was greatly encouraging. Most of the objectives had been reached ; in the north overpassed ; and even in the least favourable sector considerable ground had been gained. We had taken 6,000 prisoners, and inflicted heavy loss on the enemy. At this rate everything promised well for the slow methodical advance of the armies.

And then the rain began to fall—faster and faster, heavier and heavier, until a persistent downpour commanded the situation, and held on unceasingly for four days and nights. The heavy, low-hanging clouds obscured observation. The opening assault was brought to a halt. No further major operations could take place for some days ; though on the 10th August the 18th and 25th Divisions improved their positions by a local attack that captured Westhoek—important to the enemy for observation purposes—and also slightly advanced the line, establishing forward posts.

The next important move was made on the 16th, an assault by nine divisions launched on a nine-mile front. This followed very much on the same lines as the events of the 31st July and substantial gain was made across the flooded marshes north of Steenstraate. Langemarck was taken in the early hours of the morning, and our line pushed forward east of St. Julien as well as east and north of Langemarck, the 20th and 29th Divisions reaching their final objective at all points excepting some 200 yards of trench ; the 48th and 11th Divisions equally successful at most points. The 16th and 36th made but slight advance, and unfortunately enemy strong-points were passed and left unreduced behind them.

On the right flank and right centre the advance was once more held up. The first objectives were seized everywhere by

8 a.m., but on the desperately difficult ground about the Menin Road the tanks were unable to reach their rendezvous and the Infantry of the II Corps were left unaided to fight in this most difficult and stubborn sector. Some troops of the 56th and 8th Divisions and a brigade of the 18th on their right forced their way beyond Glencorse Wood and Nonne Bosschen and the Hannebeek. But the check on the extreme right exposed our flank. Once more artillery support was hindered by the devastating rain, and the 16th and 36th Divisions were driven back before a powerful counter-attack. This recoil of the IX Corps exposed the left flank of the II Corps, already in the air on the right, and it was compelled to surrender the position so hardly won, and to fall back also.

North of the XIX Corps the XVIII Corps had to draw back to keep touch. The end of the day was disappointing when the urgency of saving time and the threatening weather outlook are considered. But as an achievement in most adverse conditions such gains as were made were remarkable. There followed a period of more and yet more rain ; and the battlefield had become a bog into which men were sucked, where it was not a honeycomb of pits in which men drowned.

The next major operation did not develop until the 20th September, when a little drier weather had taken some effect ; but minor attacks had been carried out all through the flooded days of August by which the pill-box defence was penetrated and our line pushed forward between Langemarck and the Menin Road.

The plans for the battle of the 20th September aimed at breaking up the stubborn opposition centred about the Menin Road, and to further this the disposition of the troops was altered, so that the assaults should not be made from the flank or weakest part of an army. The Second Army was accordingly extended northwards, and when the attack was launched the battle-front was carried as far south as the Comines Canal. The Menin Road had become the centre of the Second Army, and of a single concentrated operation. The Fifth Army continued its advance in the north-easterly direction. From the 20th September to the 4th October our advance was steady, and the success of the method was proved to the hilt, rendering perhaps more bitter the disappointment when this success was annulled by the renewal of the unprecedented rainfall.

This advance opening on the 20th September was carried forward in a series of very shallow steps, which, in the better visibility, the artillery barrage was able efficiently to support ; each short step allowing that the next one could be swiftly advanced. The possible direction of counter-attacks was the object of careful forethought, and these were broken up by men who after a short advance were not already exhausted as by a prolonged struggle. So successfully did the advance proceed that Ludendorff was driven to change his tactics; but his experiment of returning to the original scheme of a strong front line with divisions in close support resulted in the most ghastly carnage from our guns, and gave the British on 4th October the most complete victory of this offensive. Our line now ran along the Ridge from Reutel by Broodseinde to Poelcappelle. And then the rain came down again. . . .

On the 9th October the troops, battling in the marsh in the centre that was a drain for the ridges, made little advance. On the higher, drier ground on the right the 2nd Australian Division reached its objective on the Ridge ; and in the north, with less opposition, the Guards and the 29th Divisions came, south of Houthulst Forest, to their final objective. And still it rained. . . .

An attempt was made two days later, but the mere assembling of troops in such a downpour was very difficult, and the ground was in such an impossible condition that the attack was broken off.

It had become evident that the wide scheme of clearing the Belgian coast could not be carried out so late in the year, and we ask why the deadly, long-drawn agony of the battle was not now cut short.

The reply of the High Command is that the tactical necessity of pinning down the enemy troops was not over. Fresh divisions were pouring in from the Russian Front, and of these some had gone down into Italy. We gave Italy in her worst hour the most valuable aid we could when two divisions were deviated to her front from Flanders. We had already compelled the renewing of the battered divisions in front of us by all troops that Ludendorff could spare, and the staggering German success at Caporetto was not carried on to the utter destruction of Italy. Pinning the enemy closely, we gave the French the opportunity to strike at Malmaison and capture the Chemin des Dames. The concentration of attention on Ypres allowed the stage to be set for the brilliant opening of the Battle of Cambrai. A final reason for the continuation of the offensive in the Salient was the effort to lift our bogged and soaking troops into higher ground for the winter. Therefore on 22nd October the British struck again, and with success, a brigade of the 18th Division, two of the 34th, and two of the 35th moving forward. A bigger operation opening on the 26th brought the great battle to a close. Six divisions attacked north of the Ypres—Roulers Railway, while the 7th Division and a brigade of the 5th made a diversion with an attack on the Menin Road ; by the 30th October we had reached the outskirts of Passchendaele. The village itself was carried by the 1st and 2nd Canadian Divisions on the 6th November. The final assault was made on the 10th by these Canadian Divisions and our 1st Division.

The end of the great offensive was disappointing, as although Passchendaele had been captured and the Ridge attained, our position was not so defensible as to be secure from danger from formidable counter-attacks, and to enable our troops to leave the swamps of the western side. Time proved that we could hold the positions so desperately won, until the German attack on the Lys in April 1918 caused the evacuation of the greater part of the Salient.

Different schools of thought will endlessly argue the wisdom of this or that war plan, and paint visions of what might have been had totally different technique informed our commanders. Passchendaele—our most cruelly costly battle—gives special temptation to such speculative dreams. What might have happened had different schemes been followed can never now be known ; what was done is ours to dwell upon.

We can but glory in the astonishing, patient courage of men who, yard by yard, broke through the colossal barricade of the German defence. We can but believe that the menace of such inexorable persistence paralysed Ludendorff's vaster schemes farther afield.

EPILOGUE

" PASSCHENDAELE. FOR CONSPICUOUS
BRAVERY . . ."

" He's gained a V.C. for conspicuous pluck ?
Well, of course, that is often a matter of luck ;
And dash and fervour of racing blood,
Will carry him through on excitement's flood."

Held in the bog that grips his thighs,
    Wet to the shuddering skin,
Weighted with pack and equipment,
    Stunned in the monstrous din ;
Visored against the goodly air,
    Sucking in acid breath.
He peers, half blind, through the swirling smoke,
    For the stabbing flash of death.

So goes he—so fights—and he is in luck,
For someone may note his conspicuous pluck.

THE LYS, 1918

As we read the history of the battles on the Western Front, the whole story falls into three distinct phases. Opening with the first struggle for tactical advantage, the War passed into a state of deadlock when for two years either side strove to wear down the other ; to destroy numbers, strength, and *moral*. During this period the most ambitious efforts to force a way through failed to break the line, and at enormous cost the attackers succeeded only in distorting the shape of the iron barrier to no ultimate advantage.

In 1918 the final phase was reached : the side that was weakening staked all in one stupendous last effort. That effort failed, and the winners, profiting by just that little extra measure of endurance and strength that was theirs, struck the final blow.

In the spring one more superb resistance against the tremendous thrust of Germany's last effort—which was her defeat : in the early autumn our break-through. Germany had struck in the Somme area with all the strength, skill, and courage of which her military nation was master, and though she had regained that ravaged battlefield, she had failed to break through our defence. But the British had turned the blow unaided by their Allies, and at so exhausting a cost that Ludendorff judged a loss of *moral* would spread through the hard-hit divisions. He granted no respite nor time for recovery, but struck again : this time in the north. Once again Germany misread the character of the British ; once again proved that with back to the wall, outnumbered, desperately crippled, British soldiers show a nobility of character that makes a last stand their most formidable hour.

The Germans opened the battle with twenty-seven divisions, reinforced during the offensive by another twenty-two—forty-nine in all, of which forty were fresh divisions. Our line, drained of every possible man to meet the shock on the Somme, was held chiefly by weary troops withdrawn from that battle. Of the whole of our fifty-eight infantry divisions on the Western Front, forty-six had been already worn down in the death-grapple in the south. Between La Bassée and the Ypres Canal six divisions were strained out, each covering over 600 yards of front, but the line had to be held.

The tempest broke in the north on the 9th April. As soon as threatening symptoms appeared, the British Command decided on the relief of the Portuguese Divisions that had been

in the line for some time through the trying winter months in
the low ground of the sector about Neuve Chapelle south of the
Salient.   This was in the area chosen by the Germans for attack,
and they assaulted with fourteen divisions on the eleven-mile
front held by three divisions, before the relief had been completed : within three hours of their assault, the Portuguese had
gone.   The result was a gap of a thousand yards torn in a line
that was already held with only the barest possible numbers,
and by the evening of the 9th April, five weary and depleted
British divisions with one additional brigade were holding about
twenty-five miles of front against sixteen German divisions.
The rupture and this subsequent lengthening of the line strained
our troops almost to the breaking-point.   But wide as was the
rent, and enormous the force of the enemy army that swept into
it, the southern flank stood like a granite cliff ; the German tide
could not overflow the Givenchy position.   Here the 55th
(West Lancashire) Division met the shock with the resources of
a highly fortified and organised defence ; and not only held their
own front but threw out a defensive flank 2,000 yards long.
During seven days of indomitable resistance the division lost
3,000 officers and men, but they had taken 900 prisoners, and
their magnificent stand was a chief factor in the final success of
the desperate defensive battle.

North of them, the 50th (Northumbrian) and 51st (Highland)
Divisions wonderfully held the enemy along the Lys throughout
the 10th April, where, stretched across eleven miles of front,
they were assailed by seven divisions.   But it was impossible
to maintain so long a line against such odds, and during the next
few days the British troops were pressed slowly westward,
though still unbroken, nearly to the Forêt de Nieppe ; it seemed
almost outside the bounds of hope that the battle-line could be
held intact.   It was at this awful hour that Sir Douglas Haig
sent out the call to every man in his armies : the appeal that
rang through those stalwart hearts with fresh inspiration, rang
a toxin of alarm through England, and—meeting with the magnificent response of that last stand—will ring through history.

" To all ranks of the British Army in France and Flanders.
" Three weeks ago to-day the enemy began his terrific attacks
against us on a fifty-mile front.   His objects are to separate us
from the French, to take the Channel Ports, and destroy the
British Army.
" In spite of throwing already 106 divisions into the battle
and enduring the most reckless sacrifice of human life, he has,

as yet, made little progress towards his goals. We owe this to
the determined fighting and self-sacrifice of our troops.

" Words fail me to express the admiration which I feel for the
splendid resistance offered by all ranks of our Army under the
most trying circumstances.

" Many amongst us now are tired. To those I would say that
victory will belong to the side which holds out the longest.

" The French Army is moving rapidly and in great force to our
support.

" There is no other course open to us but to fight it out.
Every position must be held to the last man : there must be no
retirement. With our backs to the wall, and believing in the
justice of our cause, each one of us must fight on to the end.

" The safety of our homes and the freedom of mankind depend
alike upon the conduct of each one of us at this critical moment."

.   .   .   .   .   .

In this book, dealing solely of Ypres, with Armentières as our
southern boundary, it is difficult to take up that part of the
battle which may justly be included. We can only touch on
the gallant defence of the sector in the south that culminated
in the magnificent stand in front of the Forêt de Nieppe of the
4th (Guards) Brigade, and on the 12th April swung the German
attack northward against the 29th and 31st Divisions. A gap
was opened south-west of Bailleul, and closed at once by the
19th Brigade of the 33rd Division ; but the line, fighting step
by step, was forced back still unbroken, close up to Meteren and
Bailleul. Throughout this time reinforcements were being
rushed to the danger-point by our Command, while the promise
of help in great force was made by the French. The aim of
the desperately stretched-out and exhausted British troops was
to keep the line intact until these reinforcements could arrive.

Armentières on the 7th April had been bombarded with some
40,000 gas shells and the town was evacuated. As the German
thrust developed along the front the battalions damming the
breach to the south gradually withdrew, and in the Nieppe—
Messines Sector fought their way slowly back, contesting each
step from hour to hour, and keeping in touch with the troops
on their right and left ; until on April 14th the line ran nearly
straight from the Canal near Hollebeke to Wytschaete and
Bailleul. The success of this withdrawal was due in great
measure to deeds of individual heroism, the boldest souls
creating centres of defence and fighting with utter sacrifice of
self. These heroic stands of small parties held the enemy long
enough for the line to re-form, mile behind mile, until a strong

defensive position was reached. So once again the few in number, the exhausted in body, denied the way to an enemy seemingly overwhelming in number and strength.

But a cruel sacrifice had to be made, one that might well have broken down the *moral* of an army less resolute. It had become impossible to hold that jutting line east of Ypres that outlined the Salient. The holding of the Salient had always been to our troops the severest task : it had now become a menace. To keep the line intact, to save Ypres, a deliberate withdrawal was ordered. All the ground that had been wrenched with such effort and agony from the enemy a few months before was now deliberately yielded back to him. The troops manned a battle-line closely bastioned round the ruined city, and this greatly shortened and less vulnerable line was held.

The British had by now defeated the German aim of turning the northern defences by a break-through south of Armentières, and the enemy concentrated on the capture of the high ground at Kemmel and the Mont des Cats ; to meet this menace, reserve defences were prepared from Meteren—through Dranoutre to Kemmel by the IX Corps.

On the evening of the 15th three fresh German divisions, including the Alpine Corps, entered Bailleul, crashing south and east of the town, where three and a half miles of front were defended by two brigades of the 59th Division. They got no farther : the reserve line of defence held by the 34th Division north of Bailleul stood fast. The British line, now running almost directly from Wytschaete to Meteren, withstood all attempts to break through ; till on the 17th the Germans made a determined effort to capture Kemmel Hill, attacking on either side. They attacked in vain, although they employed eight divisions, of which seven were fresh to the battle. The enemy tried again to capture the hill two days later, but again failed completely ; and now he began to show signs of exhaustion : the stubbornness of the British opposition had told. The critical hour had passed and the nation knew that its armies had responded to Sir Douglas Haig's call to the utmost meaning of those words.

The fresh Australian divisions had arrived, and were in the line to the south, and some French troops—though they had been a week on the way—had come up to the Wytschaete Sector. The slow response of the Generalissimo had been hard indeed for the British to understand. They had already withstood alone the terrific effort of the enemy to break through on the Somme, and now their hardly hit battalions were again defying the full force of Ludendorff's gigantic thrust. Yet the French

were loath to part with any reserves, and appeared to rely on
the national British characteristic of utmost tenacity, that had
been so often proved during the last four years, to weather once
again the storm.   Perhaps they were justified : when the French
troops arrived, the crisis had passed.

The British were now standing on the Meteren—Kemmel
position.   An attack was planned by the Allies for the 16th by
the French 28th Division ; but unfortunately the French assault
did not materialise, and two battalions of the 62nd Brigade,
the 7/Seaforth Highlanders, and two companies of the 39th
Division Composite Brigade (all under command of the 9th
Division), that had been allocated to support the French, attacked
alone.   In spite of the heavy fire from machine guns that the
failure of the French to advance released on this front, the British
drove through beyond Wytschaete ; but being unsupported, the
line was consolidated north of the Wytschaete position.

The Kemmel Sector was now taken over by the French, the
troops relieving each other through the nights of 18th/19th and
20th/21st April ; and by the 24th four French divisions were in
charge of some 12,500 yards from the Kemmel—Messines Road
to Bailleul.   On their right the Australian Division held with
two brigades a front of 7,000 yards.   On their left four depleted
Brigades, the 27th, the 146th, the 64th, and 26th (now forming
the 9th Division), held a front of 5,500 yards.

A short lull followed the enemy failure to capture Kemmel
Hill : then on the 25th April he launched a fresh attack between
the Bailleul—Locre Road and Hollebeke : four German divisions
assaulting the four French, and two German divisions attacking
the 9th British Division.   A very heavy gas bombardment
preceded the attack, and the fact that the French on both flanks
of the hill gave way almost at once is sometimes attributed to
their use of an insufficient gas mask.   At 9.15 in the morning
our 9th Divisional H.Q. heard that the Germans were 1,000 yards
north by east of Kemmel—2,000 yards behind our right flank.
Here the 12/Royal Scots had stopped the advance of the enemy
at 5 o'clock, and their front was intact at 7.30.   At the same
time the 6/K.O.S.B., fighting desperately on the right of our
second line of defence, could see the Germans assembling French
prisoners in their rear.   The enemy advanced to the positions
they had gained, pressing the British flank northwards, and
entirely cutting off the four front-line battalions that held the
9th Division's centre and right.   Only a wonderful feat of arms
of the 26th (Highland) Brigade that stood fast, and also succeeded
in throwing out a defensive flank, broke the enemy assault and

barred the way to the north. The French divisions now lay from the lower slopes of the Mont Noir and Scherpenberg Hills to the Kemmel Beck. Our line northward had no features favourable for defence and was dominated by the enemy on Kemmel Hill. Aeroplane observation next day reported that some posts of British trench-mortar and machine-gun units that had been attached to the French were still holding out on the hill, and a counter-attack was decided upon next day with the object of rescuing these parties and recovering the invaluable positions. The 25th British Division with some odd units, very weary from the struggle, yet attacked with such vigour that they reached Kemmel Village ; but the two fresh French divisions did not start, and our troops were compelled to withdraw.

The loss of Kemmel, that had been held by our exhausted and cruelly strained troops against the enemy's powerful onslaught only a few days previously, was a bitter blow to the British and aroused most disturbing reflections. But fortunately the end was near. Heavy fighting and hot local attacks continued for some days longer, but the enemy's force was spent. No further offensive of any importance was attempted.

And the envoi ? They had fought to the end. Every position had been held to the last man. The safety of their homes and the freedom of mankind were gained. Victory was to those who held out the longest.

EPILOGUE

1914—1918

From the first shot fired to the last bolt sped,
When the sun rose white till the sun sank red,
A cry to the living across the dead :
                    HOLD !

When your flanks are turned, and it's five to one ;
When your rifle jams and your belt is done ;
When your pals are down, and behind you—none !
                    HOLD !

When the only gun unscuppered yet
Has one round left—and you forget
When last you slept, or drank, or ate !
                    HOLD !

For Ypres is ours ; though the foe may slay
Till the bog runs red, we stand and stay,
And never in life will we yield the way.
                    HOLD !

ADVANCE IN FLANDERS, 1918

THROUGHOUT August and September the British Armies on the
Arras and Somme Fronts struck their first hammer-blows of the
last fight, the fight that broke the German Army. As the
enemy was driven inexorably backward across the battlefield
in France, his grip on the Ypres Salient inevitably relaxed.
By the middle of September he had withdrawn his troops from
the Kemmel area, and the battle-line lay through Nieppe,
Ploegsteert, Voormezeele, and east of Ypres. Our Second Army
was placed under the supreme command of H.M. the King of
the Belgians, and in concert with the Belgian forces and three
French divisions, the advance opened on the 28th September.

The operations were planned to follow much the same lines
as the battles of 1917. A direct thrust eastward from Ypres ;
then, the nearest ridges gained, an advance north and north-
eastward, the right flank resting on the Lys. But how astound-
ingly different was the development ! The enemy were no
longer in such numbers on this front ; and those weary miles
that had been agonisingly wrenched yard by yard from the
enemy through four months of battle in 1917 were in 1918 overrun
in a single day. In truth the Army swept forward with a
magnificent dash and elation that carried the very spirit of victory
over the arena of the long conflict—over the mortal resting-place
of those who died that this day might come.

But swift as was the advance, it was by no means over a royal
road of costless success : the casualties from the 28th September
till the day of Armistice reached 1,304 officers and 24,926 other
ranks.

In view of the results attained during the last hours of warfare,
the spirit, the fitness, and the power of endurance of all ranks
had proved to be remarkable. The more remarkable when we
remember that the forces had been bled white five months
before, and the ranks were filled up with recruits, many being
mere boys. At the finish an advance of twenty-two miles had
been made in two days and a few hours.

. . . . . .

The operations may be divided into three phases. First the
launching of the initial attack and the rapid advance towards
the line of the River Lys, 28th September—2nd October. In

the British Nomenclature of Battle this is called the Battle of Ypres, 1918. After this there followed from the 3rd to the 13th October a period devoted mainly and of necessity to the improvement of communications. Lastly, there is the period from the 14th October to the end of the month when the offensive was resumed and a line running along the River Scheldt was reached.

The offensive was opened by the II Corps on the left, the 9th and 29th Divisions being in line with the 36th in reserve ; and the XIX Corps with the 14th and 35th Divisions in line and the 41st in reserve. The X Corps, consisting of the 30th and 34th Divisions, and the XV Corps, including the 31st and 40th Divisions (on extreme right of Army front), were to watch their opportunity on the day of the attack, and, taking every advantage of any signs of weakening on the part of the enemy, were to press his retirement.

Complete success attended the opening stages of the offensive, and by 6.35 in the morning the 29th Division, after driving through Hooge, had gained the high ground immediately to its south, while the 9th Division captured Rabbit Villa. The XIX Corps was equally successful. The left brigade of the 36th Division captured all its objectives by 7.30 ; swept on and took Hill 60 and Canada Tunnels by storm. Shortly after St. Eloi Craters and The Bluff fell to the 14th Division.

Impelled by these successes in the north, the X Corps felt their way forward early in the day and by 7 o'clock their patrols reached Ontario Farm, Kruisstraat Crater, and Big Bull Cottage. Pushing steadily to its goal, it reached the line running from Warsaw Crater to Piccadilly Farm by 9.15.

Before midday the 29th Division had occupied Jackdaw Tunnels and Post, and established itself at Jargon Cross-roads and in Westhoek ; the right brigade of the 14th Division swooped down on its objectives, and by 12.20 the division reported its patrols established at Dome House and along the Dammstrasse. The 35th Division had also captured all the line as planned. Meanwhile Polderhoek Château and Cameron Wood had been occupied by the 86th Brigade, and Tower Hamlets Ridge and Veldhoek captured by the 87th Brigade of the 29th Division. The ground sanctified by the martyrdom of the old Army in 1914 was falling hour by hour into our hands, and now the 88th Brigade passed through and captured Gheluvelt soon after midday ; Zandwoorde and Alaska Houses had been taken while Wytschaete was cleared of the enemy, who now lined the Messines—Wytschaete Road. Progress continued to be made

throughout the afternoon. The 11th and 12th Bns. the Royal
Scots of the 9th Division captured Becelaere, while further south
the 30th Division took Petit Douve, and later on reported having
gained a line from Messines to Sloping-roof Farm.

Consequent on the successful progress of the main operations
in the north, the XV Corps pressed the enemy in the south,
with a view to harassing his retirement. The 31st Division
advanced to St. Yves, but their progress through Ploegsteert
Wood, highly organised as it was by the Germans with cunningly
concealed machine-gun nests, was hotly contested. The troops
battled through the Wood, doggedly advancing step by step,
but suffering heavy casualties, until late in the day, when they
were held up at the Railway Triangle. They paused that night
to reorganise and prepare for further attack on the morrow.
By this time the division had reached its objective on the left,
and, though counter-attacked, held the enemy, having organised
a defensive flank south along the road which passes through La
Hutte, in view of the slow progress made through Ploegsteert
Wood.

In the XIX Corps, the 124th Brigade of the 41st Division
had driven the enemy from the Warneton line, and had gained
its final objectives north-east of Kortewilde.

The 34th Division that evening reported that its right was
advancing through Scott Farm, its centre east of Onraet Farm,
and its left had reached the line Martin's Farm—Dome House,
the stream just west of La Douve.

By nightfall on the 30th September a general line had been
reached from Erquinghem along the Lys and forward, passing
Comines and Gheluwe, to a point 1,000 yards east of Dadizelle—
St. Pieters. During the 30th there had been sharp fighting for the
possession of Gheluwe, Hill 41, and Ledeghem, and the roll of
casualties became heavier, the state of the ground even worse,
and the difficulties of progress consequently greater than during
the first two days. The fighting now reached a stage inevitable
in big operations conducted in bad weather. The enemy's
resistance was increasing and he was using his reserves to counter-
attack, but his activity was a minor consideration as compared
with the problem of communications. In a considerable zone
of the conquered territory every vestige of road had disappeared,
and the ground, churned up by shell fire and drenched with
heavy rain, had become an all but impassable slough. In spite
of those conditions, guns had been advanced, supplies had been
forthcoming—the Second Army, by improvisation of corduroy
roads and by rapid extension of railway tracks, had in some

degree, though not wholly, met the difficulties. But these difficulties were still more insistent in the case of the Belgian Army, with whose rate of advance the Second Army was obliged to keep in close unison. It became necessary to moderate the pace, but on the 14th October the divisions surged forward again ; and when the last shot was fired on the 11th November the Second Army lay far off, fifty-one miles east of Ypres.

The long guard was over, and the shattered tower of Ypres still stood, the pointing witness of an inviolated charge. The curving belt of fire and steel—so often strained near to breaking-point, so often pierced but never broken—had spread wide, had gone forward.

There was no Salient.

EPILOGUE

Men of our race whose bodies circle Ypres,
We here salute you Guard of deathless might !
You held the way to Britain, and now hold
Our pledge fulfilled to stake our all for Right.

THE BATTLEFIELD OF YPRES

From the painting by Sir D. Y. Cameron, R.A. in the Imperial War Museum

THE STORIED MAP

EXPLANATORY NOTE

FOR the greater ease of those who take this book on pilgrimage to Ypres, the narratives of the battle fighting have been assembled in alphabetical order of place-names. But, to avoid losing the interest of historical sequence, they are grouped as far as possible under battle-centres with cross-references where required. For example: Mouse-trap Farm—sometimes known as Shell-trap Farm—will be found under " M " and " S " with a cross-reference to Wieltje, where the stories will be read.

Au Bon Gîte, a famous pill-box, will be found under " A " as well as under Poelcappelle, where the account of its capture is written.

Under each name the stories follow in sequence of date.

The narratives of the Menin Road—that portal to Ypres—on and about which the furious struggle of 1914 is a saga in itself, are all grouped under the one head, so as not to lose the cumulative weight of daily events.

The aim has been to give a wide variety of incidents of war, and in each category some one account will be found at greater length than others, not because it was a finer or more important event, but because this one is the fullest first-hand account that I could secure. The inclusion of some personal names results from the same accident : it is perhaps in keeping with the spirit of this history that no name, neither of General nor Private, is picked out to be particularly honoured : each is a type.

The substance of all these narratives is drawn from military records. Accounts of German treachery and brutality have been omitted from this book. The Briton is a clean-handed and debonair fighter, his hand-clasp ready after the bout. The Teuton is different.

But strong man met strong man foot to foot ; brave man fought brave man with unsurpassed valour. That the greater number, long prepared and armed cap-à-pie, did not prevail against the unprepared and lightly armoured, is the heart of the story of the Salient.

ARMAGH WOOD. (See ZWARTELEEN.)

ARMENTIÈRES. (See FOREWORD, BATTLE OF THE LYS, and under PONT DE NIEPPE.)

AU BON GÎTE. (See LANGEMARCK.)

BAILLEUL. (See FOREWORD, THE LYS, 1918.)

Bailleul (South of), 1918

In the extreme south of the Salient in the spring days of 1918 the situation was growing more and more desperate. The Germans, with a preponderance of three—sometimes four—to

BAILLEUL (SOUTH OF)—*continued.*

one, in forces fresh to the battle, were battering the strung-out
and exhausted troops that had for the most part lately come
up to this area to recuperate after the smashing attack in the
south. By the 11th April the onslaught of the enemy had
brought him south-west of Bailleul. The 1/Battalion of the
Border Regiment was placed at the disposition of the 50th
Division, then struggling to stem the tide north-west of Estaires.
Soon after midday the front of the division began to be driven
in, and herculean efforts were made to rally the troops and
form them into a new line. " D " Company, fighting hard, was
outflanked. The O.C., 2nd Lieut. Yates, was carried back
wounded, and they received the order to retire, but two platoons
could not win clear ; they were last seen as an island in the
enemy tide—still fighting. " A " Company counter-attacked
and for two hours kept the enemy back, until, when heavy
trench mortars had been dragged up against them, and both
flanks were in the air, the word was given to withdraw and form
a new line. This done, they flung back two powerful attacks
with heavy loss to the enemy. Six battalions here, including
the Borderers, made a stone-wall defence on which the Germans
made no impression until nearly midnight ; then outflanked,
the British withdrew to make a fresh line which they held, while
all next day the news of the advance and strength of the enemy
grew from hour to hour more disquieting. The officers commanding the battalion came into Headquarters with the report
of the terrific struggle ; their units reduced to thirty men . . .
to twenty men. Lieut. Chicken, himself wounded, brought in
all that was left of two platoons of " C " Company of the Border
Regiment—just three men.

These were days of heart-breaking struggle, our troops beating
out the hours of resistance to the last hopeless moment, and
then falling back to make another line : once more to face the
onrolling torrent, fight through the same round of defiance,
until once more the hard-fought ground was yielded. During
these intolerable days the C.O., Captain (acting Lieut.-Colonel)
Forbes Robertson of the Borderers, was the leading spirit that
held the line from breaking ; with resource and splendid courage
he inspired his men through all. When the troops in front
wavered, he rode forward on horseback with calm audacity into
the midst of close-range fire, and having made his reconnaissance,
he organised and led a counter-attack ; his horse was shot
beneath him, but he led on afoot and re-established the line.
Late into the evening he rode about where the danger was

BAILLEUL (SOUTH OF)—*continued*.

greatest, steadying the men, checking the least sign of yielding, and infecting everyone with his indomitable spirit, though he was wounded three times and five times brought to the ground. Through the next day he kept his men steady, forming a strong post at Battalion H.Q. as his flanks were pressed back ; and, holding like grim death, covered the retreat of troops on his flank ; then drew his troops into the line where the general plan required them. On the 13th this line was tried to the utmost. East of the Forêt de Nieppe the 29th and 31st Divisions were stretched across 10,000 yards, to be held at all costs, until the 1st Australian Division could detrain behind them ; and so —clinging to their posts, fighting back to back in the trenches, with little groups fighting to the last bullet while the enemy surged between them—so, time was saved, and the leading brigades of Australians formed up behind them. The way to Hazebrouck was closed. The dispatch of the 20th July 1918 reported : " No more brilliant exploit has taken place since the opening of the enemy offensive, though gallant actions have been without number."

BANFF HOUSE.   (See PASSCHENDAELE.)

BECELAERE.   (See MENIN ROAD.)

BECK HOUSE.   (See FREZENBERG.)

BELLEWAARDE, 1915

During the heavy fighting on the 8th May 1915 the Germans succeeded in pushing back our troops holding the trenches round Frezenberg. The effect of this was to open up the flank of the 80th Brigade immediately to the right and leave it exposed and in the air. The flank trench was held by the Princess Patricia's Canadian L.I. ; and their grand defence of it was one of the outstanding features of the fighting at this part of the line. Major Gault, the C.O., and all the other senior officers were killed or wounded and the command devolved on Lieut. Niven. Apart from the heavy shelling and the gas, the trenches were raked by machine guns from neighbouring buildings which had been captured by the enemy. The German artillery fire was so accurate that the Canadian machine guns endeavouring to reply to them were buried again and again, but were dug up and blazed out their defiance once more. Corporal Dove worked one of these guns till both his leg and his arm had been shot away. When the trenches were obliterated, the Canadians

BELLEWAARDE—*continued*.

manned a communication trench and continued the desperate resistance. The 4th Rifle Brigade sent up a reinforcement and the fight went on. Later a party of the 2/Shropshire L.I. pushed their way also into the fire-swept trenches, bringing with them a welcome supply of cartridges. The Germans made a determined charge and got possession of the trench at a point where all the defenders had been killed. The survivors in the other sections rushed to the threatened point and drove the Germans pell-mell out again at the point of the bayonet. From then till darkness set in all attacks were held at bay, and late that night the Princess Pats were relieved. Having read the Service over their comrades, many already buried by German shells, Lieuts. Niven, Papineau, Vanderburg, and Clark led back the survivors : just 150 men of a battalion that had gone into action that morning 700 strong.

Bellewaarde Spur, 1915 [1]

On the 16th June 1915 the 1/Lincolnshires took a leading part in the 3rd Division's attack on the Bellewaarde Spur. They advanced at 4.20 a.m. with the Liverpool Scots on their left and the 1/Wiltshires on their right. This line passed through the enemy's front trenches which had been captured five minutes previously by the 9th Brigade, and attacked the enemy's second line. The Lincolnshires' bombers drove the enemy at a run down the communication trenches leading back to his second line, and by 4.30 a.m. this line, running from Bellewaarde Farm to the corner of a copse in front of Bellewaarde Lake, was captured by the Lincolnshires at the point of the bayonet. The Commanding Officer, Major H. E. R. Boxer, then led a party of fifty Lincolnshires along a communication trench which led to the enemy's third line on the western border of the lake, and succeeded in bombing their way there when the British artillery recommenced a barrage which cut them off from the remainder of the battalion. Major Boxer then ordered his party to fall back on to the main body of his battalion, but he himself was mortally wounded and remained in the enemy's third line with a small escort, none of whom returned. Major Boxer's name appeared in the Gazette for the D.S.O. on this date.

The net result of the day's fighting was that the enemy's front line remained in British hands and a salient bulging into the British north of the Menin Road was flattened out. The captured trenches were consolidated and were subjected to a violent

[1] From regimental contribution.

BELLEWAARDE SPUR—*continued.*

enemy bombardment for the remainder of the day. The Lincoln-shires broke up an enemy counter-attack in the evening, dispersing his waves of infantry with rapid rifle and machine-gun fire. The day's fighting cost the Lincolnshires the loss of 7 officers and 350 other ranks in killed, wounded, and missing.

During 1915 the 1/Battalion of the Lincolnshire Regiment served 248 days in the Ypres Salient, was subjected to all the worst conditions of trench warfare, suffered the loss of 30 officers and 1,046 other ranks in battle casualties, and never lost any ground to the enemy, but, on the other hand, did its part in winning some ground north of the Menin Road and took advantage of every opportunity of inflicting the maximum amount of damage upon the enemy.

Bellewaarde Lake, 1915

A huge mine was sprung in July 1915 between Hooge and Bellewaarde Lake with the object of destroying a German redoubt and improving the position of our front line by capturing the crater and trenches alongside. The 4/Middlesex were detailed to attack, supported by other units of the brigade. On the evening of the 19th July a single shot from a 9·2 boomed the signal to fire the mine. Immediately with a dull roar the earth heaved, and with an uprush of smoke and dust, debris and bodies of men were hurled into the air, and flung so far that ten men of the Middlesex were killed by falling fragments and two store dumps were buried. The enemy replied with frenzied howitzer fire which did not cease for hours ; the Middlesex at once went over the top and forward into a blinding whirl of dust and smoke, forcing a way through to the crater, which they reached as darkness fell. From the first they were short of bombs and the advance of the column on the left was slow ; but they fought through to their objective, a German com-munication trench, which they identified in the smoke and gloom by the arrival of German bombs, flung from two directions. There appears to have been no stint of bombs in enemy hands, and it was with great difficulty that the British soldiers built a block—a very gallant achievement, as they filled the trench up 7 feet high with a barrier eight layers thick. And this was done in the midst of a violent fight. Soon after midnight a strong hostile bombing party attacked, and the British bombers, with every grenade spent, came near to being destroyed entirely, when suddenly one of the Diehards snatched up a burning " potato " bomb and flung it among the enemy party, checking their advance for

BELLEWAARDE LAKE—*continued.*

a time. The Middlesex held on with rifle fire, until a further
bombing party attacked, when very slowly, fighting foot by
foot, the Englishmen withdrew along the trench, until at last a
small but steady supply of bombs began to arrive, and enabled
a stand to be made in the next bay. Private Matthews's wonderful throwing greatly helped in the repulse of the enemy ; with
remarkable accuracy he hit every target that showed at 70 yards
from the trench. The enemy came again courageously to the
attack with the bayonet supported by machine and rifle fire ;
but just as the Diehards—left with one bomb—made ready for
a final fight to the death, the enemy checked and withdrew. At
dawn a further and last supply of bombs arrived ; so, as advance
to the original " stop " was impossible, the Middlesex blocked
the trench where they were for a solid 30 yards, working under
continuous fire. The centre column had established itself on
the eastern lip of the crater in their first advance, but the trenches
had been filled up by debris, hindering the bombers' advance
beyond. The work of sandbagging the crater's edge was slow ;
many sandbags had disappeared under the debris. The men
were unable to dig themselves in adequately before the counter-
attack started. This came at 9 p.m., and during the night
three attacks, developing into a matter of bombing duels, were
made, and every time repulsed. The right column had met
with little opposition, as the enemy trenches on their line of
advance had been obliterated by the explosion. The Diehards
consolidated the position, and handed over to the Gordon Highlanders.

Bellewaarde, 1917

The advance of the 2/Northants Regt. had not developed
according to plan, and Captain Colyer Ferguson found his company
scattered by wire and difficult ground, and himself left alone with
the sergeant and five men. He continued the attack and with
his small party captured the trench, cleared it of its garrison,
and repulsed a heavy counter-attack from the left front. To
reinforce his rather undermanned position, he advanced, helped
only by his orderly, and attacked and captured an enemy machine
gun. This he turned upon the assailants, driving such as were
not killed into the hands of the flanking British unit. Finding
this a very helpful manœuvre, he slipped out with the sergeant,
and attacked and seized another gun. By this time some
more of his company had come up, and consolidated the position
gained by his extraordinary dash and gallantry. Captain

BELLEWAARDE—*continued*.

Colyer Ferguson was soon afterwards shot down and killed by a sniper. He had received the Victoria Cross.

BERRY POST, 1917

In the middle of January 1917 Boche patrols, dressed entirely in white, crossed the snowy waste of No-man's-land and, all unsuspected, reached Berry Post and succeeded in making many casualties among the garrison. British authorities took the hint, and white patrol coats were issued from ordnance. But the thaw had come.

BLACK WATCH CORNER. (See MENIN ROAD.)

THE BLUFF, 1915 [1]

The 2/Battalion the Manchester Regiment held the Bluff for 87 consecutive days from the 15th April to the 25th July—a period of dull endurance, when no important engagement relieved the monotony of hours of trench work, though casualties occurred daily. Although there was no heavy fighting, yet of individual gallant acts there were many, and perhaps the one by which Lieut. Arthur Close-Brooks won a Military Cross is the most conspicuous. Lieut. Close-Brooks with one sergeant and one private went out on patrol in the early hours of the 10th June from their company trenches below the Bluff, to try to obtain a report of a new piece of work in the enemy's lines. They agreed that if they were discovered they would separate, and each one make his way back independently. Just before day-break a heavy fire was opened on them, and Lieut. Close-Brooks and the private, the latter wounded, got back to their trench ; but there was no sign of the sergeant. Lieut. Close-Brooks turned back to look for him. Dressed only in a mackintosh and a pair of boots, with bandages, water-bottle, and a ball of string in his pocket, he went out into No-man's-land in broad daylight. The trenches were fully 200 yards apart, but with patient perseverance he wriggled his way along the ground, and at last found the sergeant, lying dead within 35 yards of the enemy's trench. He fastened the end of the ball of string to the body and made his way back, having been over two hours on his task. As soon as it was dark he went out again, followed up the string, and brought the sergeant's body back.

The Bluff, 1916

" A " Company, 7/York and Lancaster Regiment, counter-attacked on the 15th February 1916, when the enemy, after springing a mine, had seized a crater. An officer writes :

[1] From a regimental contribution.

THE BLUFF—*continued*.

" I saw The Bluff a couple of days afterwards, and it presented a haunting spectacle. Upon the slopes of the Crater
were the dead, frozen as they had been killed, for the weather
was intensely cold. Right up near the crest was a sight which
drew famous generals to the place.

" Silhouetted against the skyline, and plainly visible from the
British line, was the figure of the only man who had looked
upon the invisible enemy. Clad in his great-coat, his shrapnel
helmet was still on his head. His right knee was bent to the
ground ; his right hand grasped the barrel of his rifle, the butt
of which also rested on the ground. He had been frozen stiff
as he had died ; turned into a piece of terribly arresting sculpture
by the frost.

" What his regiment was no one could say ; but it was agreed
that the probabilities pointed to his being one of the York and
Lancaster missing, for that was the fate of a number of them.
Anyone who saw this unknown hero will readily recall the incident, for such a one can never forget it.

" There is one other curious problem connected with this affair
at The Bluff. In every one of the neighbouring dugouts men
were to be seen sitting in strange attitudes. They had died
without wounds ; but whether from the effects of concussion
when the mine was sprung, or from exposure or gas, it was
impossible to tell."

The Bluff, 1916 [1]

The Bluff was the name given to the precipitous cliff that
ended the embankment of earth and spoil, dug out in the making
of the canal and left alongside. This Bluff end faced the enemy,
and was the highest point held by us in the district. Its value
for observation was evident, and it was subject to terrific hostile
shelling, and the Boche had put up many mines, leaving at least
three enormous craters. It was enfiladed from both flanks,
and could also be taken in reverse.

With the brigade the 2/Suffolks held this position for four
months through the winter 1915–16 ; two regiments relieving
each other, and carrying on the work of reclaiming land from the
overflowing water, and consolidating, while being subjected to
daily " strafes " big and little. " We floundered in the mud,
we endeavoured to stop or rather to divert the endless flow of
water which the Boche, being as always on higher ground than
ourselves, cleverly poured into our trenches to join streams

[1] From the regimental contribution of Lieut.-Colonel H. d'Arch Smith.

THE BLUFF—*continued.*

that flowed in from our back area. In fact we became amphibious. With keenness, ingenuity, and cunning we dug where we could, erected parapets where we could not, and filled hundreds of sandbags with a sort of porridge of mud as a foundation before anything could be built up. . . . The arrival of timber and of ready-made duck-boards helped matters, and support and communication trenches began to look as though they might resist a puff of wind, though the front-line ones had not much more strength than what the barrier of barbed wire lent them. All this work had to be carried on at night under enemy observation with an almost continuous stream of Verey lights from the Hun line that lay so very close." As the long winter drew to a close the brigade—what was left of it—was pulled out and sent back for a rest ; to refit, recoup, and make up the strength, sorely depleted by the winter-long stream of casualties.

But only a week's rest was vouchsafed before the sorry news came through that the position on the Bluff had been lost. This was followed by the order that the brigade would retake the lost ground. The troops immediately moved to a training ground, where for three weeks in snow and slush the attack was rehearsed to a plan of the well-known trenches " spitlocked " on the practice ground, until every man knew what to do blindfold. During this preparation a valuable reconnaissance was carried out by Major George Crosfield, second in command of the 2/Suffolks. He went out on the night of 27th/28th February with Corporal Lynn and Private Hailstone, and reaching the enemy's wire at the edge of the canal left the two men to guard his return, and wading through the canal round the wire, swarmed up the muddy slopes to the lip of the crater. On reaching the top he detected the enemy at work in a square patch of brightness against the inky face of the Bluff. This appeared to be the entrance to a gallery. Having learned all he could, and found also that beyond a thickening of the front wire the crater had not been put in a state of defence, he rejoined the patrol. The reconnaissance proved of the utmost importance and value, as it disclosed the presence of unsuspected and fairly strong dugouts, that were accordingly dealt with in the plan of attack.

" The brigade moved into the assembly trenches on the night of the 2nd/3rd March, and waited through the dreary eerie hours of the cold dark night in utter stillness—no smoking, lights, or talking being allowed. Zero hour was 4.30 and no preliminary bombardment warned the enemy ; the advance moved silently forward and took them unaware. At 4.35 the Boche rockets

THE BLUFF—*continued*.

went up, and a triple barrage fell across our line of attack ; but
he was too late ; his first-line trenches were in our hands before
his gunners received the S.O.S." Our men advanced as fast as
the sticky ground would allow, and the objective was reached
without much resistance except for a stubborn defence on the
left which held up our men and caused many casualties before,
being reinforced, they reached their aim. On the right the line
of attack had to go round each lip of the enormous crater at the
eastern end of the Bluff. Here the reconnaissance had prepared
us for the fortified dugouts on the western side that were in a
position to fire on our troops that passed on beyond the lip, and
so a special party was detailed under a C.S.M. to move along
the west edge and bomb the dugouts below them. The surrender
of their entire garrison removed a great danger from the advance.
" As day broke large streams of flying Huns could be seen inside
our lines anxious to give themselves up, and striving to get under
cover from the terrible rifle fire and bombardment from their
own guns, which had now reached such a point of frenzy that
you could not hear a word shouted close to your ear. Many of
these men belonged to regiments that had been against us most
of the winter, many being Würtembergers ; and one officer
paid us the compliment of saying that they expected us to come
back and retake our lines. The brilliant success of the attack
was followed by the fearful work of consolidating, which in this
case meant that you crouched behind a half-blown-away parapet
and endeavoured to make it higher by filling sandbags with mud
from under your own feet, piling these on top, and incidentally
making a pond for your own feet to stand in. And the hardest
task of all was hanging on to this precarious position under the
tremendous shelling to which we were subjected for the next
forty-eight hours. Our inter-communication was extremely
difficult—the supply of ammunition, food, and water to the
advance trenches and the bringing in of wounded." When
finally the battalion was relieved, it took a whole long night,
owing to the havoc of the ground.

Thus was the Bluff recaptured by those who had held it the
whole previous winter, at the terrible cost of 50 per cent. casualties, and this position was never again in the hands of the Huns.

BOESINGHE SECTOR, Crossing the Steenbeek Pilckem Ridge, 1917

The 29th Division, that had come to great fame in the magnificent landing in Gallipoli and had enhanced their reputation on

BOESINGHE SECTOR—*continued.*

the Somme, arrived in the Salient in June 1917 to take part in the third battle. The line they prepared was on the right of the Guards Division, and ran from the Ypres Canal north of the town eastwards toward Wieltje, at that date the extremity of the Salient. It was a heavy job getting this front ready for the big attack, a struggle with mud under shell fire, and a toil of burdened men labouring up at night. The division reckoned they shifted about 3,040 tons of stuff up to their line during the tour. It was followed by three weeks in reserve, and on the 31st July the battle began ; the divisional artillery coming first into action and putting down a successful barrage for the Guards, who made good progress during this day towards Wijdendrift and were relieved by the 29th Division on the 8th August. A young 2nd Lieutenant not twenty-one years of age—Acting Captain A. E. G. Leadbetter—had the distinction remarkable for his age of commanding " L " Battery R.H.A. (of Nery fame), and was killed during this advance. The Divisional Artillery gained the confidence of the infantry especially by silencing for ever with less than six rounds from the howitzers, the garrisons of a group of block-houses that had been a trouble to the men in the front line.

The division lay along Pilckem Ridge and went forward from here on the 16th, crossing the Steenbeek by a brilliant manœuvre, fighting across the quagmire and capturing their objective on a mile front. The speed of this advance sent the wing battalion ahead of the units alongside, and the K.O.S.B. had a hard fight, the French on their left being late in starting. The Scotsmen —battle friends throughout history of the French—were able to help them now again by enfilading the foe.

This brilliant page of the history of the 29th Division was illuminated by two outstanding deeds that were rewarded by the Victoria Cross. Machine guns from a pill-box were raking the company of the K.O.S.B. under Sergeant W. H. Grimbaldeston, a Lancashireman. He crept out and round the flank of the block-house covered by rifle fire, and coming round to the back, appeared in the entrance behind the garrison, grenades in his hands. The whole of the 36 defenders surrendered with 6 machine guns, and the sergeant had single-handed cleared the way for his company. But he was not alone in his unit in reaching the greatest honour of our armies by way of a captured block-house that day. Company Sergeant-Major John Skinner of Pollokshields rivalled him in the second advance. Fire from three block-houses was shattering the charging infantry

BOESINGHE SECTOR—*continued.*

on the left flank, and the company commander, Captain Currie, crawled as far forward as possible with Company Sergeant-Major Skinner and silenced two of the guns with their rifles. When they had gained within 70 yards of the block-houses, Skinner asked to be allowed to attempt their capture : Captain Currie covered him with his rifle and Skinner wriggled his way ahead alone round the left-hand pill-box, and bombed the garrison into surrendering. He crept on and attacked the second block-house, pushing bombs through the gun loopholes. By this time Captain Currie had signalled the company to assault the third. They did so, and, losing many in the attack, captured this one also. Sergeant-Major Skinner was later ordered while on leave to join the reserve battalion at Edinburgh. But he slipped away with his leave-warrant, and reappeared with the brigade at the front, giving as one uncontrovertible reason for this breach of discipline the excuse that he had a bet with the quartermaster-sergeant as to which of the two should receive a ninth wound first. In the Passchendaele Salient next year he heard a voice crying in No-man's-land, and went over to bring in a wounded man. A bullet between the eyes won his bet for him. The regiment gave him a remarkable funeral. He—*brave des braves* of that great division—was carried from the gun-carriage to the grave by six brother V.C.s.

To return to the advance on the 16th August, the 29th Division had carried out its programme to the full and on time, and although the ground captured at great cost was actually small, the result was viewed by Ludendorff as a " fresh great blow," and our troops were much heartened by such a successful " show." Martin Mill, Denain Farm, Cannes Farm, Craonne Farm, are names of proud memory for these battalions. But in four days from the 15th to the 18th 88 officers and 2,024 other ranks had become casualties.

Boesinghe Château, 1917

The Welsh Guards attacked from the line by Boesinghe Château on the 29th July 1917, and came to their first experience of the new German system of pill-box defence. Sergeant Bye signalised the first victorious onrush by capturing one of these pestilent strongholds. He succeeded in gaining the opening at the rear and bombed the garrison into surrendering. As the first objective was taken and passed, Sergeant Bye went on, stumbling and falling in the rough ground, reached a second pill-box and repeated

BOESINGHE CHÂTEAU—*continued.*

his gallant exploit, clearing the way for a fresh onsweep which
brought the guards to their final objective.   Alone he accounted
for over 70 of the enemy killed, wounded, or captured, and was
awarded the Cross.   There were other Welsh Guardsmen who
attacked the pill-boxes on this first day.   R. R. Jones, while
his men were waiting in the rear of a pill-box, drove the garrison
into their hands, by firing his rifle into a loophole.   Private
Hughes was personally congratulated by the French, whose way
on their left was opened by the capture of a strong-point, to which
he led the assault.

The Boesinghe Sector, 1916

Deeds of valour in the excitement of battle ! but also deeds
of valour, of very great valour, enacted in the hours of duty in
the front line of a forty-eight-hour garrison.   In the winter
months this was an ordeal of courage of a very special kind,
endured in the marsh that was the Salient.   Men stood hour
after hour deep in water and mud with feet chilled to anguish,
and in expectation at any moment of the whine and zip of a
sniper's bullet.   Gum-boots were not always high enough to
keep out the standing water, even if a man reached the trench
without their having been dragged from his feet and left behind
in the mud.   Of what use to him was foot-grease, if there was
no place to sit down that he might rub it in ?   Of what use dry
socks in support, if there were none in the lines ?   Of what use
hot food and drink, chilled before it could be brought up ?   A
fire in the trench would fatally draw the enemy's artillery.

In these surroundings, in this misery, men stoically faced the
horror of death or mutilation with no exhilaration to carry them
through.   In the sector of Boesinghe the 1/4 Duke of Wellingtons
record as typical, and no strange event, that after a forty-eight-
hour tour one officer brought back twenty-four men—one signaller
and three other ranks.   The rest were casualties.   The battalion
had endured for months the abomination of the Salient, when
on the morning of the 19th Dec., 1916, an appropriate climax was
reached.   A special artillery shoot had been planned, and as
the enemy lines were very near our own, the men were ordered
to evacuate the front trench during the day, so as to give the
artillery a free hand.   Just as these men were being withdrawn
they were overwhelmed by a sudden swirling fog of gas and a
terrific bombardment.   The warning alarm of gongs and horns
sounded, the men dragged on their gas-masks and rushed to

The Boesinghe Sector—*continued.*

their posts, but many were caught unprepared, and were struck down in the strangling paroxysms of the poison. The 6/Battalion in Brigade reserve got the warning, and came up through the hostile barrage across the Canal into their battle stations. The British Artillery, supplied, perhaps for the first time, with unlimited ammunition—flung back the challenge of the guns ; the men, labouring in their gas-masks, were able at last to return the bombardment with an equality of shells. " A " Company of the Dukes had not yet withdrawn from the front line when the first wave of gas came over. Gas-masks were pulled on so promptly that no one was affected ; the commander grasped the duty to stay and hold the position and opened with rapid rifle fire, blazing into the enemy until the rifles were red-hot. An S.O.S. got through to Battalion H.Q. and every possible man was collected and sent up, though many failed to reach the line ; the rest struggled on, and reaching the trench they clung to the position surrounded by waves of gas, and unaware of what was happening elsewhere. A trying time of waiting followed, and a volunteer was called for to make his way back through the driving machine-gun bullets, and over the Canal by the one remaining bridge that was now being heavily shelled. Private W. Bancroft, who knew the danger of the route well enough from former experience, offered to go. He succeeded in reaching Battalion H.Q. unhurt, and carried the Commanding Officer's messages back to the front line. When darkness came, the Battalion withdrew and went into relief.

BRAY FARM. (See PASSCHENDAELE.)

THE BROENBEEK. (See PASSCHENDAELE.)

BROODSEINDE POINT, where Gravenstafel Road crosses Railway

When the Germans attacked, following on the first waves of gas in April 1915, the 85th Brigade was in the forward trenches north of Broodseinde. As the 2/East Surreys came up into the line, marching through Ypres, the first battalion, who were in the town, turned out in the Place, and as the sister battalion swung past the men cheered each other—parts of a whole that had already done, and were yet to do, so much for the glory of the Colour.

The position about Broodseinde was a centre assaulted in tremendous weight by the enemy using his new overmastering weapon, and bombarding with enormous artillery. Here the

BROODSEINDE—*continued.*

2/East Surrey and the Middlesex held on until the 3rd May,
repelling again and again all attempts of the enemy to break
through, and only losing ground when the defenders were helpless,
overcome by the fumes of gas. A fine effort to recapture one
trench so lost was made by the 2/K. Shropshire Light Infantry.
Brilliant moonlight betrayed the advance to the enemy, who
waited until the K.S.L.I. came within 30 yards, and then mowed
them down. The officers only reached the parapet to be shot
down, and with the loss of all leaders the gallant attempt failed.
The K.S.L.I. were withdrawn into support, and the two battalions
of the 85th Brigade, obeying a message from General Bullfin,
who " looked to them with confidence to hang on to their position . . . to save the situation for the British in Belgium, and
to enable a victory to be won," fought and endured until on the
3rd they were withdrawn. The 2/East Surrey had suffered 441
casualties in 15 days.

Broodseinde, General Condition of Roads, 1915

Relief nights in the Salient were ordeals as cruel as battles
without the relief of dash and excitement. The only way for
the infantry across the morass was a narrow duck-board track ;
in places single tracks drew together, making a possible meeting-
and passing-place. As a battalion groped along in Indian file
in the dark through long hours, any side-step meant engulfment
in the disgusting slime, while each black moment might burst
into flaming death. Transport used the roads—such as remained
—and military plank roads. Here an overturned wagon might
be replaced, holding up traffic for seemingly endless time, but
lorries were merely pushed over the edge. Blocks when transport
was blown up were so frequent that the front line came greatly
to depend on pack-animals, as a more dependable way of getting
rations up. But at one time at a spot known as Garter Point,
one could count 250 dead horses and mules alongside the track
within a mile, all victims of shell-fire. The bottom of the
Hannebeek Valley, crossed by a duck-board track, was a target
for incessant shelling, and the whole bottom was blasted into
enormous craters—filled with putrid water—by the constant
play of an 8-inch howitzer ; while the enemy brought up an
armour-piercing gun for a month on end, and distracted the
batteries parked wheel to wheel on the west of Broodseinde
Ridge. The Germans selected spots about 200 yards square,
and plastered these with a 15-minutes area strafe when no shell
under 5·9 calibre was used and no foot of ground escaped. There

BROODSEINDE—*continued.*

was no safety when the moving battalions reached the trenches or lines of rifle pits, but at least the exposure of their deadly trek was over.

Broodseinde Sector, 1917 [1]

On the 4th October 1917 the 1/Lincolns just before zero hour took the place of a battalion that had been caught in heavy shell fire on its way to the assembly position. The object of the advance was to follow up and pass through the 3/4 Queens when that battalion should have attained Judge Trench. The Lincolns closed up behind the Queens, but a bog was reached that could only be crossed at definite points at wide intervals. The Lincolns' C.O., Lieut.-Colonel Evans, quickly realising the danger of the leading battalion, whose advance split up by these conditions offered a target to enfilade machine-gun fire, ordered the two leading companies of the Lincolnshires to push on, fill up these gaps, and, merging into line with the Queens when the bog had been passed, clear the ground in front until the first objective was reached.

On approaching Juniper Trench the leading waves passed a pill-box without encountering resistance from it, but immediately afterwards they were enfiladed with machine-gun fire which came from the north side of the pill-box and suffered some casualties. Colonel Evans rushed at the pill-box, fired his revolver through the loophole, and forced the garrison to capitulate.

The line went forward, wheeling slightly from an eastward to a south-easterly direction, past Jetty Warren, a narrow valley where another bog stream further broke up the line, and captured Judge Trench. The severity of the enemy barrage was one of the heaviest the Lincolns had experienced, and the battalion, which had gone into action 600 strong including 22 officers, now numbered 7 officers and some 400 other ranks. After a couple of hours' halt the Lincolns advanced upon the final objective, encountering more machine-gun and rifle fire than they had yet done. Colonel Evans was wounded in the shoulder, but refused any assistance, and continued to direct his battalion. The attack was carried to a successful conclusion. Colonel Evans was again badly wounded, but nevertheless continued to command until the final objective was consolidated. For his most conspicuous example of cool bravery and leadership which stimulated in all ranks of his battalion the highest valour and

[1] From regimental contribution.

BROODSEINDE SECTOR—*continued*.
determination to win, Colonel Evans received the award of the
Victoria Cross.   During the battle of Broodseinde the casualties
of the Lincolnshires totalled 16 officers and 227 other ranks.

The Australians at Broodseinde [1]

On the morning of the 4th October 1917 the Germans still
held the main height from which for two years they had looked
down upon Ypres.   In the past fortnight of fine weather the
Second Army's offensive had beaten them back from all the
nearer undulations ; and during the night of the 3rd October
columns of British, Australian, and New Zealand infantry had
been winding their way out across the crater-field to the " jumping-off tapes " from which at 6 a.m.—the hour of dawn—they
were to attack this vital objective, the Broodseinde Ridge.
Before daybreak the mass of attacking troops were lying out in
the crater-field : on the left the 11th and 48th British Divisions ;
in the centre four Australasian Divisions (the New Zealand and
3rd, 2nd, and 1st Australian) ; on the right the 7th, 21st, and
5th British Divisions.   Before the Australians the black line of
the Ridge could just be seen against the sky.

These hours were tense with anxiety lest the enemy should
discover the impending attack.   At 5.30, half an hour before
" zero," observers saw with dismay a brilliant yellow flare thrown
from the enemy's lines west of the Ridge.   It was followed by
others, yellow, red, and green, which began to go up in sheaves
along a whole mile of Broodseinde Ridge.   Within a few minutes
the barrage began to fall, swiftly increasing until from the valley
in front of the Ridge the crunch of shell-bursts became almost
continuous.

The worst fears of onlookers had been realised ; the enemy
was placing a barrage fairly upon the centre of the attacking
force.   The shell holes in which the battalions lay were continually shaken by the pounding projectiles ; the loose earth
was showered on them ; fragments of steel smacked the crater-
edges.   Here and there a shell descended on one party or another,
killing every man in the crater.   The fire fell directly upon the
line of the 1st and 2nd Australian Divisions, and though the
3rd Division escaped the fiercest of the bombardment, which
passed slightly over, casualties grew heavy.   The torment showed
no sign of relaxing.   By the end of half an hour some battalions
had lost a fifth of their strength.   The line of that barrage was

[1] From contribution by Captain C. E. W. Bean, Commonwealth Historian
for the War.

THE AUSTRALIANS AT BROODSEINDE—*continued.*

for hours afterwards marked by the dead, lying thickly. Scores of officers had been killed, among them men who were known through the whole Australian Force—Phillip Howell Price of the 1st Battalion, Errie of the 7th, Goodwin of the 8th, Brewster of the 22nd. To many of the surviving leaders it seemed that any hope of success had been shattered. Such was the position when the hour arrived for the British bombardment and the launching of the advance.

At 6 o'clock, heralded by the usual eight or ten premature discharges, the British barrage descended with a roar which instantly swallowed up the sound of the German guns. At the same instant the troops in the shell holes observed that the German artillery slackened its fire. The day was then just breaking, and it was possible to see dimly up to a distance of 30 yards. To the surprise of many of their officers, the men were everywhere rising from their craters, the survivors apparently unaffected by the bombardment, reorganising, lighting their cigarettes, then steadily advancing. The British artillery fire at this moment lay 150 yards ahead, and they had to walk swiftly in order to approach it before it moved forward ; but they had not gone far when, in the crater-field close before them, there was perceived another line of men somewhat thinner than the advancing one. And now for a few moments the two lines confronted each other, that of the enemy replying with a few scattered shots. Then it turned and ran back towards the dark rise beyond, attempting wildly to escape through the British barrage. As the light increased, other lines of Germans could be seen running back beyond the shell-bursts over the whole face of the slope.

By a strange chance the enemy had planned an attack to take place on the same morning, along part of the front on which the British attacked, and at the same time. In the early hours of the morning, unknown to each other, the two forces had been lying in No-man's-land.

The German assault was to have been solidly supported. Though the storming force—three battalions of the 212th Infantry Regiment and one of the 211th—was comparatively slender, close behind it lay the 4th Guards Division, comprising the 93rd Infantry Regiment, the 5th Guard Grenadiers, and the 5th Foot Guards.

During the first stage the enemy was carried off his feet. In vain a few of his field guns, which had been emplaced on the summit as a precaution against tanks, opened fire over open

THE AUSTRALIANS AT BROODSEINDE—*continued*.

sights at the advancing troops.   Here and there, in some of the numerous ugly block-houses which studded the area, parties of resolute Germans with their machine guns attempted to hold out.   The danger was always present that such resistance might cause part of the attacking line to lag behind and to " lose the barrage."   Such a break had resulted in the wrecking of many an assault ; but on this day all opposition was overrun.   When, for example, part of the 21st Battalion was faced by resistance from some of these shelters, Lance-Corporal Oliver, boldly walking forward and spraying the enemy with fire from a Lewis gun at his hip, kept them blinded while the line advanced to left and right, and finally closed round them.   Similar incidents were occurring along every part of the front.   Near Zonnebeke a portion of the enemy's infantry endeavoured for a time to retire in an orderly manner, by short stages, with covering fire.   Along the greater part of the Ridge they finally fled or were captured.

Thus advancing, the Australians and New Zealanders and the British on either flank fought their way to their first objective, which lay mainly along the hill-side.   But here a misunderstanding of the barrages led to formidable and unforeseen difficulties. In parts of the front it was hard to restrain the troops from moving ahead straight through the stationary protective barrage, which was comparatively thin, in pursuit of the Germans, who were fleeing in numbers up the hill or were leaving their defences on the summit.   Thus on the right of the attack a considerable part of the 4th Australian Battalion and of the 2nd Gordon Highlanders—troops who had previously fought side by side at Bullecourt—went over the crest together, through their own protective barrage, and down the edge of the farther slope. When this was discovered by the Commander of the 4th, he sent to bring them back before the heavy gun barrage that had swept forward should return to cover the second advance.   The greater part, Scots and Australians, returned together through the light barrage in good time ; but one Australian company commander, as it was then rather late, took the risk of keeping his men out in shell holes, and allowing the main bombardment to pass over them.   In the centre of the attack also a certain number of the 6th and other Brigades followed the enemy over the top of the hill, but were brought back by their officers before the second stage.

This unintended advance had, on certain parts of the front, kept the Germans on the run, and cleared away groups which might otherwise have made a stand on the top of the hill.   But

THE AUSTRALIANS AT BROODSEINDE—*continued*.

in many places the fire from blockhouses and other strong-points
on the hill-crest, unaffected by the light barrage continued without
intermission and threatened to become dangerous as soon as the
advance should be resumed.   In numerous cases this danger was
met by officers or N.C.O.s going forward with a few men through
the protective barrage, working round the flanks of the enemy,
and then taking him from the rear.   In the centre of the front,
however, the enemy was so active and defiant that stronger
measures were taken.   The opposition here came from a number
of German staff officers, N.C.O.s, and determined machine
gunners who appear to have rallied some of the Footguards in
the trenches around the staff dugouts, and especially in a crater
caused by the blowing-up of a dump of ammunition in some
previous year.   As the barrage was falling beyond them their
immediate reduction was obviously necessary.   Accordingly,
half an hour before the advance was to enter its second stage,
part of the 6th and 7th Battalions crept forward under cover of a
bombardment of rifle grenades, and rushed the position.   Both
sides fought bravely and well.   Captain Annear, commanding
one of the Australian companies, reaching the crater, walked
coolly along its edge, firing down with his revolver at the enemy
ten yards away, while they threw bombs at him, until he was
killed ; Major Taylor, leading another company, was mortally
wounded.   But the crater and dugouts were cleared and a vital
advantage gained.   Farther north, where German gun-crews and
officers from the artillery dugouts resisted strongly with machine
guns, revolvers, and bombs, the opposition was finally swept
away by a rush of the 8th Battalion.   A white flag appeared
through a steel trap in the top of a dugout and was waved to
and fro in token of surrender.

Thus by energetic fighting in the hour between the ending of
the first stage and the commencement of the second the menacing
nests of Germans which lay immediately ahead of the line were
cleared away.   When the fire of the heavies suddenly thickened
and concentrated in front of the first objective, and the second
stage was launched, the troops on right and centre swept almost
immediately over the summit.   Behind them lay the devastated
crater-field of Ypres ; but crossing the road which led along the
backbone of the ridge, they looked out on a country of green
trees, farms, and hedgerows, almost unbroken by artillery fire.
Close in front in some parts lay trenches dug in the sandy soil by
the British in the early months of the War, when Broodseinde
was still theirs.   The possession of these vital heights, which for

THE AUSTRALIANS AT BROODSEINDE—*continued.*

over two years had enabled the Germans to turn the Ypres Salient into a graveyard of British troops, had at last been won back for the Allies.

On a more northerly sector of the front this stage of the advance was not so easily accomplished.   There the troops had first to cross low boggy ground full of huge water-logged craters like the hoof-marks of gigantic cattle about some trampled water-hole.   In traversing this swamp the line, which elsewhere followed so close upon the barrage as to be practically in the fringe of it, began to fall farther and farther behind.   In the marsh were a number of strong blockhouses behind which the enemy, when the bombardment had passed over, was able to set up his machine guns to play upon the advancing men.   Lieut. Dunbar of the 42nd, which was lying in rear, observing part of the troops in difficulties in this mud, immediately took his men forward at the double across drier ground to make good the gap behind the barrage.   But, in spite of this gallant support, progress in that sector became a fight from one blockhouse to another.   Lieut. Fraser of the 41st, for example, locating one machine-gun nest by observing some of the enemy making towards it, worked forward with his runner until they were in rear of the place and then, after firing a couple of rifle-grenades, rushed it, capturing 21 Germans with their machine gun.

By such methods the crest was won.   The final objective lay some distance down the farther slope.   The farms on the other side of the valley were now beginning to burn under the fire from the heavy guns, and among the hedges in the valley could be seen numbers of the enemy's reserve troops in full equipment, mostly retreating.   That many stayed, however, was obvious from the strong fire of snipers which met the troops as soon as they breasted the summit.   At least one German battery was firing on them direct from the heights across the valley ; and at this last stage fell Captains Pearce of the 21st, and Godfrey and Harriott of the 24th, and many other leaders and brave men. But the line was carried over the brink of the hill to settle precisely as had been ordained in the old trenches and shell holes commanding the farther slope.   The enemy was disorganised, and the only counter-attack worth calling such (on the Australian front) was broken by the action of an artillery subaltern, Gordon Linsley, who, going with the infantry, observed the Germans massing on the Morslede Road, and by means of a pigeon message called down a bombardment upon them.   The enemy's aeroplanes, however, which had been waiting to follow up his expected success,

THE AUSTRALIANS AT BROODSEINDE—*continued.*

came over as soon as the objective had been reached and directed artillery fire upon the ridge ; and in front of the 3rd Australian Division, German infantry was seen moving down behind hedges into an old trench 200 yards away.   In spite of the fire brought to bear on it, the sniping from this concentration of Germans became very galling.   After the centre company of the 41st had lost all its officers, wounded, Lieut. Skewes of the support company, taking command, decided to clear the front.   Accordingly, assisted by Lieut. Butler and part of the support company, he led his men gradually forward among the hedges and shell holes until they were within fifty yards of the enemy, when he gave the word to charge.   Shouting with all their might, the handful of Australians dashed towards the Germans, who fled, a few being captured.   Skewes was killed and Butler wounded.

So, under a galling and accurate sniping fire, the line faithfully carried out its task of consolidation.   The German front was more nearly broken on that day than on any other during the Passchendaele offensive.   The German staff, waiting to watch a successful advance of their troops, had found the attacking force annihilated and the supporting battalions driven back in confusion.   Though many of the pursuing troops would have liked to press much farther the fleeing enemy, this was not the intention of the high command and the officers had properly checked and brought them back.   The day's achievement was a magnificent one for the whole of the Second Army, and, for the Australians engaged, one of the most memorable in the War. After lying for half an hour under such artillery fire as might have been expected to break any offensive, they had swept away a German assault ; and, by their subsequent enterprise in fighting during the hour when they might have been content to rest, had wrenched from the enemy one of the most important of his positions around Ypres.

BUCKS HOUSE.   (See PADDEBEKE.)

BULGAR WOOD.   (See also SHREWSBURY FOREST.)

BURNT FARM, NORTH OF ST. JEAN

An enormous ammunition dump was blown up by a Boche shell on the 1st December 1917, killing over 150 men of the Labour Company at work here.

CANAL DE L'YSER, 1917

The 51st Division arrived in the Salient in June 1917 and occupied the front line due north of Ypres. The trenches here were merely breastworks, some of those in the front line did not even hide their occupiers. There were not many shell-proof dugouts, as the enemy, who started shelling on the least provocation, took advantage of every conspicuous object. The bank of the Canal de l'Yser some two thousand yards behind the front line had become a warren inhabited by a large military population, and was a queer township made up of every kind of shelter down to the most primitive of " Heath Robinson " constructions. The position was a maze of derelict trenches, which had to be prepared as the threshold of a great battle. The plans were designed by the C.R.E., Lieut.-Colonel J. Gibson Fleming, while General Maxse, the Corps Commander, personally supervised the meticulous training of the troops. A large model—about the size of four tennis courts—was built up on which every feature of the landscape and every detail of the position were represented. The plans for the advance were rehearsed here, resulting in a clarity of idea that governed action to a brilliant issue when the battle-day arrived.

The battalion was so keen that some of the troops constructed models around their billets, and with these, and " tracing tapes " that outlined plans of the enemy trenches, a very thorough preparation was made down to the smallest detail during six weeks preceding the attack on the 31st July.

During this time the enemy launched their first wave of mustard gas, a most devilish invention by which a long agony led up to death by suffocation. Our gas-mask, mercifully, proved to be an absolute protection, but the ground retained the fumes so long that men were often overcome when working in a district hours after the actual shelling.

A form of attack known as a " Chinese attack " was found by the 51st Division to work very successfully. This consisted of a cunning manœuvre. The artillery opens by sweeping an 18-pounder barrage across the enemy trenches, feigning to prepare for an infantry attack. But instead of going over the top, the men in the front line hoist dummies up on to the fire step and the whole line bursts into an uproar. The Germans naturally leave their shelters and man their lines, when the barrage at once sweeps back, overwhelming them with shells. This ruse makes the Boche disinclined to man the fire steps too promptly, so that when the day for the real attack arrives our infantry,

CANAL DE L'YSER—*continued.*

charging close after the forward sweep of the barrage, are able
to leap upon the enemy all unprepared.

When the battle opened on the 31st July the 51st Divisional
Artillery provided an 18-pounder to every 12½ yards of front,
which, with 112 machine guns, were reinforced by mortars that
flung 206 drums of burning oil on the enemy's support and reserve
lines—a revival of very ancient tactics that had as drastic a
result now as in the days of old.

THE CATERPILLAR, South of Hill 60

On the 15th February 1917 a raid was carried out by the
6/Battalion, London Regiment, which proved the most brilliant
achievement of the 47th London Division during this winter
in the Salient. It owed its success to a meticulous preparation,
and the deception wrought on the enemy as to what was in the
air. A neatly staged dummy attack was played out in front of
Hill 60, a spot always held very apprehensively by the Germans.
A small mine was fired here in No-man's-land; trench junctions
and strong-points behind their line were aroused by heavy
barrage bombardments; the Hill and the Caterpillar were
smothered from sight by smoke bombs. The enemy sprang to
the alarm, and opened a barrage in front of the menaced sector,
where our almost emptied trenches received the attack. Salvos
of coloured rockets made a display of fireworks—equally deceptive
—on the Bluff. When the excitement had worked up to its
height, eighteen Stokes mortars, that had been collected in front
of our real objective south of the Hill, burst upon it like a hurricane, cutting the wire and driving the front-line garrisons into
their concrete dugouts. Then the 6/Battalion, under Colonel
Mildren, with six Lewis guns, backed by twenty Sappers of the
520th R.E. under an officer, and five of the Australian tunnelling
company, opened their attack. The raiders charged the enemy
trenches almost unopposed ; so great had the surprise been that
his machine guns were not ready for action. The biggest haul of
prisoners made by any single battalion throughout the War
was the result ; one officer and 117 other ranks being captured,
with two heavy and three light machine guns, and a lot of maps
and documents. Mobile charges were fired, wrecking dugouts
and machine-gun emplacements, and in the uproar, triumphant
and excited men were seen looting machine guns and junk from
dugouts where charges of ammonal were sizzling. Finally, red
rockets were sent up behind our lines guiding the attackers back

THE CATERPILLAR, SOUTH OF HILL 60—*continued.*
again, while rockets of other colours painted the night sky north
and south of the goal, and the battalion got back with very few
casualties. The enemy report is interesting : " Strong English
patrols which attempted to advance after exploding mines on
both sides of the Ypres—Comines Railway were checked by our
barrage fire. Some few did rush the German lines, but were
driven out again, losing prisoners. It is significant that the
unwounded English prisoners captured here were so absolutely
intoxicated that it was impossible to interrogate them."

The Caterpillar, 1917

During the Battle of Messines a method of making communication trenches with great rapidity was carried out. A line of
holes was bored, push-tube canisters were placed 4 feet deep at
6-feet centres, and twenty-eight charges at a time were blown
electrically. By this means two good trenches, each about
200 yards long, were made in three hours' work by fifty men.
These trenches were of use for a long time afterwards.

CHEDDAR VILLA

Cheddar Villa was a large strong-point that fell into the hands
of our troops ; it had unfortunately an exceptionally large
entrance, which in the reversed position was now fully exposed
to the enemy. On 7th Aug. 1917 the 1/Bucks 3 Bn. (Ox. &
Bucks L.I.), taking over the line, established a first-aid post in
the Fort, and a closely crowded platoon also sheltered here
in an attempt to get some hours' sleep. A hostile bombardment
opened, and the very first shell came straight into this large
opening and burst among the sleeping men. The result was
ghastly ; many were killed and a still greater number horridly
mutilated. Captain Hughes, the M.O., most luckily escaped and
worked indefatigably for hours relieving the wounded.

CHINA TRENCH. (See WYTSCHAETE.)
CHINESE HOUSE. (See PASSCHENDAELE.)
CLAPHAM JUNCTION. (See MENIN ROAD.)

CLONMELL COPSE, 1916

On the 2nd December 1916 a raid was made on Clonmell
Copse. The plan was to enter the trenches close to a German

CLONMELL COPSE—*continued.*

sap, bomb down the sap, kill the Germans, clear dugouts, and secure prisoners. Two officers with 50 other ranks of the 8/York and Lancaster made the raid. Lieut. Fitzherbert, with one N.C.O. with a Bangalore torpedo, and two men crept out of the dugout and wormed their way by a roundabout route till they reached the chosen point in the enemy's wire. It was a most unfavourable night, No-man's-land was pitted with shell holes full of icy water, and the ground was frozen hard and echoing under a night of utter stillness. The enemy seemed to be on the alert expecting an attack and opened at once on the little party with rifle fire. Corporal Murphy at 20 yards' range was shot through the jaw, but went on steadily with his job, pushing the torpedo through the wire until his officer sent him back. He then only retired as far as the main party of raiders—34 N.C.O.s and men under Lieut. Spalding, who were waiting behind in No-man's-land until the torpedo had cleared a gap in the wire. For nearly four hours Lieut. Fitzherbert lay close up to the enemy's line, under fire the whole time, working the torpedo into position. He was wounded, but kept on until at 4 o'clock the Germans laid hold of the far end of the torpedo and began tugging at it. Lieut. Fitzherbert promptly fired it, leapt forward, shooting with his revolver, and a gap of 15 yards was cleared. Directly the torpedo fired, the assault party dashed forward and, led by Lieut. Spalding, charged into the gap. Sergeant Jurley, one of the first into the trench, was pinned through the leg by a bayonet. The sergeant brought his knobkerrie down on the German's head, pulled out the bayonet, and carried on the fight. The raiders captured the trench, bombing along to right and left. Later the Germans returned heavily reinforced, and a stiff bombing fight followed ; until, to avoid being surrounded, Lieut. Spalding collected his men and withdrew steadily to our line.

COCKROFT. (See POELCAPPELLE.)

CONDE HOUSE. (See PASSCHENDAELE.)

DADIZEELE. (See LEDEGHEM.)

DEAD COW FARM. (See LA BRIQUE.)

DESPAGNE FARM. (See MESSINES.)

DICKEBUSCH, 1917

There was no safety anywhere in the accursed Salient, even for troops resting out of action, such places as Dickebusch were

DICKEBUSCH—*continued*.

no sanctuary. " C " Battery, of the 2nd City of Edinburgh
Brigade, had pulled out of the line, moving with all prudence ;
had crossed the dangerous spots of the Lille Road, and the Café
Belge, swinging safely at last into the wagon lines west of Dickebusch. The horses had barely been watered, fed, and all made
ready for the night, when a shell landed at the end of the lines.
The men were turned out and stood to the horses, taking them
off the line and ready to move off. Another shell fell in the
next field ; the horses, trembling and sweating, fidgeted about.
An anxious ten minutes passed, and then with an awful crash
another shell fell. Right in the midst of men and horses it
burst with the reek and fumes of high explosive. As the dust
cleared away it revealed a horrid calamity ; 9 men and a number
of horses were killed outright and a great many wounded by that
one shell. The centre sector no longer existed.

Dickebusch Sector, 1914

An English battery in this sector in 1914 was constantly
sought out and shelled by guns on the Messines Ridge, however
carefully their position was selected. When relieved by a
French 75 battery, they warned the officer of this suspicious
circumstance. A few weeks later the British returned to this
spot and inquired how the French battery had got on. They
were told that at first the French had been constantly shelled,
but they noticed that a Belgian farmer, riding a white horse,
passed in front of the battery every morning before German
shelling began. The French tested this discovery, and decided
it was no mere coincidence. Next morning, as the white horse
bore his rider in front of the battery, the 75s fired. Since then
the battery had not again to change its position.

DOUVE. (See LA DOUVE.)

DRANOUTRE, 1915

On the 30th April the Germans drove a cloud of poison gas
across our line, and before the warning siren on Kemmel Hill
sounded, a sentry in the front line smelled the gas. He stayed
not to put on his helmet but sprang to sound the gong. As
the gas cloud passed over, he fell dead. The few seconds he had
saved sent the warning back in time along the line.

Dranoutre—Wulverghem, 1918

Early in September an urgent call for ammunition brought Lieut. A. P. Blakiston, R.F.A., along the Dranoutre—Wulverghem Road with twelve wagons. It was well known that this road passed under direct balloon observation, and as it was a clear day the little column was not taken by surprise when high-velocity shells began dropping on its way. It moved steadily along until the fourth shell burst in the midst of the leading teams. The wagon remained blocking the road. Bdr. F. Smart, in charge of the next wagon, at once gave the order " Left about wheel—trot," and the rest of the column got out of the way, and out of immediate danger. Lieut. Blakiston was busy extricating the tangle of dead and wounded men and horses, and Bdr. Smart went back to him ; the two rendering what first aid they could, and even getting stretcher-bearers and an ambulance. The heavy shelling never ceased along the road, and two of the stretcher-bearers were killed and one wounded. Then Lieut. Blakiston sent the ambulance and all the men away except Bdr. Smart, and by themselves they carried the dead and wounded stretcher-bearers to a safe place. This done, Bdr. Smart brought up a pair of horses and drove the wagon back. But still the ammunition was wanted at the other end of the road. The shelling died down, the column formed up, and at a collected canter again moved into the danger zone. They were seen—but just too late ; and the German shells dropped just behind them all along the exposed road. " The ammunition was duly delivered in accordance with instructions."

EARL FARM. (See MESSINES.)

FITZCLARENCE FARM. (See MENIN ROAD.)

FREZENBERG, 1915

It was largely owing to the action of the artillery that the Germans did not push through the broken front of the 3rd Canadian Brigade on the 24th April 1915. Practically the sole defence of the gap was the fire of the 122nd Heavy Battery at Frezenberg, with the 37th Howitzer Battery, already made famous at Le Cateau, and the first howitzers in the British Army. They were escorted by a company of the 8/Middlesex and a section of the 6th Battery C.F.A. came up on to the Zonnebeke Ridge, firing over open sights at 1,500 yards until all ammunition was spent. When it was withdrawn, sections were brought up from the 356th and 367th Batteries from the 28th Division, and their unceasing fire, though so parlously short of ammunition, kept the enemy at bay.

Frezenberg Ridge, 1915

The 83rd Brigade held the forward slope of the Frezenberg Ridge, on either side of the Zonnebeke Railway, suffering, in the words of a battalion diary, " a hard and cruel time " while the Germans strove to overwhelm the sparsely held line that defended Ypres in April 1915, when the retirement of our Allies had opened up the flank of our army. On the morning of the 8th May the enemy opened with an annihilating bombardment of high explosives—the British were without any to speak of—and after an hour of terrible shell fire his infantry stormed against the exposed slope of the ridge where the 3/Monmouthshires, the 2/King's Own, and 1/Suffolks wonderfully drove them back. Again the storm swept up ; again it was driven back, but in the heroic stand nearly every man was killed, wounded, or buried. No reinforcement could live on the forward slopes, and after three hours an order was received to evacuate the front trenches—what was left of them. The few of the 3/Monmouths still living counter-attacked, led by Colonel H. W. Worsley Gough, and then withdrew to the support trenches behind the Ridge.   Lieut. A. R. S. Martin was killed commanding the King's Own, his men clinging on to the front line until they were overwhelmed, when the survivors also moved to the support trench. On either side the Germans could come no farther in face of the rifle fire and shrapnel that met them as they topped the Ridge. The 2/East Yorkshires, only 228 strong, and the 5/King's Own pushed up in support, and the report went up that the battalions were to retire to G.H.Q. line. Some parties received the order, but the greater number did not, and fought on desperately until they were surrounded. These battalions had been called on by General Plumer to hold on at all costs, and magnificent was their response, though by this time there were many half-trained and inexperienced officers and men among them.

That night the 3/Monmouths mustered 4 officers and 130 men ; the 2/King's Own 4 officers and 94 other ranks ; the 1/K.O.Y.L.I. had lost 427 all ranks.

Between Frezenberg and Mouse-Trap Farm

Terrible disaster overwhelmed the 84th Brigade on the 8th May 1915, where the British battalions clung to their trenches under enormous shell fire from Zonnebeke Ridge. The 2/Cheshires were annihilated. Major A. B. Stone and all the three companies in the front line were killed or captured with nearly the whole of the battalion headquarters. One hundred men under

FREZENBERG AND MOUSE-TRAP FARM—*continued.*

two 2nd Lieutenants mustered in G.H.Q. line. The enemy
infantry, following on the devastating shell fire, worked forward
where the 1/Suffolks were fighting tenaciously in small detachments isolated in the front line, until their C.O., Lieut.-Colonel
H. B. Wallace, with 11 officers and 432 men were casualties.
One officer and 29 men mustered next day. The 1/Monmouth-
shire, attacked on right flank and rear, threw back a defensive
flank. The Germans trained a machine gun upon them from a
house which overlooked their trench, but nothing could shift the
gallant miners who formed the greater part of the battalion.
Colonel Robinson was shot dead while passing his men down
the trench one by one in the hope of forming a new front. Half
the officers and men were already on the ground. The Germans
stormed on the top of them with cries of " Surrender ! Surrender ! "—" Surrender be damned ! " shouted Captain Edwards,
and died firing with his revolver into the field-grey masses.
Only 120 men out of 750 reassembled that night.

While these battalions were fighting to the death on the
forward slope, the 12/London (Rangers) were sent up to reinforce
them. They were but 200 strong, but they went through the
barrage of H.E. shells, and over the flat top of Frezenberg Ridge,
falling in heaps by the way, never halting for a moment, and
some of them even succeeded in joining the Monmouths in their
desperate stand. The crew of their one machine gun was wiped
out, and a Monmouthshire officer worked it successfully, covering
the exposed flank until it was put out of action. But this gallant
Territorial battalion ceased to exist as a unit on this dreadful
field, and after three weeks in the Salient, only 53 men of the
Rangers, under Sergeant Hornall, survived to answer the roll-call
that night.

Frezenberg, 1915

On the critical day of " Second Ypres," the 8th May, the
3/Monmouth were in the apex of the Salient east of Frezenberg
between the 2/King's Own and the 1/K.O.Y.L.I. The brigade
had not been out of the line since the 17th April, and its numbers
were already greatly reduced. It was a thin line—only two
divisions, the 27th and 28th—between the enemy and Ypres.
Our position was rendered more desperate by shortage of heavy
artillery : " It is now authoritatively stated that during the
second battle of Ypres we had one 9·2 howitzer, eight 60-pounders,
four old 6-inch howitzers, and twelve 4·7's. Against these twenty-
five guns . . . the enemy brought into action 183 guns, consisting

FREZENBERG—*continued.*

of one 16-inch howitzer, twenty-four 8-inch howitzers, eighty-four 6-inch howitzers, eight 5·2 guns, and forty-eight old heavies."

The enemy guns opened a bombardment early in the morning of the 8th May, and attacked with infantry once and again, only to be twice driven off. Another hour's terrific shelling wiped out our front-line trenches, and about 10 a.m. the Monmouths received orders to evacuate. The survivors of " A " Company began to withdraw, but were swept away by machine gun and shrapnel, Captain Baker being killed with his men. A few under Lieut. Read never got the order, and with some machine gunners gallantly carried on, fighting to the last, until Lieut. Read was killed. No officer of " A " Company and only 13 men mustered after the battle. " D " Company held their line indomitably, their only officer, Captain Lancaster, and every sergeant killed ; only 16 men survived. But few of the machine gunners came out of the slaughter, and they brought back the lock of one gun ; the other was destroyed. Colonel Gough gathered up " C " Company that had been forced back from support owing to the exposure of their left flank, and with some stragglers collected by Sergeant Jenkins, led a counter-attack reaching the western edge of Frezenberg. Here they held up the enemy's advance until Brigade orders came to fall back on G.H.Q. line near Potijze. The M.O.s of the 3/ and 1/Monmouths (in action farther north), Lieut. Maclean and Lieut. Marrack, stuck to their dressing-station east of Verlorenhoek long after the order to retire came, while stretcher-bearers kept bringing in the wounded. They carried on till the Germans reached the village, when Lieut. Maclean was hit. In the afternoon the remnants of the battalion went up in support of a counter-attack, and reached a line from Verlorenhoek to the railway. Fresh troops came up in the night, this line was consolidated, and was held as our front line until our advance two years later.

The 83rd Brigade had lost between 23rd April and 8th May 128 officers and 4,379 men. The 600 left were formed into one composite battalion under Lieut.-Colonel Gough, and on the 11th May marched back to bivouac in fields east of Poperinghe.

Frezenberg, 1915 [1]

On the night of the 12th May the Queen's Bays, together with the rest of the 1st Cavalry Brigade, moved into the front line in the Ypres Salient. The line held by the regiment was on the left of the Ypres—Verlorenhoek Road in the immediate

[1] From regimental contribution.

FREZENBERG—*continued*.

neighbourhood of Frezenberg, about half a mile in front of Potijze Château.

On taking over the line it was found that the trenches were shallow, the parapets not bullet-proof, and there was a complete absence of wire. On completion of the relief, work was immediately started on improving them ; but having deepened them by about a foot, this had to be stopped owing to the fact that the water level had been reached, and the presence of a number of corpses. The night was exceedingly quiet, and our covering parties and patrols encountered no German activity, and before dawn on the 13th stand-to took place without incident

Shortly after dawn, however, a series of green lights were sent up from the German front line. Immediately following this signal a terrific bombardment of our trench line commenced ; all calibres appeared to be firing, but the proportion of heavy howitzers was very marked.

Their fire was unpleasantly accurate, and by 7 a.m. the whole of the left half of " B " Squadron's trench had been blown in, all No. 1 Troop being killed with the exception of the troop sergeant and one man, while many of No. 4 Troop were killed and buried.

The fire continued with increasing intensity, the enemy scoring continuous direct hits on the trench line held by the regiment.

The steadiness of the men under these trying conditions calls for the highest praise, especially since they had no opportunity of retaliation, and they knew that our artillery support was of the feeblest nature, owing to lack of ammunition. At about 10 a.m. the enemy's infantry were seen to be advancing, and the order was given to fix bayonets and to open fire.

All the morning the greatest difficulty had been experienced in keeping the rifles in working order, owing to the clouds of mud thrown up by the bursting shells which clogged the bolts. The men were therefore ordered to tear pieces off their shirts in order to clean and protect them.

The regiment, who had been holding the position on the right of the main road, were now shelled out of their trenches, and retired ; but Major Ing gallantly got out of his trench and, standing on the main road in the face of a terrific fire, shepherded them into our trenches, where they were used to fill up the depleted ranks of " B " Squadron.

For this fine action Major Ing was awarded the D.S.O.

By this time the fire was intense and parties of the enemy were observed working round our right flank. The 10th Hussars

FREZENBERG—*continued.*

were sent up to counter-attack and establish the line on our right, which with the aid of an armoured car they endeavoured to do with the greatest gallantry, but could only succeed in occupying a line somewhat rear of our flank. In the meantime, however, the enemy were observed advancing on our immediate front, and fire was straightway opened on them, the men cheering at having at last an opportunity of retaliating, after the hours of enduring an appalling hail of shells. Unfortunately, at this juncture, the regiment on the left of " B " Squadron retired, having been shelled out of their trenches, and the whole of our left flank was exposed.

So successfully was the fire directed that the enemy were frustrated in their effort to occupy the vacated lines, and though they succeeded in reaching at one point to within 150 yards, they were compelled to retire after a few moments. The German infantry did not again attack, and though a very heavy bombardment of our line continued until 5 o'clock, contented themselves in consolidating their original advanced positions. The action of the regiment in holding its ground, and beating off a determined attack while both its flanks were unsupported, without doubt saved a very dangerous situation.

The Queen's Bays suffered severely during its gallant stand, 2 officers and 28 other ranks being killed and 1 officer and 28 other ranks being wounded, while the total strength did not amount to more than 250 all ranks on going into the line.

In addition to these casualties mention must be made of a detachment of the 19th London Sanitary Section, R.A.M.C., T.F., consisting of one officer and twelve other ranks who were attached to the Bays for anti-gas measures. Each man was equipped with a Vermorel sprayer ostensibly to clear gas from the trenches, and while probably quite efficient in this rôle was not a very efficient weapon with which to help repulse an attack of the German infantry. The whole detachment were killed at their posts.

At nightfall the remnants of " B " Squadron were relieved by " A " Squadron. Luckily the whole of the next day was quiet, and on the night of the 14th/15th May the 1st Brigade was relieved by the 9th Cavalry Brigade and went back to Vlamertinghe for a well-earned rest.

Frezenberg, 1917

General Thuillier brought the 15th Division up to the battle of 31st July in a condition of freshness and vigour that bore

FREZENBERG—*continued.*

marked result in the attacks of the day. To achieve this, he
planned and carried out the very ticklish manœuvre of keeping
only two battalions in the front line for two days before the
battle, the remaining troops resting in bivouac until the last
moment. He relied on these troops to make their way up
into the line just before zero hour ; and in spite of the difficulty
of following tracks in the dark through the shell-swept zone,
they carried the plan out, and were at their battle positions at
the given hour. At 3.45 in heavy thundery weather the advance
was launched and moved forward rapidly, capturing the first
objective, the German front line having been demolished by our
shells. Soon after 5 o'clock the advance swept on to the second
objective, a line east of Frezenberg. This village and North
Station Buildings presented a strong front, but wire around
them was well cut, and the Black Watch and Gordons fought
through the heavy fire, captured Frezenberg, and came to the
objective " black line." A tank named Challenger succeeded in
coming up through the quaking mud, and dealt drastically with
the fortified houses—a great help in gaining the village. Most
of the other tanks were bogged, and smashed by gun fire.

Frezenberg Redoubt was gained by the K.O.S.B. after severe
fighting ; this concrete emplacement lay behind the Ridge, and
the Borderers met tremendous fire as they topped it. Held up
in the direct line, a company worked round, and captured the
strong-point from the north. The fresh advance at 10.18 drove
on to the final objective—from Potsdam to Gallipoli Copse.
The 6/7 Royal Scots Fusiliers on the right, and 6th Camerons on
the left, led off; with the 11/Argyll and Sutherland Highlanders
and 13/Royal Scots in support. The Camerons met a horrible
obstacle east of Beck House, a belt of uncut wire 2 feet high and
10 yards thick, and the leading waves very remarkably cut their
way through, keeping up with the barrage. They reached the
objective " green line " against a strong resistance, and when
their C.O., Lieut.-Colonel J. C. Russell and his Adjutant were
killed, they fought on, clinging to the position they had gained,
without any orders, for many hours. The Royal Scots Fusiliers
found their right flank uncovered as they advanced, and gained
a precarious position above Potsdam and Bremen Redoubt.
At midday the Camerons also found themselves outflanked, from
the north, and fell back until Colonel Hannay with two and a
half companies of the Royal Scots came up, threw out a defensive
flank, and ordered the line, now east of Beck House, to be held
" no matter what happened on either flank." Vickers guns were

FREZENBERG—*continued.*

sent up, and the 12/Highland Light Infantry were ordered to
support if required, in reply to a call for reinforcements. The
heavy fire of this mixed force held the enemy, and towards evening
all attacks died down.

Next morning it was found that there existed a gap between
the Royal Scots and the Seaforths at Berry Farm, and before the
latter could close up an enemy attack was made in great strength
and pierced between the battalions. Captain Christie of the
Royal Scots flung out a defensive flank with every rifle he could
collect, facing south from Beck House ; and held on till he was
wounded and Captain Logan killed, when the party, gradually
overwhelmed, fell back, the enemy retaking Beck House. Two
Vickers guns remained behind covering the Royal Scots, and
only one man of the teams came back. He had last seen his
officer standing firing his revolver at the enemy within a dozen
yards. Colonel Hannay at Square House Farm immediately
formed up his headquarters staff to counter-attack, with eleven
guns from the 46th Machine-gun Company. The Scots Fusiliers
and the Argylls, the former reduced to 130 all ranks, were sent
up to recapture the " black line," hold, and consolidate. The
Argylls, exhausted and soaked to the skin, attacked in the darkness, gained the position, and dug in. They held the whole front
line all next day, the remnants of the Royal Scots and Camerons
being withdrawn.

During these events on the left, the flank of the battalions on
the south had been exposed, and the right of the 8/10 Gordons,
fighting hard, moved back to the crest of Frezenberg Ridge ;
their left and the Seaforth beyond them standing firm. The
Adjutant, Lieut. Geddes, in Battalion H.Q. behind the Ridge,
gathered every available man, and made a defence about North
Station building ; only thirty men of this party survived, and
the Germans came within 200 yards of the crest. At this moment
the leading company of the 7/Camerons (coming up in support
under Captain Symons) appeared on the Ridge, and the reserve
company of the Seaforth under Lieut. Brodie arrived from north-
west. Lieut. Geddes mustered his remnant, and together all
the Scotsmen charged the right flank of the Germans ; the
artillery drew the barrage close in, and the enemy, taken utterly
by surprise, broke and fled.

The battle died down that evening, and when the division
was relieved the front line had been advanced 2,000 yards, and
Frezenberg Ridge held and securely consolidated, but the
battalions were reduced to skeleton strength.

Frezenberg, Beck House Farm, 1917

The 42nd East Lancashire Division made a very gallant but abortive attack on the 6th September on the fortified posts known as Iberian, Berry, and Beck House Farms. The German positions were known only very vaguely, and Sergeant Finney, of the 8/Lancashire Fusiliers, went out to reconnoitre in broad daylight, with a rifle grenadier and two Lewis gunners. They got to within 25 yards of Beck House under observation of the enemy for the final 100 yards ; they worked forward until rifle fire forced them to withdraw and lie down in No-man's-land. Alone next night Sergeant Finney returned to this post, and lay for hours studying the enemy movements during the night. Not only did he gain valuable information, but the enemy seemed to have been disturbed by his bold advance, and sent up so many fireworks in the dark hours that the German dispositions were brilliantly illuminated for our observation.

In this area a covering party found a wounded private of the Inniskilling Fusiliers lying out in No-man's-land. He had been there for thirty-one days. He was without food, and only just able to creep laboriously from one poor body to another, managing to live on just such meagre rations as this dolorous pilgrimage discovered.

FROST HOUSE. (See PASSCHENDAELE.)

GAPAARD. (See WARNETON.)

GHELUVELT. (See MENIN ROAD.)

GLENCORSE WOOD. (See MENIN ROAD, " Nonne Bosschen Battle.")

GLIMPSE COTTAGE. (See MENIN ROAD.)

GLOUCESTER FARM. (See POELCAPPELLE.)

GRAND BOIS. (See WYTSCHAETE.)

GRAVENSTAFEL, 1915

The Buffs, after their engagement at Wieltje in April, rejoined the 85th Brigade at Verlorenhoek. Reinforcements came out from home, much needed by the hard-hit battalion. On the 1st May a draft arrived, and there being no time to detail the men, they were all put together in a new support trench in front of a wood. There followed the most scathing ordeal for fresh young soldiers, without the stiffening of any veteran fighters. An

GRAVENSTAFEL—*continued*.

extraordinarily violent storm of shell fire burst upon this trench
the day after their arrival, one trench mortar concentrating on
the position.   The parapet was blown to pieces, and an attack
in force surged into the line where were very few of the English.
Eighty of " C " Company, under Captain Howard Smith, had
been overcome, nearly all killed or wounded and missing.   The
enemy were all round the trench firing from a wood in the rear,
but were held up by a few of the Buffs and a company of Royal
Fusiliers.   The trench was valiantly held under enfilade fire
from Heavies of all calibres, and at last the Buffs were obliged
to retire along the line.   Steadily they moved down, the Germans
pressing upon them until they had come within a few yards.
Men were falling rapidly, the odds were too great, and the little
company fell back.   Then Company Sergeant-Major Port and
Private Campbell turned back and stood to cover their retirement and intrepidly held the enemy back until the rest had got
away.   They both very wonderfully escaped with their lives.

It was impossible after these days of fighting to ascertain
the exact casualties, and in the case of the new drafts so hurriedly
rushed into the battle, the names were not even known.

Gravenstafel, 1915

In April 1915 the line between Zonnebeke and Polygon Wood
was held by the 28th Division.   North-west of the Canadians
was the great gap left by the French Colonial troops when overwhelmed by the first gas attack ; and five reserve battalions
were sent up on the 23rd April as our first reinforcement.   The
3/Middlesex attacked and Colonel Stevenson was killed, calling
out to his men at the last, " Die hard, boys ! Die hard ! " The
division was in a very weakened condition owing to the withdrawal of the troops to the emergency point, and for the following
four days the line was manned with one man to each twelve
yards.   The battle here reached its crisis on the 25th April,
when the 85th Brigade with the Middlesex on their left fought
fiercely round Gravenstafel, and by evening had to draw back a
little distance near Broodseinde.   A short lull followed, to be
broken on the 1st May by a tremendous bombardment that
burst upon the line between Gravenstafel and Zonnebeke.   The
Germans came to within ten yards of our trenches, and under
great difficulties our bulging line was shortened, and straightened
out on Frezenberg Ridge.   Another terrific bombardment and
very heavy attack followed on the 8th, and some ground was
lost, and regained by a furious attack of the brigade.   The

GRAVENSTAFEL—*continued*.

Middlesex recaptured their trench, led by a sergeant with the cry, " Never say die, Middlesex," and a yard at a time they forced their way ahead and regained their position. As they got into the trench the sight of their comrades lying unwounded and dead—suffocated by the first gas—drove the men to a reckless fury that swept the enemy away, and won back the line. When the division was relieved, four days later, only one battalion had a colonel in command, many being now in charge of captains.

Gravenstafel Ridge,[1] 1915

The 1/Hampshires were part of the 11th Brigade whose eight-day defence of Gravenstafel Ridge under unceasing and terrific bombardment in April 1915 has been described in the Foreword to Second Ypres. An officer who was present contributes the following account of the stand :

" In the afternoon of the 26th April the expected bombardment started. The most polished writer can never describe adequately a really big shelling, because such a thing is indescribable. For eight days in succession, for hours on end, several batteries concentrated on our line. With every advantage of position and observation, and with little or no retaliation, the German gunners had the time of their lives. Every type of gun, from 8-inch downwards, was employed, and ' stink-shells ' were freely used. It was amazing that the trench and its occupants were not blotted out, for entire batteries of those magnificent 5·9 guns would be directed on a small sector.

On the first day there were about a hundred casualties, and the trenches were badly damaged. Headquarters had a narrow escape, the C.O., Adjutant, and some orderlies being half-buried by the explosion of a big shell. At nightfall there was much to be done. The trenches had to be repaired and improved, water, rations, and ammunition had to be fetched, and the wounded had to be collected and carried back many miles, for no vehicle could approach our position. It was a strange sight to see the ' Verey ' lights almost completely in a circle around us. It was only towards dawn on the 27th that the rest of the brigade came up on our left and effectively closed the gap.

The enemy made no attempt at infantry attack, possibly because of our tenacity, but we always had to be ready.

On the 29th the bombardment increased in intensity and casualties were again severe. The whole position was clearly untenable.

On the 3rd May the German artillery surpassed itself. From

1 From regimental contribution.

GRAVENSTAFEL—*continued.*

3 a.m. our whole position was subjected to a most terrible bombardment. For hour after hour and from every angle, tons of metal were hurled upon us. There was practically no reply from our own guns. It was obvious that an infantry attack was in preparation, and at 3 p.m., after twelve hours' bombardment, it came. For some minutes previously the enemy had concentrated his fire on the Buffs, and he then assaulted and carried the wood in spite of a gallant resistance. An attack was then made on us, and on the Fusiliers on our right. It melted away before our fire, for the men were fully prepared. The enemy had been seen erecting his gas apparatus, but whether on account of our fire or because the wind was unfavourable, the gas failed to appear. The attack had been beaten off decisively and it was not repeated, although the heavy bombardment was maintained for some hours. Captain C. F. H. Twining was killed during the evening.

That night the withdrawal was made to a shorter line previously ordered by the Army Commander, for it had been recognised that the exposed salient could not be held. A few weeks later Sir John French told us on parade that ' No finer work had been done in the War than the defence of the Gravenstafel Ridge.' "

GROENBURG FARM. (See SHREWSBURY FOREST.)

HALF-WAY HOUSE. (See ZONNEBEKE.)

HELL FIRE CORNER. (See MENIN ROAD.)

HERONTHAGE. (See MENIN ROAD.)

HILL 60, 1915

THE CAPTURE AND DEFENCE OF HILL 60

[The Queen's Own Royal West Kent Regiment, the Duke of Wellington's Regiment, the East Surrey Regiment, and the Bedfordshire Regiment have contributed accounts of their share in the capture and defence of the Hill, as being an achievement in the Salient in which they take a special pride. The following narrative has been compiled from these accounts, chiefly descriptions by officers who were present at the battle ; and from other sources.]

" Hill 60 " in 1914 was merely a low ridge some 150 feet high, and 250 yards from end to end, formed artificially when the

HILL 60—*continued*.

railway cutting was dug ; receiving this name from our troops
as signifying its height in metres on the contour map. Its
military importance was due to its being the highest point in
this area, and consequently commanding views in every direction.
The Germans had captured it from the French on 10th December
1914, and soon after the British had taken over from the latter,
in February 1915, it was decided to recapture the position, as
from it the Germans could completely overlook our defences
and detect our movements in this part of the line. The 13th
Infantry Brigade, under Brigadier-General Wanless O'Gowan,
which formed part of the original B.E.F. and had been through
a trying time of hard work and exhausting trench warfare, was
ordered to make the attack, and carried on after very thorough
preliminary preparations.

During the night of 16th April 1915 the Brigade took over
the trenches. The 1/Royal West Kent, detailed to capture the
hill (which had previously been mined by the 171st Tunnelling
Company) and the 2nd K.O.S.B.s were in the front line; the
2/Duke of Wellington's in support near Zillebeke Lake, and the
2/K.O.Y.L.I. in reserve.

April 17th was a quiet day of hot and brilliant sunshine ; not
a shot on either side disturbed the stillness. Suddenly, at
7.5 p.m., the ground shook as with an earthquake, with a tearing
roar clouds of earth and stones rose from the summit of the
hill, and a deafening crash of bombardment broke the silence.
Two pairs and one single mine were exploded at ten seconds'
interval, and simultaneously, in one mighty salvo, the guns of
the 15th and 17th Field Artillery and 9th Heavy Artillery
Brigades, the 130th Howitzer Battery, the 28th Heavy Battery,
with two batteries of French and three of Belgian artillery opened
fire. As the last mine was fired, "C" Co. of the R.W. Kents
sprang from their trenches with a cheer, and charging straight
up with fixed bayonets, stormed the hill, whilst sappers of the
2nd Home Counties Field Company, detailed as a working party,
also swept into the charge, fighting with picks and spades. The
success was complete, and within three minutes the crest was
occupied with few casualties on our side. The effect of the
mines had been practically to demolish the top of the hill, the
enemy's trenches having given place to great craters on the lips
of which our working parties started with vigour to throw up
the necessary defences. The German garrison had been almost
wiped out ; such as remained greeted the attackers with cries
of " West Kents ! West Kents ! " showing that the attack had

HILL 60—*continued.*

been expected and the name of the assaulting regiment known. Some of the wounded had been nearly buried, and seemed to think they would be shot instead of being dug out. One pleaded for mercy, saying that in the days of peace he used to bake bread in the Old Kent Road.

" B " Company of the R.W. Kents now joined " C " on the hill, and a trench was dug along the easternmost brow. At about 10 p.m. the German artillery started shelling the hill, and the bombardment gradually increased until fire from some 54 different gun-positions was concentrated on the captured ground. The work of connecting the flanks with our old trench line was proceeded with, and by 2.30 a.m. the position was reported as having been consolidated. The artillery bombardment, however, was but the prelude to a counter-attack. The Germans naturally knew every inch of the ground, and creeping up from all directions, started an attack with hand grenades of the " hair-brush " pattern, whilst on another part of our front they launched a bayonet charge. Meanwhile the fire of their artillery was lifted to prevent supports or reserves reaching us, most of their shells falling in our recently vacated trenches. The bayonet attack was more easily dealt with than the bombing, as the enemy got our bayonets in return for theirs, the result being that in that sector the German casualties were heavy, whilst ours were very small indeed ; the bombing attack was harder to deal with, as the night was dark, " Verey " lights were few in those days, and the enemy could not be seen clearly enough to bring effective fire to bear, though one of our machine guns was doing good work, and the men shooting wherever they could see a target.

During the early morning of the 18th the K.O.S.B.s were sent up in relief, and at this critical moment the Germans launched a further counter-attack under a storm of artillery fire, in which the R.W.K.s suffered their heaviest casualties. Those of " B " and " C " Companies who were left stayed on the hill, and continued to share the defence with the K.O.S.B.s. One platoon of " C " was practically annihilated, and " D " Company was sent up to reinforce as the German attack became more violent. " A " Company also went up, taking a large quantity of ammunition of which the K.O.S.B.s were running short. The two largest craters were desperately contested, but the battalions held on with indomitable gallantry under an ever-increasing intensity of artillery fire. High explosive, shrapnel, trench-mortar bombs, hand grenades, machine-gun and rifle bullets

HILL 60—*continued.*

swept and searched the hill, but the attack was repulsed, and still the defence held.   Over 50 per cent. of the officers and men of the R.W. Kents had become casualties, and at length the remnants of the battalion were withdrawn.

Sir John French in a speech to the troops said : " The two battalions held that hill throughout the long night.   In the morning they had to throw back a series of the most violent counter-attacks of the enemy, who knew the worth of that hill when he was turned out of it ; he used every means to get it back. . . . At last it was necessary to relieve them ; they had done enough, their time had come ; but I am convinced they would have stayed till the last man."

On the 17th April the 2/Duke of Wellington's Regiment was billeted in Ypres, where life hitherto (with the exception of periodical shelling of the cathedral and the fine old Cloth Hall) had been comparatively normal.   As the mines under Hill 60 were fired, orders were received to move up to Zillebeke in support of the attack.   At 3 a.m. on the 18th the leading company (" A ") was ordered up into the line and took over the advanced craters, and at 6 a.m. the remainder of the battalion relieved the R. West Kents and the K.O.S.B.s.   " A " Company in its advanced position suffered badly owing to the proximity of the enemy, who had gained a lodgment on the hill ; but the weary men, supported on their outer flank by their fellow-Yorkshiremen of the 2nd K.O.Y.L.I., continued to hang on stubbornly. During the morning the C.O., Lieut.-Colonel Turner, with his Adjutant, Lieut. Ince, with a couple of orderlies, visited these advanced trenches—a most precarious journey, as the shallow communication trench leading to them was blocked with dead and wounded, and for part of the way they were in full view of the enemy.   None of the small party, however, was hit, and on his return Colonel Turner ordered " B " Company, augmented by one platoon from each of " C " and " D " Companies, to reinforce " A," which by this time had been nearly wiped out.

The rest of the day was spent by the Germans in strengthening their hold, and by the British in preparing for a renewed assault.   This second assault, more formidable in many respects than the first, since it was undertaken against an expectant enemy, was fixed for 6 p.m.   At this hour " B," " C," and " D " Companies, with two companies of the K.O.Y.L.I., at a given signal rose to their feet, and with a rousing cheer rushed forward. The losses of the storming party were heavy, but nothing could stop them.   " B " Company, only, reached its objective without

HILL 60—*continued.*

much difficulty, but lost Lieut. Owen. " C " had to charge
over some 50 yards of open ground, and suffered very heavily,
only Captain Barton and eleven men being left out of a hundred ;
but none the less they captured the trenches allotted to them,
killing and taking prisoner a number of the enemy. Privates
Behan and Dryden of this company particularly distinguished
themselves, taking charge after their platoon officers and sergeants
had been killed or wounded. They both received the D.C.M.
" D " Company, in touch with their comrades of the K.O.Y.L.I.,
had some distance to charge over the open, and lost all their
officers at the start, Captain Taylor, Lieut. Thackeray, and
2nd Lieut. Croft being killed, and 2nd Lieuts. Crisp and Cheetham
wounded. After a fierce struggle the Germans were once more
ejected, and the whole crest of the hill held by our troops. Their
losses had been grievous, the various craters formed by the
mines and heavy shells being desperately fought for by either
side. About 7 p.m. the Yorkshiremen of both regiments drew
together in the dusk and made an organised charge across the
whole length of the hill, sweeping it clear of the enemy from
end to end, while the sappers of the 59th Company R.E. worked
vigorously in helping to consolidate the position. It was a
desperate tussle, the men fighting hand-to-hand, and hurling
bombs at a range of a few yards into each others' faces. Seldom
in the War had there been more furious fighting. By this time
the men were utterly exhausted, but the German defence being
for the time completely broken, advantage was taken to send
up fresh troops. The casualties already numbered some 50
officers and 1,500 men, and they lay, with as many Germans,
within a space no larger than an ordinary-sized meadow.

The 1/Battalion East Surrey Regiment, which belonged to
the 15th Infantry Brigade, commanded by Brig.-General Northey,
took over the defence at 5 a.m. on the 19th, relieving the Yorkshiremen, and at once set vigorously to work to clear the trenches
of dead and wounded, and as far as possible to improve the
defences, the latter a somewhat hazardous task, as within 20
yards of our trench lay a German strong-point provided with
steel loopholes from which any man who showed over the parapet
was at once sniped. Five men in succession were shot through
the head while attempting to bring rifle fire to bear on this point.
As soon as it was full daylight and the morning mists had lifted,
a furious bombardment was directed by the enemy over the
crest and reverse slopes of the hill—a bombardment which
wrought great destruction among our already sorely battered

HILL 60—*continued.*

defences. During the afternoon a new phenomenon was observed
for the first time—an indication, had it been realised, of what
was to come later. Officers and men seated in a dugout behind
the fighting line experienced a strange feeling of suffocation, and
were driven from their shelter, some lighted candles in which
were extinguished by noxious fumes, whilst shells, bursting on
the hill itself, set the troops coughing and gasping for breath.
It was the first German experiment in the use of poison gas.
Attacked by this new and unaccountable scourge, the battalion
nevertheless still held on, and during the night carried on the
work of repairing their ruined trenches to the best of their ability.

The 20th April was a further day of furious bombardment,
many trenches being obliterated, and men killed and buried by
the explosions. One shell alone that morning blew in a parapet
and buried Lieut. Watson with 20 men. At the height of the
bombardment Captain Wynyard, seeing some men helping the
wounded in a particularly exposed spot, ran to them, moved
them away from the danger-zone, and returning, attended to
the wounded men himself until he was killed by a shell. At
3 p.m. the enemy attempted an advance from a saphead, and
protected as they were by the snipers in the strong-point, things
for the moment looked dangerous at this point of the line.
Private E. Dwyer,[1] however, saved the situation by leaping
boldly right on to the parapet and flinging bombs into the strong-
point. This enabled his comrades to man their parapet and
repulse the attack. The top of the hill was now in an appalling
state, enveloped in the flame and smoke of shells which burst
incessantly. Trenches had been battered out of existence, bits
of wire, broken equipment, and debris of all sorts littered the
ground, whilst on all sides lay the bodies of the dead and wounded,
crushed into the mud. Every telephone line was cut hopelessly,
and all communications ceased. The Headquarters dugout of
the battalion was hit by a heavy shell and destroyed, the commanding officer and second-in-command being killed, and only
a corporal and one signaller left fit for duty. In the advanced
line " A " Company, under Lieut. Roupell, suffered heavily, the
platoon on the right flank having been buried by an explosion
which had wrecked their trench, whilst reinforcements coming
up under Lieut. Abercrombie had actually to cut their way
through the remains of this platoon in order to connect up the
trench, many men being lost from shrapnel fire while doing so.

The 1/Bedfords, who, after having spent twenty-four hours on

[1] He was awarded the Victoria Cross.

HILL 60—*continued.*

the hill on the 19th, had been withdrawn into support, now arrived at the foot of the hill in the nick of time, having been sent forward to reinforce the woefully depleted defenders ; and a party of them worked their way up and occupied one of the craters. Joining up with two platoons of the East Surreys, the Bedfords attempted to get through to " A " Company in the advanced trench, but were unable to do so. This trench was most gallantly held by the Surreys, the few survivors again and again stopping the assaulting Germans by their rapid fire. 2nd Lieut. Geary,[1] with a platoon of " C " Company and the men of the Bedfords, held the craters, repelling all attacks made on them. Corporal Adams, though single-handed owing to the rest of his team having been killed, and himself severely wounded, with part of his jaw shot away, fought his machine gun for over half an hour until he too was killed by a bullet through the head.

By 7.30 p.m. the enemy's bombers had worked their way into broken ground within 20 yards, and began a most harassing attack, which tried the half-stupefied troops to the utmost, but was nevertheless held at bay. When darkness set in, and the shelling had diminished somewhat, Lieut. Roupell, though wounded in eight places, succeeded in making his way back to the headquarters of the sector to explain the desperate situation, then gallantly went forward again to resume command of " A " Company, being the only officer left.[2]

Soon after midnight on the 21st the Brigadier received a report that the 1/Surreys in the trenches to the left had lost all their officers except one subaltern, and that there was a rumour that the company was falling back. A message, based on this supposition, eventually reached them, and brought forth the curt answer : " We have not budged a yard, and have no intention whatever of doing so." At 2.30 a.m. the situation seemed very precarious, so fierce was the assault and so worn the defence ; but this was the culminative point of the German effort, the fury of the battle gradually died down, and at 6 a.m. these trenches were handed over to the 1/Battalion Devonshire Regiment, and the survivors, weary but singing ragtime music, limped back to their rest-camps in the rear.

Throughout these hours the 1/Bedfords, assisting in the defence, hung grimly to their trenches through a hail of shell fire. They were on the Hill under Colonel Griffiths from 2 p.m. on the 20th when, during the height of the bombardment that was sweeping

---

[1] He was awarded the V.C.   [2] Also awarded the V.C.

HILL 60—*continued.*

over the ground, news was received that the C.O. Adjutant, and
all the senior officers of the East Surreys were killed, and assistance
being asked for, the Bedfords came forward just in time to meet
a German attack. The bombardment of the hill continued all
day and through the night, ceasing occasionally to enable German
patrols to work forward to see if any British were still living.
They advanced with bombs and machine guns, only to be
repulsed every time. The hill had become a shambles ; the
fire concentrated on it swept men away by groups, but others
at once filled the gaps without waiting for orders. An exaltation
seemed to possess them. Lieut. Webb of the Bedfords, going
forward to certain destruction, was heard to exclaim : " Anyway,
it will be a glorious death." Major Lees arrived with a company
of the 9th London Regiment (Queen Victoria's Rifles). They
were really a carrying party, and had no bayonets. It being
imperative to drive the Germans from a trench they had taken,
and only a few Bedfords being left, Major Lees gallantly led
forward the Q.V.R.s, headed by the survivors of the Bedfords,
and regained the trench, but at the sacrifice of his life. It was
on this day that the Q.V.R.s, under Colonel Shipley, added lustre
to the reputation of the Territorial Army by their admirable
steadiness. At one time during the day a handful of Territorials
of the Q.V.R. under Lieut. Woolley were the only troops on the
actual crest of the hill, but they held it against all attacks, Lieut.
Woolley being the first Territorial officer to win the V.C.

And so the struggle went on during the night ; enemy machine
guns enfiladed and even took one part of the hill in reverse,
trench mortars and mine throwers fired incessantly, whilst field
guns, brought within 300 yards, fired point-blank at the parapet,
blowing it to pieces and flinging shattered khaki figures in all
directions. At one moment, during the early morning of the
21st, the front line wavered, and by sheer weight of numbers
was on the point of being pressed back. Only 20 Bedfordshire
men were left in reserve, but with a cheer they ran forward, and
the line held firm. British guns, which had by now, with infinite
toil, been run up to close range, silenced the German guns for
the time being, and drove their infantry to cover, thus bringing about a definite lull in the fighting. With daylight the
1/Devons took over the defence, and an hour later the hill was
clear of the enemy once more, save for a few snipers concealed
in the north-west corner. The death-roll by this time had been
doubled, 100 officers and 3,000 of our men being the price paid
to hold that little ridge, now littered with bodies and red with

HILL 60—*continued.*

blood from end to end. In vain the enemy tried again and again to win back a foothold, but nothing could shift the tenacious Devonshire men. The German field guns, brought within close range, fired at the hastily repaired parapets, but the Devons lay flat and held tight. The British guns which had been run up during the night opened fire once again, and finally and completely silenced those of the enemy, whilst bombers who still lurked in the craters were routed out with the bayonet. At last the battle was drawing to a close. During the afternoon of the 21st hostile fire gradually died away, and the enemy's assaults came to an end. On the morning of the 22nd the 2/Cameron Highlanders, under Colonel Campbell, took over the trenches, and the hill remained intact in British hands.

Such is the story of Hill 60—a spot to which the words of Napier in regard to our " astonishing infantry " at the battle of Albuera, 104 years before almost to a day, may fitly be applied ; for there, if anywhere, was seen " with what a strength and majesty the British soldier fights."

EPILOGUE

Through the wild days of furious battle already related, the contest for the hill had been an epic of valour, when man met man in desperate fight ; and the British soldier established his ascendancy over the Prussian and once more proved his capacity to stay it out to the bitter end, though tried to the uttermost. In fair fight the British soldier had won the hill ; in fair fight he could not be dislodged from it—the sequel tells how he was at last overcome.

On the evening of the 1st May 1915 a greenish-yellow vapour came swirling slowly from the German trenches, drifting with the wind, curled round the base of the hill, and, gradually rising, engulfed the summit. The hill was held that day by men of the 1/Dorsets and the 59th Field Company R.E. There, facing the oncoming death, they clung to their trenches and were suffocated as they lay. When the fumes cleared away, reinforcements which came up found that one officer and 50 men had gone to their last account, while four officers and 150 men had collapsed in the agonies of choking.

This essay by the Germans was probably of an experimental nature, as it was not followed up by any attack by their infantry. The real attempt was made four days later, on the 5th. Early that morning the now familiar cloud was seen once again, and the hill, now held by the 2/Duke of Wellington's West Riding

Hill 60—*continued.*

Regiment, was rapidly submerged in it—and so the end came.
" There appeared staggering towards the dugout of the Commanding Officer of the Duke's in the rear two figures, an officer
and an orderly. The officer was pale as death, and when he
spoke his voice came hoarsely from his throat. Beside him his
orderly, with unbuttoned coat, his rifle clasped in his hand,
swayed as he stood. The officer said slowly, in his gasping voice,
' They have gassed the Duke's. I believe I was the last man
to leave the hill. The men up there are all dead. They were
splendid. I thought I ought to come and report.' That officer
was Captain Robins. . . . They took him and his faithful orderly
to hospital, but the gallant officer died that night." [1] His two
subalterns both remained in the front trench until they died.

So ended the fighting at Hill 60. What with the shelling and
the effect of the mines, little of the original hillock remained.
The British still held the lower trenches, while the Germans
occupied the summit—such as it was. Our losses on these two
days totalled nearly a thousand officers and men, practically all
from the effects of gas.

It is doubtful if anything in history is more striking than the
patient and disciplined endurance with which men of our race
uncomplainingly faced a death of horrible torture in those early
days when no form of protection from poison gas had been provided for them—the shattered heap of rubble that was once
Hill 60 stands as a token to keep our memory alive of what
those men did, and how they died.

Hill 60 District

Horribleness was added to the difficulties of defence work.
An officer writes of Hill 60 : " The place was practically a ceme-
tery, and hundreds must have been buried on the ground, it
proving impossible, when digging trenches, not to disturb some
poor fellow in his last long sleep." Everywhere it was the same.
The walls and parapets of trenches contained perforce these
gruesome reliquiæ.

> *When you drive the spade in the fragrant loam*
> *And disturb the gleaming bulbs that lie*
> *Of lily and tulip and daffodil,*
> *While a robin flutes their lullaby,*
> *Can you forget ? . . . Ah !*
> *How your tool hacked through, and the rank clay gave*
> *Where the base of the trench was the roof of a grave.*

[1] From *The British Campaign in France,* by A. Conan Doyle.

Hill 60.   (See Caterpillar.)

Hill 60 (Line South of, 1915)

The permanent way, that should have been a line for transport
from the horse-transport dump, south of Ypres in July 1915,
had entirely ceased to exist, and the 6/South Staffords, in the
trenches at Hill 60, found it an exhausting and dangerous route
to stumble along ; yet all material and rations, including water,
had to be carried up along the devastated track.   They decided
to mend the permanent way.   Lieut. Ashford, with a party,
searched the ruined station at Zillebeke, the shattered cutting,
and land around ; salving therefrom a trolley or two, piles of
sleepers, spare rails, and even a set of navvies' tools.   With
much strenuous toil the old twisted rails were torn away, holes
filled up, and a new line laid.   The work was done at night
while bullets glanced round the working party, flicked off the
rails, and struck sparks from the metals.   But the work was
done, and the " Hill 60 express " rumbled triumphantly up with
the stores ; thenceforth the work of an entire company in
transport could be expeditiously carried out by half a dozen men.

HOLLEBEKE CHÂTEAU, 1914 [1]

" Hollebeke Château was a detached post linking up the line
of the Ypres Canal with the Zandwoorde Ridge.   On the 30th
October it had been garrisoned by ' A ' squadron (Major Dorring-
ton) the Royal Dragoons for the last four days with the help of a
machine-gun section.   A nerve-racking position, as it was isolated,
and the presence of constantly increasing numbers of Germans
on the front had kept the garrison on the *qui vive*.   On the
previous day Lieut.-Colonel Steele, after inspecting the defences,
decided to remove the horses except the M.G.   This was done
under shell fire.   The Germans opened battle on the 30th
October, their patrols advancing only to be repulsed, until at
8 a.m. a regular and heavy bombardment burst over the château
and surrounding enclosures, smashing the troops in the shallow
trenches of the perimeter, while the enemy attacked intermittently
in considerable force but made no progress against the well-
directed fire of ' A ' squadron.   Meanwhile, farther to the left,
the I Cavalry Brigade had been overwhelmed on the Zandwoorde
Ridge and the enemy were seen advancing in masses over this
rise, while their field guns came into action on the ridge itself.
The position of the château garrison became critical ; ammunition was running short.   The stand of the right flank that had

[1] From regimental contribution.

HOLLEBEKE CHÂTEAU—*continued.*

been hotly engaged became increasingly difficult, as the 4th Hussars, who had been at Hollebeke Village, were withdrawn to the canal cutting farther north. This had enabled the enemy to work their way into the village and expose the right flank of the garrison. At 11.30 the remainder of the regiment, ' B ' and ' C ' squadrons, were moved up in support into the woods behind the château ; and under heavy shelling, ammunition supplies with two troops of ' C ' squadron succeeded in coming up to reinforce. By 2 o'clock ' A ' squadron was still holding on doggedly, with only ten rounds a man left ; on the right every man of one troop had fired 350 rounds in these few hours. The stand of the château garrison had delayed the powerful German attack for several hours at a critical time, enabling reinforcements to be brought up, and prevented a break-through at a point that would have made the further defence of Ypres impossible. When General Makins ordered the Hollebeke position to be evacuated, the regiment withdrew to a straight line taken up 1,000 yards in the rear."

Hollebeke Area, 1914 [1]

The 20th October found the 4th Q.O. Hussars in Hollebeke, entrenching the east side of the village ; next day they received orders to withdraw which were presently cancelled, and the trenches remanned under heavy hostile infantry fire. After a night of labour improving the shallow trenches and a day of sniping, the 129th Baluchis came up and took over the line, and the Hussars moved to the Canal, where they spent three days shifting about before they settled into the trenches along the Canal. A reconnaissance was made by Lieut. Sherston and Corporal Evans ; and they narrowly escaped capture as the Germans pretended to be Baluchi troops, and the ruse would probably have succeeded but for Lieut. Sherston's knowledge of Hindustani. On the 30th information was received that the château north of Hollebeke was in the possession of the enemy, and the regiment was at once ordered to advance, dismount, and retake it. They reached the place under heavy shell fire and found it occupied by the Royals and 10th Royal Hussars ; " A " and " B " squadrons took over the trenches covering the château, in relief of these units. Soon after midday the Indians in the village, having lost all their white officers killed or wounded, and finding themselves left with flank in air, went to pieces and could be seen trickling back from Hollebeke.

1 From regimental account.

HOLLEBEKE AREA—*continued.*

The machine guns of the regiment, under Lieut. K. C. North, had been assisting the Baluchis in the defence of the village. He and a few men practically single-handed put up a most magnificent stand, and after all other troops had left, kept the advancing lines of German infantry at bay for an hour and a half, literally mowing them down in heaps. It was not until the whole of his ammunition was expended, and the advancing infantry within a hundred yards of him, that he retired, bringing back both his guns successfully in a wheel-barrow. For this very gallant act he was recommended for the Victoria Cross, but he was killed in action next day, to the regret of the entire regiment. His memory will always be kept very green amongst those who served with him ; he was a very gallant gentleman.

The Hussars held the position until the French relieved this part of the line, when the regiment, less " A " squadron, was withdrawn ; but, as the French did not arrive till next morning, " A " squadron held the line single-handed under heavy fire throughout the night until they were relieved. From the 19th October to the 31st the regiment, with no rest to speak of, had held this section in the Salient ; such rest as the men were supposed to have had had been employed in improving entrenchments or digging new ones. They had been subjected to heavy shelling the whole time.

Hollebeke, 1914

Near Hollebeke on the 30th October a battalion of Indian Infantry was sent up in support behind the 5th Lancers. These men, shivering in the misery of autumn chill in Flanders straight from the hot weather in India, and sent up against the withering bombardment, were almost at once despoiled of their officers and left like sheep without a shepherd. They got among the ruins of some houses, seeking what cover they could find. Corporal Colgrave of the Lancers could speak Hindustani, and he ran among them, encouraging them, cheering them on, and finally formed them up to follow him. Seeing a wounded Indian officer, he picked him up and carried him out under the terrific fire. This act seemed to bring the Indians back to themselves, and they rallied and followed him. He was awarded a D.C.M.

Near Hollebeke took place a great fight of an Indian regiment, the 129th Duke of Connaught's Own Baluchis, and with them Sepoy Khudadad—a Pathan—gained the first V.C. for the Indian

HOLLEBEKE—*continued*.

Army. His detachment was rushed by the enemy in over-powering numbers. It was a fight in the dark. Six British officers and five Indians fell, six being killed outright, and over 200 were killed in the ranks. Khudadad, left alone, kept his machine gun working, the only man alive of the detachment. He was grievously wounded, but fought to the last possible moment, then crawled back and escaped with his life.

HOOGE. (See MENIN ROAD.)

HOOGMOLEN (near Courtrai), 1918

Lieut. David Stuart McGregor, a machine-gun officer of the Royal Scots, was in charge of a section attached to the right flank platoon of the battalion assaulting near Hoogmolen on the 22nd October. He concealed his guns on a limber under the bank of a sunken road as the troops assembled. The battalion advanced and came directly under intense enfilade machine-gun fire from Hill 66 on their right flank. Lieut. McGregor went forward fearlessly, and when he had located the position of the enemy guns, he realised that as the ground was raked by fire, and bare of all cover, it would be impossible to get his own guns forward either by pack or by hand without great delay. He found a more covered route round to the position, and ordered his men to take it. Then he himself mounted the limber, and galloped the gun straight through the fire-swept zone till they reached cover 600 yards ahead. The driver, horses, and limber were all hit, but Lieut. McGregor got into action, opened fire, and beat down the enemy while the advance of the battalion was resumed. He continued quite unafraid to order and control the fire of his gun, exposing himself without heed, until an hour later he was killed. "His great gallantry and supreme devotion to duty were the admiration of all ranks." And for these he received the Victoria Cross.

HOUPLINE. (See LYS.)

IBERIAN FARM. (See FREZENBERG.)

INVERNESS COPSE, 1917

The 7/Queen's were given the well-nigh impossible task of capturing Inverness Copse on the 10th August, assaulting the strong and elastic defence with depleted troops. The enemy wire was very close in front of our forming-up tape, and when

INVERNESS COPSE—*continued.*

the first ranks stole out in the darkness they clanged into the posts. Instantly green lights shot up with the crash of rifle shot, and a barrage came down on the attackers. The line was shattered, but the surviving officers gathered the remnant together and jumped off on time. The ground was meshed with wire, studded with the stumps of old trees amid bogs of mud and water, and all was riddled with machine-gun and rifle bullets. It is hardly strange that the attackers lost cohesion and gaps appeared. The south-west corner of the copse was reached by part of the Queen's leading platoon, and all but one man were killed or wounded by a machine gun as they charged into the trees. Farther north 2nd Lieut. J. H. Wilson, the only unwounded officer of the assaulting companies, followed the barrage up, and, being without support and his left flank exposed, withdrew, carrying out a successful attack on a concrete emplacement from which a murderous fire had withered our men. He reached the north-west corner of the copse, drew his party into Jasper Lane, and held on here with the help of two Vickers guns for eighteen hours, until relief came. Lance-Corporal Jelly of the Queen's distinguished himself that morning with a Lewis gun. He carried his gun, in answer to the S.O.S. of another Lewis gunner, across forty yards of open bullet-swept ground. He got another gun into action, and kept his own going in face of all assailants until the battalion was relieved next day.

In the meantime a superhuman feat had been asked of the 7/Bedfords and the 11/Royal Fusiliers : to clear their way up to Glencorse Wood across a quagmire hampered with half-sunk derelict tanks ; put a row of ten pill-boxes out of action ; fight through the wood, and close up on the Nonne Bosschen. The battalions formed up near the Menin Road, and at 4.35 in the morning the Bedfords went over the top with magnificent dash and into the wood, fighting through the stark mutilated trees with bomb and bayonet, and came to their objective. They dug in and stretched out to link with the Fusiliers, who, having lost nearly all their officers, had not come up so far. The wood had become a very unpleasant salient enfiladed all day from pill-boxes to the south, and a strong counter-attack threatened from Polygon Wood. But the Bedfordshires had consolidated, ammunition and machine guns had arrived, and the Boche attack was withered by an outburst of fire. The battalion held this line until they were relieved. Captain Driver, commanding the left company, received a Military Cross for his deeds of leading and reconnaissance. He was finally shot through the jaw

INVERNESS COPSE—*continued*.

and tongue, and lived to hear the report of his death being dictated to the sergeant-major.   He struggled to turn over and, speechless, scribbled on a bit of paper : " I'm not dead, blast you !   Give me a bandage."

Inverness Copse (Ritz Street Area), 1917

A strong-point south of Inverness Copse was the scene of a very fine counter-attack on the 10th August by the 8/Norfolks under Lieut.-Colonel Ferguson. The strong-point had been seized by the enemy, who had made a sudden raid in force just as the Bedfords were being relieved by the Norfolks. There were six hundred yards of bullet-swept ground, rough and difficult ground, to cover. Being a sudden affair, there was no artillery preparation or barrage. Led by Captain Morgan, and joined by a platoon of the 6/Berkshires, the Norfolks charged in sectional rushes, and recaptured the strong-point. It was but a little by-show that was specially commended for the daring and gallant manner in which it was carried out on the initiative of the Commanding Officer on the spot.

POMMERN REDOUBT

The 6/Staffords recall here an enemy attempt to strengthen a pill-box close to our line under cover of a Red Cross flag and a stretcher party. Within a short time the Padre and M.O. of the battalion were killed by one shell.

JAP AVENUE.   (See MENIN ROAD.)
JASPER LANE.   (See INVERNESS COPSE.)
JUMP POINT.   (See MESSINES.)
JUNIPER TRENCH.   (See BROODSEINDE.)

KANSAS HOUSE, 1917

One of the most formidable of the German strong-points was Kansas House, a huge fort of concrete roofed with steel, armed with machine guns, heavy and light, and manned by quite a big garrison. It stood in the first wave of the advance of the " Robin Hoods " in the battle of 26th September 1917. The men had been waiting shivering in the shell holes, pinned to one spot by the enormous volume of enemy shell fire, until at dawn our own barrage dropped, and our troops moved forward to the attack. The bombardment had pulverised the ground out

KANSAS HOUSE—*continued.*

of all recognition, and the units came near losing direction, as, mingling in the dark among the craters and marshes, they trudged forward into the rifle-swept zone between our barrage and that of the enemy. Kansas House brought devastating fire to bear upon the Sherwood Foresters, but Captain Spinar, manœuvring brilliantly, got Lewis guns, bombs, and rifles into action until in a surprisingly short time the garrison surrendered, and the fort passed into our hands, Captain Spinar falling in the moment of victory. The line was held throughout a day of continuous fighting—attack and counter-attack. The system of grouping the men in irregular posts instead of regular lines saved many lives under the terrible barrages. One enemy attack in great force threatened to outflank and overwhelm the battalion, but the S.O.S. was sent up and a barrage wonderfully placed by our guns and kept on for an hour and a half checked the attack, while the Commanding Officer, Lieut.-Colonel Martyn, went into the front line and stayed there, heartening and steadying his men. The M.O., Captain Carr, worked on without food or rest, dressing wounds in the open, and when stretcher-bearers were out of action he went out, collected, and brought in his wounded himself. Padre McIlwaine was badly gassed at the first-aid station and sent home, where he endured a long illness. He was later given a convalescent post on a hospital ship that was torpedoed on his first voyage, and sank with all hands. The line was held by the Robin Hoods until the 29th, when they were relieved.

KEERSELAERE [1]

On the 22nd April 1915, a lovely spring day, the 2/Buffs were bivouacked in the fields round St. Jean and, with the Middlesex, were due to relieve the other two battalions of the 85th Brigade about Zonnebeke that night. An outburst of enemy fire at about 5 o'clock in the afternoon, a distant cloud of greenish smoke, and the arrival through the lines of a rout of panic-stricken Africans (of the Moroccan Division) without officers, altered all ready-made plans. The French—assailed by the sudden devastating horror of an unknown element—had gone ; and from the Canal to where the Canadians formed the left of the British line (on the St. Julien—Poelcappelle Road) was a gap of several thousand yards. Only the Buffs, Middlesex, and King's Own stood across the open way to Ypres. The Buffs, who were standing coolly about the streets, were fallen in and.

[1] Account, approved by the regiment.

KEERSELAERE—*continued.*

marching through the stream of retiring Africans, took up a
line facing north astride the cross-roads at St. Jean. The
Middlesex came in on their left, with the King's Own in reserve.
As Colonel Geddes, of the Buffs, was the senior officer on the
spot, he was very soon directed to assume command of all troops
in St. Jean ; the command of his battalion thus devolving on
Major Power. "Geddes's Detachment," at first consisting only
of the three battalions already mentioned, had increased by the
next day to seven battalions, but he had not even the staff of a
brigade to help him during the days that followed.

During the night the Canadians, whose left flank was in the
air, sent for help, and "B" Company of the Buffs was sent up,
though they could ill be spared. This company reached the
front line shortly before dawn, and as they filed along the trench
to reoccupy a portion lately given up, the enthusiasm with which
they were welcomed was proof of the gravity of the situation.
There they stayed throughout the day, suffering many casualties,
especially from the flank and rear, until just after nightfall they
were ordered to side-step to the right and throw back a flank
towards St. Julien, their right resting on the apex of the angle
thus formed. But the end was at hand, for soon after dawn on
the 24th the Germans opened a furious artillery bombardment
and at the same time launched clouds of gas on the flank. As
the attack developed and the position became hopeless, the
Canadians eventually decided to retire, but the order to do so
failed to reach Tomlinson's company of the Buffs and the two
platoons of the 15/Canadians which were with it in the apex.
Left isolated, they held out until after 9 a.m., when, with ammunition exhausted and most of them wounded, they were surrounded
and captured.

Meanwhile the rest of the battalion had advanced to Wieltje
and thence northward, to gain touch with the left of the 3rd
Canadian Brigade. The Buffs closed up behind a hedge, beyond
which was open country, and, deploying, they attacked at the
double, platoon following platoon where there was no cover
whatever, while the Germans met them with machine-gun and
rifle fire from trenches 1,200 yards ahead. Many fell in the
charge. They reached a farmhouse and a frail fence, and from
here Major Power observed a fresh danger to the east, where a
quarter-mile space was held by but a few gallant French in three
parallel trenches, running from the G.H.Q. line and facing
north. The Buffs again dashed across the open, again losing
heavily, and in short rushes reached and manned the trenches.

KEERSELAERE—*continued.*

Some Zouaves retired and the Buffs were now alone filling the gap in the Canadian line. These trenches had been the last line of our defence ; and that they had now become our front showed the success the enemy had gained. But he came no farther, and the brilliant action of Colonel Geddes and the valorous fighting of the regiments had stayed the Germans from pressing home the advantage gained by their first dastardly use of poison gas. The battalion was relieved on the 27th April and Geddes closed his headquarters the same night. Unhappily Colonel Geddes, who had handled his detachment with such consummate skill and by his judgment and coolness, where all was utter confusion, saved an apparently irretrievable situation, was killed as he was leaving St. Jean on the morning of the 28th.

Keerselaere, near Gravenstafel

Near Keerselaere during the frenzied battle that followed the first gas attack on the 22nd April 1915 the Canadian troops had a desperate struggle to maintain the Gravenstafel position. The 7th Battalion was outflanked, and the full force of the enemy broke on their line. Captain E. D. Bellew brought his gun into action to save the flank. The enemy were within a hundred yards, and no help came ; reinforcements had been surrounded and destroyed while trying to come up. A shell burst, killing all the detachment, and Captain Bellew was left alone to keep the gun firing. He fought on stubbornly until another shell dropped and smashed the gun to pieces. Then he snatched up rifle after loaded rifle where they lay within his reach, and kept up unceasing volleys of rapid fire. He fell wounded, but struggled to his feet, and kept the enemy at bay until the gas fumes overcame him, and he was taken prisoner. At Staden he stood an amazing trial—incredibly sentenced to death for breaking the laws of war " in that he continued fire after part of his unit had been forced, by exhaustion of their ammunition, to surrender ! " The officer in charge of the firing party hesitated when the prisoner stood with his back to the wall, and sent him back for another trial. The death-sentence was not again passed, and Captain Bellew lived to wear the V.C. three years later.

KEERSLEERHOEK MOUND. (See PASSCHENDAELE.)

KEMMEL. (See FOREWORDS, 1914, 1918. See MONT ROUGE.)

Kemmel, 1914

In November 1914 one of those batteries of Field Artillery of the 5th Division that had covered the right wing of the II Corps at Le Cateau in a fight *à outrance* was attached to the Cavalry Division. It was parked west of Kemmel Village when the major on the Lindenhoek—Wytschaete Road sent the senior subaltern back with the urgent order to bring the guns forward into immediate action. The direct road was a target for the havoc of shell fire, and the way round Kemmel Hill meant delay. The subaltern balanced both routes, discarded both, and led his guns over the hill and straight down its eastern slope in the face of the enemy. So insolent a defiance of observation proved the greatest protection. The guns came into action with unhoped-for swiftness, and not a man nor horse had been hit.

KITCHENER HOUSE. (See STEENBEEK.)

KITCHENER WOOD, 1915

On the 22nd April 1915 the 2nd London Battery, a heavy battery of Territorial artillery armed with four 7-inch guns which had been placed in action at Kitchener Wood behind the French position, was overrun, but the gunners remained with their guns until the German infantry were close upon them, when they rendered the breech-blocks useless so that the guns could not be fired, and withdrew. Both young officers present, Lieuts. Sandeman and Hamilton Field, died beside their guns, according to the tradition of their regiment.

Kitchener Wood, 1915 [1]

" The 1/Battalion Royal Irish Fusiliers were ordered up to the battle from Merris, and on the evening of the 24th April came up west of Ypres. They advanced at midnight. To avoid the burning city the column moved north of Ypres, and in a workman's cottage in the village of St. Jean orders were issued for the attack. The inhabitants had fled. A shell had partially wrecked the cottage, and rain dripped on the little household goods ; a canary was dying in its cage in the window.

The Fusiliers were to attack in the direction of St. Julien, with their left on the Hannebeek, and as dawn broke it was found that the enemy were holding posts in advance of St. Julien. These posts were driven back, and the battalion deployed for attack.

Although unsupported by artillery, the Faughs moved forward

[1] From regimental contribution.

KITCHENER WOOD—*continued.*

with their usual dash, and by about 6.30 a.m. had reached a line about seventy yards short of the village. Here they were held up by heavy machine-gun fire, the enemy in the village having been heavily reinforced. In spite of losses they held on.

It was at this time that the writer saw the troops, who were attacking Kitchener Wood some distance to the left, begin to withdraw. This was due, apparently, to the shells of a British heavy battery falling amongst them. The withdrawal gradually spread to the right and reached the Fusiliers, but their advanced lines did not withdraw ; they lay dead on the glacis-like slope in front of St. Julien, where they remained till buried by the enemy.

This attack was a feat of arms of which the battalion might well be proud, but it was not till some weeks later that the soldiers learned how well they had fulfilled the purpose of the Higher Command.

Private Robert Morrow, who had earned the V.C. at Messines, died of wounds received in this action before he knew of the award. Private J. Copeland, who had saved Captain Wright's life when that officer was wounded near Houplines, was killed whilst carrying Lieut. Davison to a place of safety.

It was on the afternoon of the 2nd May that the Faughs experienced their first gas attack. After a heavy bombardment, a high wall of yellowish cloud rolled over the position. The only protection at the time were pads of cloth to be held in front of the mouth, but the mixture in which they were to be soaked had not yet been issued.

In spite of the suffering caused by the gas, the Faughs stuck to their trenches, and as the gas slowly rolled away and the enemy's infantry were seen advancing, they were received by so hot a fire that the attack withered away.

The gas turned everything, including vegetation and even the men themselves, an ashen-grey colour.

On the 3rd May, in order to shorten the line, the trenches on which so much labour had been expended were evacuated at night. Before doing so, the defences were cleaned up as for General's inspection, as a hint to the enemy that they had not turned us out."

Kitchener Wood, 1915

On the 25th April 1915 the 10th Brigade made that great attack which perhaps because it was a forlorn hope was only the more magnificent. It was in the terrible battle of St. Julien,

KITCHENER WOOD—*continued*.
when British units were being desperately rushed up to stay the advance of the Germans through the gap on the French front.

The 10th Brigade were given the impossible task of dislodging the enemy from a position in houses bristling with machine guns, and supported by tremendous artillery. The British brigade had no time to reconnoitre, nor to rendezvous commanding officers, and was without any adequate artillery support. In the front line were the 1/Royal Irish Fusiliers, 2/Royal Dublin Fusiliers, 2/Seaforth Highlanders, and 1/Royal Warwicks. They passed forward through the wire in the mists of early morning, and opening out, moved straight on in perfect fighting formation, and in short rushes gained to within 100 yards of St. Julien. Then they were pinned down by a withering storm of machine-gun fire that for twenty minutes devastated their ranks ; there they fell and lay, long swathes of dead men across the battle-field. The following lines tried to come up, but it was beyond endurance, and they took cover in the folds of the ground.

The enemy made no forward movement ; and it appeared, from the cessation of their shelling, that they were content with the arrest by their machine guns of so nearly successful an attack. The line that was organised by the British after this heroic assault was never moved until the deliberate withdrawal of the whole line on the 4th May. The 10th Brigade lost 73 officers and 2,346 other ranks in this grand attempt.

Kitchener Wood, April 1915

The Northumberland Brigade (first Territorials to go into battle as a brigade) lost over two-thirds of its strength in a desperate attempt to second the charge of the Lahore Division on the 26th April 1915. They charged grandly up to the enemy, who met them by machine-gun fire from the houses, and they could not make any great advance. But they reached a point from which no enemy could force them to retire, and they hung on, digging in as best they could, until withdrawn next morning.

The officer commanding the battery of artillery in action in the vicinity thus described the charge at the time : " The Northumbrians had only just arrived from England. They were rushed up to the front to assist in the defence of Ypres. I don't suppose any of the men of this gallant Territorial division had ever been under fire before. The first shell that fell among them will be stamped for ever on my memory. As their leading lines topped the Verlorenhoek Ridge some 2,000 yards behind our battery position they came into view of the German artillery

KITCHENER WOOD—*continued.*
observers, who opened on them with heavy and light artillery.
At a steady pace with perfect intervals they advanced. It
flashed through one's mind as to how these untried troops would
stand their first baptism of fire. Would they face the great
ordeal without flinching? Looking at them with powerful
glasses at this short range, the sight was truly inspiring. Not
a man altered his pace or his direction, except those who were
left lying on the ground. As steadily as the oldest veterans they
continued their advance without a falter. The dead and wounded
were left for the stretcher-bearers. How often during this battle
had we seen the Germans bolting from our artillery fire, and
the German is a brave soldier. It made one proud indeed to
see our young Territorial troops go through their first ordeal
with a courage, a steadiness, and a perfect discipline which could
not be surpassed. It encouraged one at a time of great strain
to feel that such men could not be defeated."

Kitchener Wood. (See also Second Ypres Foreword.)

KLEIN ZILLEBEKE, 1914

The King's Royal Rifle Corps were holding a section of trenches
at Klein Zillebeke when the Prussian Guard attacked. The
machine guns were in charge of Lieut. Dimmer. Across No-
man's-land, hideously littered with the dead bodies that had
lain, singly or in heaps, since the great battle of the 31st October,
the enemy were dug in along the edge of " Brown Road Wood."
All through the 11th heavy shells broke down the riflemen's
parapets, and on the 12th machine guns poured a stream of
bullets through the gaps.

At 1 o'clock the Prussian Guard attacked in mass formation,
and Lieut. Dimmer opened on them, firing one of his guns himself, flailing the enemy ranks until the gun jammed. Without
hesitation he climbed up right on to the emplacement in full
view of the enemy, and with a large spanner put the gun right.
He was hit in the jaw, but kept the gun firing steadily until he
had been wounded five times. Faint and spent, his face spattered
with pieces of broken metal, he stuck to his post until the Germans
—coming within fifty yards of the trench—broke and ran back
to the Wood.

Then he fainted, but on coming-to insisted on reporting in
person to Headquarters before he collapsed, and was taken to
the dressing-station. He received the V.C., and later the M.C.,
and was twice mentioned in dispatches.

KORTEKEER CABARET, 1914 [1]

In October 1914, at the cross-roads about a mile and a half north of Pilckem, where the road from that place leading to Houthulst Forest crosses the Bixschoote—Langemarck thoroughfare, stood a country inn known as the Kortekeer Cabaret, insignificant in itself, but destined to play an important part in the making of history.

During the 22nd October the right of the I Corps, which had taken over on the previous night, repulsed all attacks made on it fairly easily. Its left, held by the 1/Infantry Brigade, was not so fortunate, being attacked in great force at Pilckem from the direction of Staden. The Germans, who were new mobilised troops, advanced about 3.30 p.m. with the utmost determination and with a complete disregard of danger, singing " Die Wacht am Rhein " and waving their rifles over their heads. According to the German view, our troops had, technically speaking, been annihilated, and it was only necessary to overrun the few mentally and physically exhausted survivors, and the way was clear to Ypres. The focus point of the attack was the Kortekeer Cabaret, which, placed as it was at the cross-roads above mentioned, occupied a position of great tactical importance, and was held by the 1/Cameron Highlanders. By sheer weight of overwhelming numbers they were forced back from their trenches, but not before they had taken an appalling toll of the enemy, 1,500 of the latter being found dead on the ground next day.

The Germans, though meeting with a certain success at this point, had failed to dislodge the Black Watch, who were holding the line on the right of the Camerons. But the enemy troops were now lodged in the centre of our defensive flank, and about 6 p.m. the 1/Northamptons, who were acting as Divisional Reserve, were ordered to retake the right section of the lost trenches extending from the left of the Black Watch to the Kortekeer Cabaret. The C.O., Lieut.-Colonel Osborne Smith, thereupon charged the trenches with two of his companies, and attacked the cabaret and adjoining buildings with the remainder of his battalion. The trenches were successfully carried and occupied ; but the inn itself proved to be very strongly held, and, hampered by the rapidly increasing darkness, which made it practically impossible to keep touch and direction, the first attack on it, though pressed with the utmost gallantry and determination, failed—the Northamptons losing 5 officers and over 100 men.

[1] Compiled from contribution of the Loyal Regiment and other sources, by Lieut.-General Sir H. Uniacke.

KORTEKEER CABARET—*continued.*

Meanwhile the 1/Loyal North Lancs and the 2/K.R.R.C. were ordered up to St. Jean, leaving the 2/Royal Sussex to hold the village of Boesinghe and guard the Canal crossings. With midnight came orders to move forward to Pilckem, which place was reached just after 5 a.m. on the 23rd. Here, in a little estaminet, the 2nd Infantry Brigade Commander, General Bulfin, met the C.O.s of all units which had been placed under his orders for the task of recovering the lost trenches.

With the first sign of dawn the troops moved forward to their allotted positions, the N. Lancs, in the van, deploying into battle formation soon after crossing the Ypres—Staden railway-line. The battalion was commanded that day by Major A. J. Carter, D.S.O.,[1] and the second-in-command was Major H. Powell, D.S.O., who, suffering from a badly sprained ankle, was so determined to be with his battalion that he fought through the action with the aid of a chair, and on reaching a hedge would mount it to get a view of the enemy. He managed to carry on like this, and would not leave the field until severely wounded late in the day.

The advance went forward as steadily as on the barrack square, but after the first half-mile it was somewhat broken up by orchards, plantations, and hedged ditches ; by 11 a.m. the whole battalion was in line, and established within 300 yards of the enemy. By this time the men were very weary, and a pause was necessary to let them get some physical rest from movement, and to give them a chance to eat such rations as they had with them—they having had no food since the night before. Moreover, it was essential to beat down the German rifle fire, which was very heavy, and coming from trenches difficult to locate ; also, to allow the five batteries of R.F.A. supporting the advance time in which to master the German artillery, which was in considerably superior strength. So a furious and sustained fire battle, gradually swelling in its intensity, arose and raged all along the opposing lines. Meanwhile, shortly before noon, the Queen's began their direct attack on the cabaret. Advancing with their customary dash, in four lines, they passed round the right of the North Lancs and gained the trenches to the south-east of the inn, which were only some fifty yards from the enemy's position, with little loss, being admirably supported by our guns, which were putting in some very good work. There they estab-

---

[1] He was killed on 10th November 1914. He was the third C.O. of the Loyal N. Lancs to lose his life in action, Colonel Lloyd having been killed on 14th September, and Colonel Knight at the Battle of the Marne.

KORTEKEER CABARET—*continued.*

lished themselves and awaited the development of the attack on the left, according to plan.

Major Carter had established his headquarters in a farm enclosure in the centre of his line, and, while sitting under a tree sheltering alike from the German rifle fire and the hot sun of a perfect autumn day, and incidentally sharing a tin of " bully-beef " with his second-in-command, found that he was receiving the persistent, if unsuccessful, attentions of a German sniper. After the fifth or sixth bullet had missed by some feet, the instincts of the erstwhile musketry officer were aroused, and he remarked casually : " That fellow is shooting at me. I should classify him as a third-class shot."   Time was now getting on ; the men had had some rest and eaten what little food they had on them. As heavy rifle fire was coming from the German trenches, Major Carter ordered a platoon of " A " Company to try to close in on the enemy's position from the extreme left of the North Lancs line, while the machine-gun section was to come into action still farther to the left, to support it. The machine guns succeeded in taking up a very advanced position from which they could enfilade the right of the German trenches, but with such heavy casualties among the detachments that at one gun there was no one left to work it, and it could not be kept in action. Lieut. V. Henderson, the machine-gun officer, and his N.C.O., Lance-Corporal Puttrell, fought the remaining gun with the utmost gallantry and ability until the close of the fight.

The right flank of the North Lancs was now reinforced by " A " and " D " Companies of the South Staffords, and his left flank being effectively protected by the K.R.R.C., who were thrown back at an angle to it and had entrenched themselves, Major Carter determined to seize the first favourable opportunity to charge home with the bayonet. The fury of the fire fight rose to its height about 2 p.m., when Germans were noticed to be slipping away from their trenches in twos and threes. " They appeared like so many rabbits running from their holes ; and as they ran, so we took pot shots at them "—the enemy was wavering. The crisis was at hand, and from instinct and from training the men knew it. " The men longed to get at them ; and gradually, without any word of command being given, you could hear the click of the bayonet as each man, on his own, drew and fastened it hard on his rifle." Major Carter, watching the situation intently, judged that the time had come to drive home the attack ; so word was passed round to get ready, and a weary dry-lipped bugler was found and asked if he could blow

KORTEKEER CABARET—*continued.*

the " Charge." " I dunno, sir, but I'll try," was the answer,
and up he stood in the line with Major Carter, making noises
which would have made any self-respecting sergeant-drummer
writhe in agony. On any ordinary occasion his performance
would have seen him into the defaulters' book, but to-day it
was good enough—its impulse sped swiftly along the tensely
waiting line, and in response to it the tired men rose with a
hoarse roar and charged straight for the enemy's trenches. On
the left a party of the K.R.R.C., in the centre the Loyal North
Lancs, on the right the South Staffords swept over the German
position with surprisingly little loss ; while to the east of the
Pilckem Road " D " Company of the Queen's, flanked by a company of the Northamptons, drove home the assault simultaneously on the cabaret itself. The Kortekeer position was recovered.

When on the next day it was decided that the bulge in our
line created by the Kortekeer position was a danger from every
point of view, with no advantage, the line was withdrawn. At
first sight it might seem that all the blood and effort spent on
that day was wasted fruitlessly. The answer may be found in
the following extract from the German Official History of the
War : " With the failure of the 46th Reserve Division to gain a
decisive victory between Bixschoote and Langemarck on the
22nd and 23rd October the fate of the xxvi and xxvii Reserve
Corps was also settled. For the time being any further thought
of a break-through was out of the question."

No additional argument need be advanced to prove that those
very tired men who, determined to carry on at all costs, laid
down their lives that day died not in vain.

KRONPRINZ FARM. (See ST. JULIEN.)

KRUISEECKE. (See MENIN ROAD.)

LA BRIQUE, 1915

When the 2/Battalion Leinsters came to La Brique in June
1915 they had spent seven months in the neighbourhood of
Armentières, where, in spite of abnormal wet weather, the conditions, compared with the Salient farther north, gained for their
division the nickname of the " Cushy Sixth." On reaching La
Brique they were astounded at the continual and heavy shell
fire that unceasingly bombarded Ypres. An old hand remarked,
" Faith, Mick, Armentières was cushy compared with this spot.
Sure, the shells down there were only connecting files, but here,
bedad, there's battalions of them—and in column of route too."
A very illuminating description of shell fire in the Salient.

LA BRIQUE—*continued*.

The Irishmen gave fancy names of their own to the shells, whose various sounds soon became familiar. A 12-inch that made a whirring noise was called the Roscrea Mail. A 17-inch that was heard occasionally was called the Burooty Express, Burooty being their slang for Birr.

LA DOUVE, 1915 [1]

The first V.C. gained by the Faugh-a-Ballaughs was won by Private Robert Morrow when the enemy started to smash the front line at " Dead Cow Farm." Private Morrow, of his own accord, went into the wrecked trenches in search of the wounded men, while the enemy kept up heavy fire. He dug among the debris and succeeded in rescuing several of his comrades, carrying them back to places of comparative safety. This act, following on a short career of conspicuous bravery, gained for Morrow the V.C. He was quite a lad, and no great soldier in peace-time, but War discovered his lion heart. Among the stories of his courage that became legends in the battalion, one tells how, when water ran short in the trenches, Morrow took an empty rum-jar, and went to fill it at the pump of a farm behind, passing under fire all the way. As he regained the trench the jar was hit by a bullet and smashed to pieces. Morrow perseveringly collected some water-bottles, crossed the fire-swept route again, and returned safely. One day his C.O. inquired as to the wherefor of a rent in his slacks, and he gently replied, " Only a piece of shell, sir." Morrow was of those who died in action without knowing of the supreme reward.

LANGEMARCK (Au Bon Gîte), 1917

On the 14th August 1917 the 10/Rifle Brigade crossed the Steenbeek under an artillery barrage described by Lieut.-Colonel Troughton as " the best he had ever seen." They were mown down by machine-gun fire from the pill-boxes, but waded through the stream, some carrying down light bridges and crossing by these. They fought hand-to-hand until they had established a position 250 yards beyond the stream. Lieut. G. Chapman, Intelligence Officer to the Brigade, went ahead with Rifleman Moore to find out the position in front. He advanced in full view of the enemy and under a fusillade of bullets succeeded in making a valuable reconnaissance, and in writing all the information down. He was killed, but the rifleman succeeded in rescuing his papers and got back with the report.

[1] See also pp. 122 and 123.

LANGEMARCK (AU BON GÎTE)—*continued.*

The left company of the 11/Rifle Brigade fought through the swampy ground, and after a hand-to-hand combat on the east bank, reached Au Bon Gîte under heavy machine-gun fire, captured the mill and some small dugouts ; but the strong-point that had withstood bombardment by our Heavies could not be taken. The Germans shut themselves in with iron doors, and though our men swarmed all round and over it, they could not get in that day.

On the 16th a fresh assault was made by the Rifle Brigade and a party of the 83rd Field Co. R.E. as part of the general attack on Langemarck. The advance was covered with standing and creeping artillery barrage, with smoke shells and machine guns. The very difficult manœuvre of crossing the stream and forming up within 100 yards of the enemy was carried out during the night. Major Norman, of the 84th Field Co., crossed under fire and laid the tapes to mark the positions. The 60th and 61st Infantry Brigades attacked as daylight broke, behind a beautifully timed curtain of artillery. Bombers of the 11th Rifle Brigade, who had crawled up and lay hidden in shell holes, threw smoke bombs on to the enemy. The rest of the company dashed forward, and the Bon Gîte was captured with a garrison of an officer and fifty men. The rest of the infantry brigades passed on, but no rapid charge was possible over this crater-pocked ground, and the troops wound their way between the water pools and holes in small columns. The 7/K.O.Y.L.I. came up against a solid defence of concrete block-houses west of Langemarck, and the men—losing nearly all their officers—fought on with splendid dash and initiative, with bomb and Lewis guns. Private Edwards won a Victoria Cross : " Without hesitation he dashed forward at great personal risk, bombed through the loopholes, surmounted the fort, and waved to his company to advance." The first objective, the road west of Langemarck, was gained before 6 o'clock and the troops advanced on the town. Here the 12/K.R.R.C. were held up by machine guns from another block-house, and Lieut. E. Cooper gained a V.C. by charging it with four men. He ordered these men to lie down and fire, himself ran straight forward and emptied his revolver into an opening. The machine guns were silenced and the garrison of forty-six men with seven machine guns surrendered. The rest of the brigade continued to advance, turning out all dugouts and shelters, and Langemarck was reached. The losses had been very heavy, especially among the officers, some battalions being left with none.

Langemarck, 1917

The long tense struggle to cover the low ground of the Salient, and win to Passchendaele Ridge, consisted of an endless number of short and fearful battles, engagements that ended in a change of position that was practically negligible ; each one appallingly costly, with very little apparently gained to balance the loss. The 5/Battalion of the Royal Warwicks aver that August 1917 at St. Julien was the worst month that they ever passed through —a time when strong bodies of enemy troops defended concrete fortresses, against weak bodies of troops that floundered in a sea of mud. The tanks, on which such high hopes were shattered, were bogged at the start. After rest and training at Nordasques, the battalion came again into the battle when the line in October had been pushed forward to the slopes of Langemarck ; and took part in the attacks on Winchester, Wellington, and Kronprinz Farm across the Steenbeek and up the next rise. This attack was much more hopeful than the struggle of 22nd August. There were enough troops in hand, and the advance was highly organised. Communication, that had so exasperatingly broken down before, was now ensured by seven different methods. There were runners, contact aeroplanes, telephones, visual signals, buzzers, messenger dogs, and carrier pigeons. All had been most carefully prepared ; but the plans came very near an untimely end, as the enemy suddenly took fright that there was something in the wind, doubled their front-line posts, and dropped a barrage twenty minutes ahead of ours. It was an icy night, and to the men waiting, chilled to the bone, rum had just been issued, and was steadily sent down in spite of the dropping shells. At six o'clock the first of four separate British barrages fell and swept forward, and the troops went over. The advance was almost immediately split up into a number of small separate engagements between isolated parties fighting through a 300-yard belt of ground, in which every crater and shell hole held machine gun or sniper. This brought about terrible losses. In the first half-hour " B " Company lost every platoon commander and eleven of the twelve section commanders. " D " Company lost all its officers, but still the troops fought on valiantly, drove through the murderous belt and gained their objective, consolidating on the Ridge.

Langemarck, 1917

The 7th York and Lancaster Regiment [1] were sent into the area to open up railway communications between the backward and

---

[1] Contributed by an officer of the regiment.

LANGEMARCK—*continued*.

passable areas west of the Yser Canal and the area forward of Langemarck.

For months they had laboured night and day, until at length a circle of light railway was laid, and in operation, from Elverdinghe along the track of the old broad-gauge, up to Langemarck ; and back over the Steenbeek, which had to be bridged in two places.

The main line was the one on the site of the broad-gauge, and the other had been made with the double object of simple utility, and to mislead the enemy should he be led to inquire into the question of communication and supply.

The main line must be kept a vital secret : and infinite pains and varying methods were taken to deny that it was there. It ran down the enemy side of the Pilckem Ridge and under direct observation from them. Every old sleeper taken away, every large stone or obstacle removed, had to be replaced without impairing the efficiency of the new track, and as nearly as possible in its original position. All the work here had of course to be done by night : and not a yard of line laid but had to be paid for with blood.

Each piece had to be covered with camouflage specially designed for the purpose ; and so, when trains began to run from Elverdinghe to Langemarck, the camouflage was stripped after dark, and returned again before dawn.

The trains were of course miniature electric tractors and small wagons ; but heavier tractors and two-ton wagons were used later. Upon these every kind of material, including artillery, was transported forward for the grand offensive.

The trains were escorted by repair parties of the York and Lancasters, as well as by loading and unloading parties of various troops.

The Germans, though they had no real knowledge of what was being done, nevertheless subjected the railway to continuous bombardments, it being the only reasonable approach for troops over the Pilckem Ridge.

On one occasion Sergeant Edge and a party of about ten or twelve went as escort to an ammunition train of several wagons. The trucks were two-ton, and every one had bogies, which rendered the operation of replacing them in case of derailment doubly difficult.

The train left the depot after dark, the tractor pushing the trucks, and managed to cross the Steenbeek ; then, within short distance of Langemarck station, two of the trucks came

LANGEMARCK—*continued.*

off the line.   They were laden with shells of all kinds, including gas shells :   and Edge was confronted with a difficult problem.

The wheels had sunk beyond hope of recovery ; the night was nearly spent ;   every trace of the labour had to be removed before daylight ;   and the camouflage had to be laid on the line for about a mile back.

The trucks must be removed also, or the secret of the railway would be no secret.   If, also, the enemy decided to shell Lange-marck, and the deadly freight of which the sergeant had charge were hit, then there was the end of him and every man in the neighbourhood.

With his small party he set to work.   First of all he sent the tractor back over the second line, letting it take pot-luck, so to speak.   If it proved unable to do the return journey that way it would not matter so much.   Then he sent a few of his men to camouflage the main line ;   and with the remainder unloaded the two wagons.   One by one the shells were with difficulty unloaded and hidden by the line.

Then something had to be done with the tell-tale wagons. Edge had recalled that some twenty or thirty yards off were some old broad-gauge wagons, upturned and ruined, as they had been left at the opening of the War.   The idea seized him to get his own wagons alongside the derelicts :   but how it was done no one could say.   Edge himself modestly confessed that by a series of tumbling movements, just as if he were dealing with heavy boxes, his men managed to heave the wagons in succession from place to place, till they were lying beside the old ones.

Done at the end of the night's labour, and when he and his men were already fatigued, it was a memorable feat ;   and one that stands out in the memory of those who know of it.

LA PLUS DOUVE, 1914

A gap a mile wide between the left of the 4th Division and the right of the cavalry was made by our deliberate retirement from the Messines Ridge on the 1st November 1914, and the Inniskilling Fusiliers were ordered to form a flank south of the Douve.   Only a squadron of the 19th Hussars was available to cover the opening, and the 1/Dorsets from the II Corps were sent for, and came up as far as Neuve Eglise.   The Germans report that they had orders to press with the I Cavalry Corps and the 40th Division round Ploegsteert Wood and capture our

LA PLUS DOUVE—*continued*.

guns on Hill 63. They say, however, that " on account of the
strongly prepared enemy positions, an advance here was impossible without abundant artillery support." Indeed the
massed engineers of eight cavalry divisions sought to break down
the meagre strands of wire that were all the defence the British
had. Yet the enemy was thrown back and made no success,
confessing to heavy losses.

La Plus Douve Farm, 1914

The German Guard Cavalry Corps were sent forward by
special order of the Kaiser to seize the moated farm called " La
Douve," north-west of St. Yves, which, had they but known it,
was ungarrisoned by our troops. The patrols of the 2/Inniskilling
Fusiliers sometimes visited it. Two companies of this battalion
had failed to get the order to form the flank beyond the river,
and were lying all day in shallow, water-logged trenches, west of
this farm. The Germans began to pound the buildings with
heavy howitzer and mortars, but the Inniskillings replied with
continual bursts of rapid fire, and kept up this fire all day, their
whereabouts remaining unknown to the enemy, who failed to
capture the farm. Along the 4th Divisional front they made no
advance, kept back by rifles, machine guns, and artillery fire.

La Douve River, 1915

The 1/Faugh-a-Ballaughs were north of the River Douve in
April 1915, and here the Battalion Grenadiers practised a primitive form of bomb-throwing. With a catapult, a jam-tin full of
explosive was hurled, its extreme range being forty yards. Surely
the shades of the Romans who subdued the Gauls some two
thousand years ago, perceiving these things, would smile. But
this was the second infancy of a very useful arm.

LEDEGHEM, 1918

On the 1st October the 50th Brigade R.F.A. close up to our
infantry were trying to silence the enemy machine guns, that in
great numbers defended the village. Lieut. R. V. Gorle swung
his gun into action fully exposed to the fury of bullets, and,
firing over open sights, shot down machine guns within a range of
only 500 yards. Three times he repeated this daring manœuvre.
Still the hostile fire grew more intense, and presently the line of
infantry wavered. Without pausing a moment Lieut. Gorle
galloped his gun forward, swept in front of the leading companies, and unhooking in the open knocked out the machine

LEDEGHEM—*continued.*

guns that were holding up the line. The infantry rose to this
magnificent example ; charged and recaptured the northern
end of the village. Lieut. Gorle was awarded a V.C.

Ledeghem, 1918

The 9th (Scottish) Division headed the advance into Ledeghem
in October 1918, where the British were bursting through the
bounds that had made the Salient ; the Scots had their right
flank in the air, and the troops on their left echeloned back to
conform to the Belgians. Stiff fighting had brought the 27th
(Lowland) Brigade to Dadizeele, the Boche being well provided
with guns of every calibre, whereas the division had none at all
on its right, the terrible quagmire having thwarted every effort
to bring up the guns, and even hampered the Lewis guns.

" ' Back each other up,' were the orders we got that day,
and—well, it was just like nothing on earth that we had ever
done ! For the whole division went streaming off into the blue
hunting the Boche away from any position in which he might
have held us up for weeks. Nothing could stop our men that
day. . . . We had broken right through one of the most important defence systems in those regions, and as we walked up
over the Strooiboomhoek Ridge we were lost in admiration of
the gallant manner in which our lads had rushed this extremely
strong natural position, made doubly so by hedges of wire and
well-sited trenches. . . . The Menin—Roulers Road exactly
resembled high-water mark on the beach, for west of that road
the land was all shell-pitted ; east of it there was scarcely a
scratch and all the land was under cultivation, all the farms were
snug and comfortable and civilians everywhere." [1]

The 12/Royal Scots, who had captured Becelaere, led the way
through Ledeghem. During the attack a gunner officer ran a
field gun close up to a strong pill-box known as Baum Farm,
opening fire at a range of 200 yards, afterwards tackling another
pill-box in the same fashion under heavy machine-gun fire all
the time. [Lieut. Gorle—see above.]

Ledeghem (Raymond Farm), 1918

The attack on the 14th October 1918, that, driving the Germans
backward, gathered impetus hour by hour until the Salient was
cleared, opened splendidly, although, true to tradition, a dense
fog smothered the first advance. In the approach to Ledeghem

[1] *Three Years with the 9th Scottish Division*, by Lt.-Col. W. D. Croft.

LEDEGHEM (RAYMOND FARM)—*continued.*
a house was held by the enemy as a fortress, bristling with
machine guns and rifles. Private Martin Moffat raced through
their fire, reached the back door and forced the enemy to surrender. Having made his own bag of 120 prisoners, he determinedly marched them back himself, delivering them and receiving a receipt from the Provost Marshal before he rejoined his
battalion. He also received a V.C. Another V.C. was won in
the battalion by Sergeant O'Neil, who showed great bravery
on this day. And four days later he heard that his brother,
serving with a division on the right, had been killed. The
sergeant, worked up to a passion of grief and fury, dashed ahead
of our attack, outracing the barrage. He led the way into every
village and hamlet that the Leinsters reached, fighting with a
reckless abandon that cleared the enemy from the houses, giving
and asking no quarter. He seemed to bear a charmed life and
lived to wear the V.C. that he earned.

A private of the Leinsters being separated from his platoon
was captured by some Boche machine gunners, who kept him in
their dugout on the ridge. One of them spoke English, and
Private Hurley spent the hours of the night in beguilement,
with so much persuasion that the party decided to surrender.
Hurley returned with his captive captors, and rejoined his
battalion at dawn.

Ledeghem, 1918

Thomas Ricketts, aged fifteen, joined the 1/Battalion Royal
Newfoundland Regiment, announcing his years as eighteen.
On the 14th October his battalion was being shot down by a
battery at point-blank range. Private Ricketts volunteered to
go with his section commander in an attempt to outflank the
battery, and they advanced with a Lewis gun, till, within 300
yards' range, ammunition ran out. At this moment the enemy
were seen to bring up their gun teams. Private Ricketts raced
back through a 100-yard zone of machine-gun fire, dashed back
again with ammunition, and firing the gun with unerring accuracy
drove the enemy gun teams away. His platoon then attacked,
capturing four field guns and four machine guns. When the
King invested him with the Victoria Cross it was as " the youngest
V.C. in my Army."

LE GHEER, 1914

The 4th Division, in spite of its weak and perilous position,
had been called on to send every possible reserve to the north,

LE GHEER—*continued*.

in view of the smashing blows that were falling on the cavalry.
The enemy seized the moment to start bombarding the front of
the 11th Brigade and attacked in force. The 1/Hampshires were
here holding 2,000 yards of the usual intermittent trenches from
the Douve to Le Gheer and had every man in the firing line. The
weight of the enemy crashed into the left centre trench. Immediately a magnificent counter-attack was launched from the
Brigade Reserve, the Germans were driven out of the trench,
and hurled back. Brigadier-General Hunter Weston's report
was : " Major Prowse and the 1/Somerset Light Infantry, God
bless them, have restored the situation." Of the platoon of the
Hampshires in that centre trench, every man was found dead at
his post.

Le Gheer, 1914

The 1/East Lancashires were holding a front-line trench near
Le Gheer, when, in the extremity of the sorely pressed Cavalry
Division, the 4th Division strained out and took over the defence
of this part of the line. The 4th Division was weak enough,
heaven knows, and they were weary men who watched in that
trench on the night of the 1st November. Drummer Spencer
John Bent was disturbed by the sound of the men retiring, and
found that orders to evacuate had been received. He turned
back to fetch a French trumpet which he had collected somewhere
as a souvenir, and met a sergeant who told him that the order
was a bogus one. Bent jumped out of the trench, ran after, and
recalled the men of his company. Next morning the Germans
attacked in force, and all his officers being killed or wounded,
Bent took charge of the platoon, led them with great calmness
and gallantry, fought off all attacks, and held the trench until
he was relieved. This was the consummation of a story of
conspicuous bravery, and Bent was awarded the Victoria Cross.
One of his earlier deeds was the rescue of a man lying wounded in
front of our line. Bent found that he and the wounded man were
a target for bullets, so he lay on his back and with his feet hooked
under the other's armpits, worked his way back into safety.

L'ENFER WOOD. (See MESSINES.)

LOCRE, 1914

Who that remembers '14 will ever forget Locre, town of tragic,
glorious muster ! Town into whose streets there marched a
procession of greater pomp than any Cæsar's triumph ! Procession of men whose unshaven faces, grey and powder-flecked, bore

Locre—*continued*.

the haggard lines of a most dire experience ; from whose red-shot eyes sleep had been withheld till they carried the vision of things unutterable. They marched into bivouac ; their feet for three weeks or more had not known release from their boots ; their clothes were filthy, torn, and verminous ; there were crimson bandages. So they marched in, remnants of great regiments whose tradition of training and drill, of punctilious smartness upon parade are bywords. Oh, forspent procession of victors ! . . .

We see them marching into the town, so crowded that they have nowhere to lay their heads, and the church is thrown open to them. In the church sleep the 1/Grenadiers, the battalion organised as a single company under a captain, but—the skeleton battalion went through an hour's steady drill. Here come the Scots Guards, and the commander of the III Corps, Lieut.-General Pulteney, comes up to meet his old regiment, and rides with them into Locre—one captain and 69 men.

The tatters of the thin red line, that infantry whose valour and endurance, whose almost incredible—to the enemy wholly incredible—skill of musketry had defeated the training and valour of that enemy's enormous army, came to Locre as to other places of bivouac ; and in every battalion the greater number did *not* march in.

LYS, NORTH OF THE RIVER, 1915

In January 1915 this part of the line near Houplines, held by the 1/Queen's Westminsters, was peculiarly inadequately defended, and the trenches were dug in such a swamp that the weight of sandbags was too much for the foundations. A form of camouflage was erected which at least deterred snipers, bags filled with straw being laid on top of the traverses. The River Lys rose rapidly in January, and listening posts and trenches had to be evacuated, while a sudden flood through a culvert betrayed an enemy attempt to flood our line. Lieut. Henderson Scott (a professional mining engineer) got a party together and fought a racing battle against the flood, filling sandbags with semi-liquid mud and piling them on the banks. The water was held back, but the collapse of the trenches left our men still further exposed to rifle fire.

Here on 8th January a corporal while crossing the open for water just before dawn was shot down ; and when daylight came he was seen lying out in full view of the enemy, at about 100 yards' range. Defying almost certain death, Rifleman Tibbs,

NORTH OF THE LYS—*continued.*

a stretcher-bearer, and Rifleman Ponchot crawled out to him, and under fire of the enemy, who opened on them at once, reached the corporal, only to find that he was dead. Rifleman Tibbs knelt by the corporal till a bullet laid him dead across the body of him he had come out to succour. Rifleman Ponchot, seeing nothing could be done, managed to crawl back to safety.

LUNN FARM. (See MESSINES.)

MENIN ROAD

The name has in its very sound the tone of a deep bell pealing, a fateful note. It calls us to remember one of those dramatic achievements that in the light of every day are reckoned impossibilities.

In October 1914 the German Army was a weapon of weight and fine temper thrusting towards the vital place of paramount strategic importance—the Channel Ports. Battering the whole line, the point of that weapon drove in along the Menin Road. The spear-point found a vulnerable spot, and with all the weight of Germany's long-prepared military force behind it, drove onward seeking to widen the gap and crash invincibly through. But the gap closed, and the living, suffering bodies of men created a barrier, pitifully slight in substance, but unsurmountable. The spear-point was broken on the Menin Road, and the weapon was withdrawn.

The triumph gained by the higher forces of spirit and mind was marked for history by a curious significance of date. On the 11th November 1914 the spear-point broke, and presage was given, though hidden then from our eyes.

The narratives begin when the battered 7th Division is astride the road east of Kruiseecke, the sudden menace of great and unexpected enemy forces having on the 20th October thrown the British Army on the defensive. The 2nd and then the 1st Divisions come up in support, and later units of the II Corps.

Reutel Ridge and Southern End of Polygon Wood, 1914

On 24th October the 2/Battalion Wiltshire Regiment with flanks in air was overwhelmed on Reutel Ridge—only the quartermaster-sergeant-major and 170 other ranks answered the roll-call next morning. The enemy having broken into Polygon Wood, the 2/Warwicks were called upon to counter-attack. They had been fighting for four days on the ridge and were so weary that they could hardly keep awake while digging trenches

THE HARVEST OF BATTLE.

From the painting by C. R. W. Nevinson in the Imperial War Museum.

REUTEL RIDGE—*continued*
in the rear of Zonnebeke. These weary men charged into the
wood, Colonel Loring, already wounded, riding at their head.
Twice his charger was shot under him, and at last he fell himself
while fearlessly leading the assault. The Northumberland
Hussars arrived in support from Hooge. They tell how, when
the orders came : " There was not a moment to lose. A hurried
gallop up the Menin Road and an advance in open order across
the usual sticky turnip-fields brought us to the forefront of
the battle. . . . Soon the Yeomanry were lying down maintaining
a steady fire. The situation was perilous. Every available
man, including the personnel of the Divisional H.Q., was in the
line, there was no reserve, each did the work of ten. Still those
grey masses advanced to the attack ; when they succeeded in
getting a footing in Polygon Wood the battle seemed as good as
lost, but the thin line held out." [1] Combining with the Warwicks,
the Hussars checked the enemy advance, this being the
first engagement of any Territorial unit. The 2/H.L.I. and
2/Worcesters now arrived to reinforce the hard-pressed troops.
The Germans were quite close and the battalions were ordered
immediately to counter-attack in a north-easterly direction
through the Wood, though it was so dense with undergrowth
that it was very hard to keep direction. Suddenly the Race-
course came into view and the enemy clearly seen in the open.
The Worcesters charged into them, firing from the hip and
using the bayonet. There were a few moments' tense, stubborn
hand-to-hand fighting, and then the enemy broke, and the
British, cheering, hunted them out of the Wood.

This charge of the Worcesters was as brilliant a feat of arms
as their more well-known charge that saved Gheluvelt on the 31st.

Kruiseecke, the Cross-roads, 1914

By the 25th October our line here formed a sharp salient.
During the night the enemy in greatly superior numbers got
into the village of Kruiseecke, and cut off two companies of the
Scots Guards, calling for Major Paynter by name. The other
two companies counter-attacked and, fighting from house to
house, captured nearly 200 prisoners and restored the line where
their comrades, surrounded by the enemy, still held on. Next
morning these trenches were completely destroyed by a tempest
of shell, including 8-inch howitzer, and many men were buried.
A little later the trenches of the 1/Grenadiers on the north face
of the salient, and of the 1/South Staffords and 2nd Border

[1] *The Northumberland Hussars' History.*

KRUISEECKE, THE CROSS-ROADS—*continued*.

Regiment on the south were also blown in. The line held under
the deadly destruction of shell and machine-gun bullets for three
hours, when by a ruse of the enemy behind them shouting
" Retire," a few of the South Staffords obeyed. The enemy
broke in at this point on the south face of the salient, overwhelmed
the Border Regiment, and swept behind the Scots and Grenadier
Guards. The three companies, who had been told to hold the
line, clung to their positions. The Scots were entirely cut off
and captured in small parties. Lord Dalrymple, who had relieved
Major Paynter, had only five men left alive, whom he ordered
to smash their rifles before they surrendered. Part of the King's
Company—the Grenadiers—were more fortunate, and with
magnificent audacity cut its way through the enemy behind it
under fire from both sides, and escaped, with the sacrifice of two
platoons, isolated and cut off.

A new line was flung across the Kruiseecke Salient with the
supports and remnants of the Scots Guards, Border Regiment,
and South Staffordshires, and the enemy advanced no further.

Kruiseecke Ridge, 1914 [1]

The 2/Battalion Royal Scots Fusiliers had already been in
action from the 19th till the 27th October, and being withdrawn
to rest, mustered less than 500 all ranks. It had landed from
England at war strength. There was, however, to be little rest ;
on the 28th the battalion moved into a new position opposite
Kruiseecke just captured by the Germans. Kruiseecke Ridge
lay like a bastion between Gheluvelt on the north and Zandwoorde on the south, and its shape with the woods just beneath
it prevented the enemy from guessing the feebleness of the thin
line here opposed to them ; on the contrary, they seemed convinced that, as it was an important tactical point, it must be
strongly held.

The Ridge was held by " B " and " A " Companies, with
" C " echeloned in rear of the right, linking to the line southward.
" D " Company was kept in reserve. The weather was wet and
foggy, and men who had now been in the trenches for the best
part of ten days were physically exhausted, though in good
spirits ; but even during this comparative lull, one day's casualties alone cost four officers and over fifty men.

Before dawn on the 29th those who were on watch on the
Ridge heard an ominous rumbling of wheels away in front—the
German artillery taking up a forward position under cover of

1 Epitomised from a regimental account.

KRUISEECKE RIDGE—*continued*.

darkness.   Daylight came with a thick mist ; the men stood to
arms, stiff and shivering after their cheerless bivouac in the wet
trenches, expecting to see at any moment the forms of advancing
enemies, but at first only an intensified sniping broke out.   There
were as good or better marksmen among the Scots and this was
soon checked.   North and south of the Ridge the German attack
was strongly pressed ; as the mist slowly cleared away it could
be seen that the British line had been bent back on the left.
At about 8 o'clock two thick lines of field-grey infantry came
pouring over the slope from Kruiseecke towards the vacant
trenches north of " B " Company ; a section of machine guns
came rapidly into action, not 300 yards away, against the
flank and rear of the Ridge position.   Part of " B " Company
turned about to meet this danger, but at that moment the
attack against the front began in earnest ; the crisis had come.
Amidst the cross-fire, the whistling impact of bullets from front
and rear, the men of " B " Company shot fast and steadily ;
but the enemy machine guns were taking a heavy toll, and the
commander began to wonder how long it would be before his
exposed flank would be rolled up, and he and his men overwhelmed.   He scribbled a short report to the C.O., and asked
for instructions.   This message, put into a weighted purse and
thrown from trench to trench, reached Captain Le Gallais ; he
sent it on by runner, who carried it to Battalion Headquarters
over some 300 yards of open fire-swept ground.   He reached the
C.O. and brought back the answer.   This man, with two or
three others, continued that day and the next to carry orders
and reports backwards and forwards, till one by one death over-
took them.   None had deserved better of their country.

" B " Company was by now a third of its strength, but full
of fight, steadied by the older reservists in the ranks ; and the
enemy in front hesitated, in spite of their overwhelming numbers,
to cross the few hundred yards of ploughed ground, where they
could so easily have rushed the position.   But a chance turn
in the fortunes of the day gave the defenders a little much-
needed relief.   The intolerably severe fire suddenly ceased.   A
misdirected shell from a German howitzer had fallen in the
midst of their machine-gun section, and wiped it out.   Then a
body of some 300 German infantry advancing was badly led into
the open, and halted as though bewildered.   A British machine
gun hidden close to " B " Company's left flank opened fire on
the German mass, while the men in the trenches followed suit.
To the company commander watching, the German soldiers

KRUISEECKE RIDGE—*continued*.

seemed to lie down to avoid the fire ; till one of his men said to
him, " Sir, they're a' deid."

Although a British counter-attack on the left had some
success, the general line now lay about half a mile behind on the
north, " B " Company remaining in the air. Possibly there was
a general impression that the Ridge was no longer held. Through
the afternoon the trenches were raked by shell fire. It did not
seem possible to any of the four surviving officers on the Ridge
that evening, that the position could be held much longer without
reinforcement or protection to the exposed flank. In any case
there was nothing that the battered, exhausted survivors crouching in the blood-soaked trenches could well do that night but
try to snatch a little sleep, after disencumbering themselves of
the wounded, the dying, and the dead.

With the first streak of dawn the Germans renewed the attack
with fresh troops, among them some of the best Prussian and
Bavarian divisions, and getting into Zandwoorde they began a
murderous cross-fire against the right of the battalion, whilst
away on the other flank their infantry poured forward north and
south of the Menin Road. Still the invisible and imaginary
forces holding the Ridge kept back the Germans whose task was
to capture it ; but the cross and enfilade fire of guns and rifles
sweeping the reverse slope pinned the defenders to their trenches.

About eleven o'clock definite orders were received by the
battalion to withdraw to a new position, but the runners sent
forward never reached the Ridge, and by evening the flash of
enemy rifles was seen right and left, shells were bursting behind
the Ridge, and the three companies holding the forward position
were practically surrounded. Night fell ; the sky to westward
red with conflagration, above the glare of which the starlike
bursts of stray shells marked the tireless efforts of some German
batteries. Round the Ridge a curious calm seemed suddenly
to descend, broken only by the tragic undercurrent of groans
and calls for help, uttered by a multitude of wounded lying on
the wide battlefield. But in front the darkness was full of
menace ; how long would it be before the massed enemy would
come to complete the work with their bayonets? The four
officers, after some hesitation and argument, decided there was
only one thing left to do—to attempt a withdrawal, if indeed it
were not already too late. Major Burgoyne gave the necessary
orders, and started back with Captain Fleetwood and such
wounded as could walk or help each other along. As they
approached the farmhouse where they had last seen the C.O.

KRUISEECKE RIDGE—*continued.*

they walked straight into the enemy, who were now occupying the building, and were captured. Captain Le Gallais, now the only officer left with " A " Company, fought his way back— a scrambling fight in darkness and confusion, and only two small parties reached Battalion Headquarters.

The survivors of " B " Company, some twenty men under Lieut. Bowen, slipped away from their Prussian neighbours in the trenches and found the British line some time later. Probably not till next morning did the enemy discover that the Ridge was untenanted, save by the corpses of those who had given their lives to hold it.

This dogged resistance long after any hope of support had gone, gained in this part of the battlefield some twenty-four hours at a time when every extra hour that the enemy could be checked was priceless. Of the defenders of the Ridge only some 120 wounded men remained to share in the battle next day.

Well might a German General say to his prisoner, Major Burgoyne : " Your men are warriors." [1]

Gheluvelt Cross-roads, North of the Road, 1914

The 29th October opened in thick fog. North of the Menin Road two companies of the 1/Coldstream, with one of the 1/Black Watch on their right, were holding part of a most inadequate trench line ; there were no traverses, no communication trenches ; one strand of wire slung with tins full of pebbles was stretched in front of them. The two companies of Coldstreamers did not number the strength of more than half a company. In the dense fog of early morning three battalions of the 16/Bavarian Reserve Infantry Regiment advanced up the Menin Road, and came unseen within fifty yards of the trenches. They were held back by rifle fire for a short time ; but two British machine guns jammed, a quantity of cartridges proved to be ill-fitting, and there was no artillery support. Reduced to an allowance of nine rounds per gun, our artillery had been ordered to concentrate on the guns of the enemy that morning.

The Germans broke in near the road, and attacking the Black Watch and Coldstream from the flank, killed or captured nearly the whole of these companies. To their left No. 3 Company and left flank of the Coldstream and the second company of the

[1] This account of the stand made by the 2/Battalion Royal Scots Fusiliers, compiled from the vivid account of Lieut.-Colonel A. G. Baird Smith, D.S.O., is included at greater length than most, as being typical of the stand made by the whole Army.

GHELUVELT CROSS-ROADS, NORTH OF ROAD—*continued*.

Black Watch broke the German attack as they charged three times against their front. When they saw that the troops on their right were overwhelmed, half of No. 3 Company of the Coldstream turned, fighting to their rear ; a small party formed a flank and the Germans were held.

Gheluvelt, South of the Road, 1914

On the south of the road and on lower ground the 1/Grenadier Guards, owing to intervening houses and fog, knew nothing of the disaster that had overwhelmed the Coldstream to the north. At 7.30, with heavy bombardment, the enemy rushed upon the Grenadiers in masses, enveloping their left flank. The support swung to the rear and the battalion fought back to back with direct thrust and parry. As the enormous pressure began to tell on the gallant few, they drew together and charged the enemy, making two counter-attacks in which the Gordon Highlanders joined.

The Gordons were led by Lieut. J. A. O. Brooke. He had been sent along the line with a message, and reached the spot where the Germans were breaking through. Acting with the greatest promptness and ability, he gathered about a hundred men together and led them in a splendid charge, driving the enemy back. He recaptured one of our trenches, the Germans still holding a fire trench within a couple of hundred yards. Lieut. Brooke dashed across the open to send a message back, while the bullets spattered red dust off the cottage walls as he passed. Twice he made the perilous journey, and a brother-officer tells how a Grenadier exclaimed : " My God ! who is that ? He's a devilish brave fellow." He was killed, but what he had done so well and so gallantly had not only linked together the breaking line, but had saved many lives. He was awarded the V.C. and promoted Captain after his death.

In spite of the overwhelming numbers of the enemy, the Grenadiers held on to the ground they had recaptured, and the end of the day found the line intact with the loss of scarcely a hundred yards of ground. Twelve of their officers had been killed and eight wounded, including their Commanding Officer, Lieut.-Colonel M. Earle. As he lay wounded, he saw a German soldier shoot down the medical officer kneeling beside a wounded man, and then approach and look to see if he was alive. The soldier then deliberately raised his rifle and shot the Colonel. This time he was hit in the leg and later in the day was taken prisoner.

GHELUVELT, SOUTH OF THE ROAD—*continued.*

The battalion of the Grenadiers had lost 470 men, mustering only 5 officers and 200 other ranks that night. The Gordons lost about 100 men.

Near Gheluvelt Château, 1914 [1]

"The 1/Battalion Scots Guards had been holding the line near Gheluvelt Château since the night of the 26th October. The night of the 27th to 28th was spent in exploring the hastily dug trenches already in existence. No movement was possible by day and there was considerable shelling and sniping on the night of 28th/29th. Shortly after dawn on the morning of the 29th the Germans attacked in force on a wide frontage. We withheld our fire until the leading wave was about 300 yards away, and then opened bursts of rapid. Germans fell in bundles, but wave after wave pressed on, some of them getting to within 10 or 15 yards of our trenches. Our men were cool and collected and their fire was causing deadly destruction. Eventually the attack died away. I was in command of 'Left Flank' at the time and sent a message back to Battalion Headquarters to the effect that the attack had been repulsed and that the Germans had lost very heavily, to which I got an answer from Captain Stephen, our Adjutant, 'Well done, Left Flank; other companies doing like you.' I could count approximately 400 to 500 dead Germans within 200 yards of my company's trenches, and as 'Right Flank' and 'C' Company had been attacked equally strongly, it is no exaggeration to say that the battalion had so far killed about 1,000 to 1,500 Germans that morning. Our own casualties up to then had been slight ; we were shelled continuously, but our trenches were well concealed and the enemy's shell fire was only fairly accurate. Our men were in the highest spirits and delighted with the result. Shortly afterwards we heard heavy firing which seemed to be coming from our right rear ; there was a hedge between Left Flank and 'C' Company which obscured our view, so I ran across to find out what was happening. I found 'C' Company having a desperate fight with a large force of Germans who were trying to work round their right. Captain Stracey, who was in command of the company, had formed a defensive flank with three of the platoons, as he realised that the Germans had broken through the line somewhere on our right, and this small party was now holding a line at right angles with the rest of the battalion. I

---

[1] From regimental account, by Lieut.-Colonel Sir Victor McKenzie, D.S.O., etc.

Near Gheluvelt Château—*continued.*

could hear ' Right Flank ' under Captain de la Pasture still fighting hard. I spoke to Stracey, who was in splendid spirits, and asked him if he would like any help from my company. He said that he would, and it certainly seemed necessary ; so I brought up two platoons of ' Left Flank ' and prolonged his defensive line to the right. An enormous number of Germans were killed, and after an hour or two they withdrew. One of the battalion machine gunners named Clancy inflicted terrible losses with his Vickers gun—a very gallant man who was killed shortly afterwards. ' Right Flank ' fought to the last man and last round, and practically the whole company was killed or wounded. Two platoons of ' B ' Company, under Lieutenant Campbell, which had been sent up earlier to their assistance, suffered the same fate. The gallant fight put up by ' Right Flank ' and these two platoons of ' B ' Company helped greatly to stem the German outflanking movement, and there is no doubt that Captain Stracey's action in forming a defensive flank finally stopped it. It was a particularly difficult movement to carry out, as it entailed moving his men out of their trenches and lining a hedge at right angles to them under fire, with the extreme probability that this hedge would be enfiladed as soon as the enemy discovered his action.

Captain Stephen had in the meantime ridden back to Brigade Headquarters and explained the situation, pointing out that a large gap existed on our right. It transpired that the Germans had broken through somewhere on the right, where the 1/Black Watch and 1/Coldstream had been wiped out after a most gallant fight.

Captain Stephen personally led up two other battalions to fill this gap, and the situation was saved and the line again intact. Stephen's very strong personality and dauntless courage were most inspiring throughout the day. He was shortly afterwards mortally wounded by shrapnel just outside Battalion Head-quarters. There is no doubt that the 1/Battalion Scots Guards saved the day and that the Germans would have penetrated the British line on a wide frontage but for the gallant fight made by all ranks. The battalion was under the temporary command of Major B. G. Van de Weyer at the time, Colonel Lowther having been wounded at the battle of the Aisne and Major Carpenter Garnier, second-in-command, having been killed at the same battle.

During this day the wounded of all ranks numbered 150, but double that number laid down their lives. Captain and Adjutant

NEAR GHELUVELT CHÂTEAU—*continued*.
A. A. L. Stephen, D.S.O., Captain C. E. de la Pasture, Lieut.
the Hon. G. Macdonald, Lieut. C. F. F. Campbell, 2nd Lieut. Sir
Gilchrist Ogilvy, and 300 other ranks were killed.

The battalion remained in the line until the end of the first
Battle of Ypres, and was reduced in numbers by then to one
officer and 69 other ranks ; the officer being Captain R. G.
Stracey, and he was killed about a month later."

Kruiseecke Area [1]

For seven days in the end of October under heavy shell fire
and against constant attacks the 1/Grenadier Guards held a
dangerous salient inclusive of the village of Kruiseecke, and had
it not been for the two machine guns which remained in position
during the whole period under continuous fire and fired 56,000
rounds, their losses would have been enormous.

It is difficult to make invidious distinctions and select any
particular company or platoon for special notice when all must
have fought so gallantly, but perhaps mention may be made of
two platoons that were sent up to hold vacated trenches a mile
to the left of the battalion. This particular part of the line
proved to be the objective of two German battalions supported
by machine guns, but these two platoons succeeded in holding
the line, and never gave an inch although they were nearly all
killed, including the two officers, 2nd Lieut. Walter and
2nd Lieut. Somerset.

Very gallant, too, was the counter-attack carried out by
No. 4 Company under Major Colby on the 26th, which was specially mentioned by Major-General Capper in his report. The
Germans were trying to break through the line between the
Grenadiers and Yorkshire Regiment, and this company was sent
up to restore the line. In spite of heavy enfilade fire and exceedingly difficult wired ground, they succeeded in driving back a
much larger body of the enemy with the loss of all but one
officer and 45 men.

But perhaps, if the truth could be known, the most heroic acts
of bravery were performed by men in the isolated bodies which
were occasionally cut off—acts that must necessarily remain
unchronicled and unrewarded since all were killed. Some of
these men must have fought on gamely until overwhelmed by
masses of the enemy.

[1] From regimental account, by Sir Frederick Ponsonby, G.C.B.

South of Menin Road

On the 31st the 1/Grenadiers were employed for a counter-attack which had far-reaching effects, and which was described by Major-General Capper as being mainly instrumental in restoring the battle south of the Ypres—Menin Road.

The 1/Battalion was sent up hurriedly to reoccupy some lost trenches and stop the Germans who were breaking through. Owing to the advance having to be made under heavy fire, hardly fifty of all ranks reached the trench, but these sufficed to hold the enemy in check.

Gheluvelt, 1914, " The Critical Day," 31st October

The name Gheluvelt will for all time recall one of the most critical and one of the most dramatic days in the history of our nation. The Kaiser had proclaimed an intention to join his Forces for a triumphal entry into Ypres. Gheluvelt denied him passage.

Our line was held by the dwindling battalions which had been fighting night and day, with ever fewer men to guard the road. And of the ways converging on Ypres, the Menin Road was the straightest and the best approach for the enemy armies.

On the morning of the 31st October our line lay across their path, just east of Gheluvelt on the forward slope of the slight rise, very exposed to bombardment, but of value to us for observation.

On the road itself—400 yards east of the church—the 2nd Welsh Regiment covered the village to the north, and to their left were the 1/South Wales Borderers, the 1/Scots Guards, 1/Cameron Highlanders, and 1/Black Watch, in this order up to Polygon Wood. From the road southward were extended three companies of the 1/Queen's, the 2/K.R.R.C., the fourth company of the Queen's, two companies of the Loyal North Lancs, and the Royal Welch Fusiliers.

As daylight broke, the whole of this line was attacked by infantry, and the assault was repelled, the 1/Scots Guards even capturing half a hundred Bavarians, being themselves so few in number that they borrowed an escort for their prisoners from the South Wales Borderers, in support. In only one spot had the enemy any success ; they got into a little orchard between the Queen's and the K.R.R.C. This success, however, was calamitous to our sparse defence, as the enemy were able to enfilade the Queen's, and the violent, systematic bombardment which by now was ravaging the front stopped any counter-attack from expelling him.

GHELUVELT—*continued.*

At 9.30 the Welch had been actually blown out of their trenches ; and a company of eighty of the Gloucesters, coming up in the gap, numbered only fifteen by the time they arrived. Thirteen battalions of the enemy troops had come to the assault, cheering and singing with great enthusiasm, while two batteries of their artillery blazed high explosive and shrapnel at close range. One thousand men—barely that number—met the tremendous attack, met it with such a storm of rapid rifle fire that the Germans reported afterwards to have met " machine guns behind every bush, hedge, and fragment of wall," " counter-attacks by fresh troops," and strong defences.

For five hours of bulldog endurance the line was held, while the salient was cut off from the outside world by a curtain of shell fire.

The Queen's were now enfiladed from either flank, but valiantly reported that " it was quite all right." A farm in their projecting line caught fire, and the blazing heat and flames added to the horror of the hour. Their C.O., Lieut.-Colonel B. T. Pell, had been mortally wounded, and Major Watson, now in command, formed up for a counter-attack. Before orders could be carried out, the enemy was seen to be behind " D " Company. Major Watson collected what men he could find. A storm of fire was bursting on them from the front and either flank, and yet there was no one visible on whom to retaliate. Lieut. Boyle took charge of " a motley throng from various regiments " with only Sergeant Butler and thirteen men of the Queen's amongst them, and fell in along the line of hedge just south of the Menin Road, while Major Watson made his way back under heavy fire to report to H.Q. He returned, and at 11 o'clock searched all round the 3rd Brigade to find any more of his men, but in vain. In this day 624 had been killed, wounded, or were missing.

On the 1st November the 1/Battalion of the Queen's consisted of thirty-two men, including cooks and transport.

Gheluvelt itself was by now a shattered ruin, with tumbling masonry and houses in flames, and the few men left alive of the K.R.R.C. and the Loyal North Lancs fell back to the road running south from Veldhoek, in touch with the Gloucesters on their left.

The enemy attacked south of the road, where about 400 men of the 2/Royal Scots Fusiliers and the other two companies of the 1/Loyal North Lancs held over half a mile of front in a line of small pits, some 15 yards apart, two men in each. They had orders not to retire ; they stood till noon, shooting down every

GHELUVELT—*continued.*

German who showed himself, until at last the enemy were round
them and the end came.

Terrible as was the report of the loss of Gheluvelt—the news
was carried back that men and guns had retired by order, and
there was no debacle. A counter-attack was attempted by the
last reserve, three companies of the Gloucesters and a party of
the Welch, and the surviving K.R.R.C. and Loyal North Lancs
who had joined them.

North of the road what was left of the Scots Guards with the
last company of the Welch and the South Wales Borderers were
fighting a desperate battle against four times their numbers ;
only eighteen rifles of the Welch were firing, and these were overwhelmed, and the two right companies of the Borderers smashed
back by shell fire through the Château grounds. The Scots
Guards with the remainder of the Borderers all mixed up together
held to their post, with the Camerons and Black Watch beyond
them.

As the overwhelming assault drove through the Château
grounds, the shattered remnant of the Borderers and the Scots
Guards, under Lieut.-Colonel Leach of the Borderers, charged
with the bayonet. The enemy fled, dropping arms and equipment, and our line was restored as far south as the village ;
and a message passed through to General FitzClarence asking
for any possible reinforcement to retake the place and stop the gap.

He galloped back to his headquarters on the edge of Glencorse
Wood, and reported to General Lomax, who agreed that he should
call upon the reserve—three companies of the 2/Worcestershire
Regiment, waiting for such a crisis in Polygon Wood. General
FitzClarence spread a map upon the ground and planned the
attack, then sent the orders to Major Hankey of the Worcesters,
and went himself to see the charge.

In the meanwhile General Lomax rode back to Hooge Château
and reported briefly : " My line is broken." This was the worst
hour of those dark and awful days, an hour when the fate of
Britain—aye, of the world—trembled in the balance. And
then came the miracle. Charging down from Polygon Wood,
across a thousand yards of open country, devoid of any cover,
came the men of the Worcesters—357 in all. They swept across
the ground towards flaming Gheluvelt ; high explosive and
shrapnel burst over them ; the wounded they met cried of the
certain death awaiting them ; enemy fire was redoubled upon
them, but they rushed on—over a hundred men were down
already—they burst upon the Germans and drove them out of

GHELUVELT—*continued.*

Gheluvelt, fighting from street to street. They gained touch with the remnants of the Scots Guards and South Wales Borderers, who, almost surrounded, still fought on in the Château grounds.

Then General FitzClarence galloped back a second time and the magnificent message went through : " It's all right. My line holds."

Hooge Château, 1914

At the critical hour of that most critical day the 31st October, the Headquarter Staffs of the 1st and 2nd Divisions gathered in the annexe of Hooge Château to discuss the almost desperate situation. Low above the house an enemy plane wheeled, and not long after the throb of the engine had died away a shell crashed into the grounds. A second fell on the annexe building, and burst in the middle of the conference. Major-General Lomax was so severely wounded that he never recovered, and died in England some time afterwards. Six of the Staff Officers assembled were killed on the spot ; four were wounded, and yet another mortally wounded by another shell. General Monro escaped with his life ; he had been standing in the doorway. Though badly stunned, he continued to command his division. Only one officer of the party was unhurt.

It was at about this time that Sir Douglas Haig was seen trotting slowly and steadily eastward along the Menin Road towards Hooge, followed by most of his staff as at an inspection—a sight most cheering to the fighting men at that desperate moment.

Hooge Château, 1914

In his book " 1914 " Sir John French describes his visit to Hooge on the 31st October 1914. The spectacle on the road " filled him with misgiving and alarm. It seemed as though the whole of the I Corps were about to retreat in confusion. In the press of wagons, ammunition-carts, all going westward, the most sinister sign was the movement of heavy howitzers retiring at the trot. Shells were screaming overhead and bursting all around." He received from Generals Haig and Gough the news of the disaster to the second divisional staff at Hooge Château, and of the " serious position, as the 1st Division had broken back and were in full retreat only a mile or so from where we were standing, with the Germans at their heels. What grieved me more than anything else was that the I Corps should at last be forced back after the glorious stand they had made.

HOOGE CHÂTEAU—*continued.*

I felt that they had done far more than could be expected of any men, and that even if they were driven to the sea they had earned their country's lasting gratitude for the determined fight they had made. No shadow of blame could be laid on them or their comrades." A further stand seemed impossible. Sir John French felt " as if the last barriers between the Germans and the Channel sea-board were broken down." He finishes this record by saying : " It was a dramatic half-hour, the worst I ever spent in a life full of vicissitudes such as mine had been. . . . It was a truly dramatic climax. At about 3 p.m. a staff officer galloped up with the news that the 1st Division had rallied, and again moved forward. Gheluvelt was once more in our hands."

Gheluvelt, 1914

During the afternoon of the 31st October an exciting gunner duel took place on the Menin Road. The enemy brought a piece up and prepared to come into action on the road at 1,000 yards' range. A gunner subaltern—Blewett, of the 3rd Brigade R.F.A.—whistled up an 18-pounder on to the road. The two guns faced each other, and both fired off the first round at the same moment. The Germans had the range wrong, but the British were right. With the second round of high explosive the German gun and detachment were blown to pieces.

Molenaarelsthoek, 1914

Battery Quartermaster-sergeant Moss went out with the 70th Battery R.F.A. in August, and on the 1st October put up the one star and took command of a section in his battery. On the 31st October an enemy gun was reported to be in action and doing considerable damage, just behind the German trenches to the south. After reconnaissance with the forward observing officer he informed the O.C. that the Boche gun was plainly visible, and that he could get one of our 18-pounders to within 500 yards of it. Major Stanley Clarke had just received an issue of 24 rounds of H.E. and he ordered the limber to be filled entirely with this. 2nd Lieut. Moss led the gun forward until they got on to the Passchendaele—Becelaere Road, unhooked, and the section man-handled it along to the chosen spot, where they pushed the muzzle through the hedge. There was another hedge a little way in front that masked the enemy's trenches, and to this crawled 2nd Lieut. Moss carrying a reaping-hook ; arrived, he cut a neat hole in direct line from gun to gun. He returned and, taking the place of layer, pulled the fire lever,

MOLENAARELSTHOEK—*continued.*
and fired his gun over open sights, timing his shot to catch a
party of Germans who, all unaware, were advancing from their
trench with fixed bayonets. The first shot hit the gun ; the
second and third completed its wrecking, and 2nd Lieut.
Moss used the rest of his ammunition to crump the trenches and
houses near, that belched machine-gun fire. He withdrew his
gun safely at dusk ; and the twisted remains of the German
piece could be seen lying on its side, and in front of the trenches
three heaps of German dead. This was the first use of H.E. by
18-pounders in the War.

West of Gheluvelt

On the 2nd November three companies of the 1/Battalion
King's Royal Rifle Corps here held a shallow, disconnected
trench without wire ; they had definite orders not to retire.
Two hundred men of the 1/Coldstream, with two officers—all
that remained of the battalion—lay on their left. The enemy,
strongly reinforced and covered by a curtain of artillery, advanced
like a rising tide and overwhelmed them. Half the Coldstream
were killed or captured, and the men of the Rifle Corps, machine-
gunned and bombed from front and rear, fought to the terrible
end and were never seen again. To right and left the Royal
Berkshire and 1/Scots Guards stood fast, and the Black Watch,
fighting their way up company by company, and with numbers
reduced to 75, filled the gap and stopped the thrust on the road.

Gheluvelt Château [1]

" We found the infantry in position in the garden of a château.
Their coolness was admirable. They had been under constant
fire for several days, were ragged, unkempt, and grimy, short of
rations and ammunition ; but not a man appeared to be weary
of the fight. Above the appalling din could be heard the cool,
concise orders of the officers, not less ragged than their men,
but undaunted and equal to any emergency. In front was
Zonnebeke Church surmounted by a German Red Cross flag.
Black Marias would come over in groups of four and burst with
a villainous roar and clouds of yellow smoke."

Zonnebeke—Becelaere Road [2]

On the 8th November 1914 the 2nd South Staffordshire Regiment, the old 80th (Staffordshire Volunteers), was holding the

[1] *The Northumberland Hussars' History.*
[2] Contributed by the regiment.

ZONNEBEKE—BECELAERE ROAD—*continued.*
most advanced line of the whole British Army.   The Germans,
in great force, attacked the French on their immediate left, and
broke through.   The South Staffords were ordered nevertheless
to hold on, and did so against repeated attacks on their left,
little groups of desperate men holding their positions to the
very last. » Among them was the litle group of twenty men holding
an island redoubt in a spinney 300 yards west of the Zonnebeke—
Becelaere Road, to whom the verses written by Lord Gorell
refer.

HOW THE SOUTH STAFFORDSHIRES HELD THE TRENCH [1]

Nineteen men and a sergeant stood
Grimly to arms as the word was passed !
" We can spare no more ! you must hold this trench ;
Stick to it, cling to it right to the last."

Nineteen men and a sergeant watched
With smothered jest as the dawn drew nigh
Cruel and cold, like a patient ghoul,
Till a man could see to struggle and die.

Out of the silence, out of the gloom,
Came with a scream the ranging shell,
First of the furies, till with the day
The twenty were crouched in a battered Hell.

Cavernous, pitted, the Belgian fields
Stretched in their ruin before the light ;
And the tumult sank, with a remnant left
Ripe for the thrust of the foeman's might.

On and on in their hosts they came
As the sun strode over the surging field,
Withered and broke and rallied and came
At the handful ignorant how to yield.

And the dusk stole down and the hosts drew back
Baffled and bitter and reeling and thin,
Sank to the arms of the pitiful night—
And the dead were too many to gather in.

[1] Contributed by the regiment.

" Not a word from that trench the whole day long
And still at night not a word to me !
Go, bring me the truth ! " the Colonel said ;
And they crept through the ruins of earth to see.

Silence ! nought else through the field, in the trench,
And never the murmuring more in jest !
Crushed but unbroken, dead, unsubdued,
Nineteen men lay bosomed in rest.

They came to the last—till his watch was done
His shattered body had death defied ;
And, roused by the voice of an English friend,
" We have held it as ordered," he said—and died.

Polygon Wood, 1914 [1]

" The part taken by the 1/Battalion Coldstream Guards differed from the work the 2/ and 3/Battalions were called upon to carry out in the final stages of the first Battle of Ypres. They belonged to the 1st Guards Brigade, and were involved in the heaviest fighting that took place at that critical time. After the severe fighting at Gheluvelt on the 30th October the battalion had lost all its officers and only 95 men came out of the battle. On the 1st November a draft arrived for the 1/Battalion consisting of 2 officers and 80 men ; they were thrown straight into the fight and were practically wiped out.

The 2/ and 3/Battalions reached Polygon Wood on the 25th October. The orders of the 2/Battalion were to link up on their left with the 1/Battalion Irish Guards, and on the right with the 2/Battalion Highland Light Infantry. The position of the enemy on the left was not known beyond the fact that he held Reutel Spur ; there was no time to be lost, and it was essential to fill the gap at once, and to march in file along narrow tracks through thick plantations was the only way to do the task. The line to be held could not be selected, being governed by the two flanks, and was a very extended one. The three companies in the front line dug themselves in, all available wire was used, and a very strong abattis of felled saplings made the position such a strong one that though several attacks matured during the next three weeks, they were easily repulsed by the deadly rifle fire which was then at the height of its effectiveness.

[1] From regimental contribution, by Major-General Sir Cecil Pereira, K.C.B., C.M.G.

POLYGON WOOD—*continued*.

The 2/ and 3/Battalions met at a right angle, so both battalions were subject to an enfilade fire, whilst the 3/Battalion on the left of the 2/Battalion had open level ground in front of them. The fact that they had several times been the best shooting battalions in the Army made a successful attack on their front very problematical ; they were on high ground and had dry trenches.

The position of the 2/Battalion was one of extreme discomfort. Their trenches, being on the lower slopes, held water permanently. The casualties in the 2/Battalion averaged nearly twenty a day for the twenty-four days that they held the position.

It is not everyone who realises the great advantage this naturally strong position was and its great importance, as behind the Polygon Wood reserves could be concentrated in perfect security, ready to counter the continual German thrusts down the Menin Road.

When first in the Polygon Wood our patrols could move freely to the front, and many were the horrors they discovered that made it a gruesome place. Three dead Germans were found tied to trees, three others were found hanging from trees. Wounded were brought in : two Germans who had lain out two days, a corporal of the Worcesters who had been wounded five days previously, and two days later a private soldier in the Worcesters who had actually been lying out there wounded for seven days. Once or twice German patrols had threatened him with a rifle, but one good German Samaritan had given him food, and as he was near a stream he could dip his water-bottle in it. Strange to say, he was cheerful when brought in and immediately asked for a cigarette, but his wounds were in a shocking state. There were numbers of dead bodies, both our own and Germans.

On the 5th November the survivors of the 1/Battalion under command of the battalion quartermaster, Captain Boys, were attached to the 3/Battalion, and so for a short while the whole regiment at the front was under the command of the senior Lieut.-Colonel. On the 12th November a gale laid low the Wood in front of the 2/Battalion ; the trees had been pierced with countless bullets. This unfortunately removed every vestige of cover we had had until then. Wet, and in the foul clothing we had worn for several weeks, we were relieved by the French on the 17th November and quitted the loathsome wood."

In a letter to Lieut.-Colonel Pereira, Lord Cavan, who commanded the 4th Guards Brigade, writes : " I should like to put on record that for the past four weeks they [the Coldstream]

POLYGON WOOD—*continued.*
have held their line intact under hardships and strain that it
is impossible to describe. . . . It is not too much to say that
the whole safety of the line has depended on their staunchness,
and truly worthily have they held it.   Their trenches, dug on a
hill of natural springs, have been undrainable and constantly
full of water above the knees for twenty-three days.   The gale
of about the 2nd November cleared the wood in which they
were of every particle of cover, the trees having all been pierced
by shrapnel and bullets. . . . They finally rejoined the Brigade on
the right flank of this part of the British line on the 17th November in as good heart as the day they left England.   I am more
proud to be their Brigadier than any words can possibly express,
and I owe them undoubtedly, with their comrades of the Grenadier
and Irish Guards, the satisfaction of handing over our line to
the French intact and unconquered."

NONNE BOSSCHEN BATTLE, Nov. 1914

The battle-ground which was the arena whereon our soldiers
were proved against the Prussian Guards covers a line northward
from the middle of Shrewsbury Forest, across the Menin Road,
east to Veldhoek, Glencorse Wood, and Nonne Bosschen, to the
south-western corner of Polygon Wood.

At 9 a.m. on the 11th November after two and a half hours of
terrible bombardment, twenty-five battalions of the most famous
regiments of the Prussian Army, at full strength and fresh to
the battle, attacked along and on either side of the Menin Road.
They numbered at least 17,500 infantry, and between them and
crowning victory there stood one thin, unsupported line—in
all 7,850.   These few men had not ceased fighting day and night
for three weeks, and now opposed the glory of Prussia, worn out,
half-fed, unshaven, in rags.   Such was the material barrier, but
who can fully comprehend the spirit that animated the defenders.

The Prussian legions were broken and exhausted.

Veldhoek Wood

The Fusilier Battalions of the German 2nd Guards Grenadier
Regiment entered Veldhoek Wood, and reached the Château.
Here the 2/Duke of Wellington's (a depleted battalion from the
II Corps) fought them hand to hand in single combat until they
became a disorganised crowd, and were reduced to a remnant of
their proud strength.   A charge of the reserve company drove
the survivors out of the Wood, but the English battalion had
lost 7 officers and 380 men.

Stout Wood

The great attack of the Prussian Guard on the 11th November made no impression whatever on the war-worn brigades under McCracken and Gleichen, who had come up from the II Corps at La Bassée with one day's rest. The German official account was most flattering to the men who held the usual inadequate defences : " Great difficulties were encountered. Deep trenches, broad obstacles, and enfilade machine-gun fire combined to make progress slow."

There was no progress, and though the Prussians advanced again and again in consecutive lines, they fell back again and again, and not a German got anywhere near the trenches.

Becelaere

In the early morning the enemy, having sapped close up in dense fog, rushed a trench held by the Highland Light Infantry. A hand-to-hand mêlée followed in mist and darkness, Captain Brodie leading his Highlanders with the bayonet. He killed eight men, fell, lay pretending to be dead, crawled back and brought up some more of his detachment. The trench was cleared and fifty-four of the attackers were taken prisoners. Captain Brodie gained the V.C., and after distinguished service was killed in command of a battalion of his regiment in August 1918.

East of Hooge, South of Menin Road

At dawn of the 11th November the front-line trenches held here by the Royal Fusiliers were hammered to pieces and many men buried. No one could carry messages through it, as it was impossible to live under such bombardment. The first shock of the attack by the 4th Queen Augusta's Guards Grenadiers was met and held back by the bayonet. Only one Fusilier officer was left, and he wounded in the head. In a second charge some of the Germans got through to the supports in the rear—a draft arrived the previous day, and not yet formed into a platoon. Colonel McMahon ran to rally them when he was hit in the leg, fell to the ground, and was killed directly afterwards by a shell. He had been promoted to a brigade, but could not be spared from the regiment at this critical time to take up the post. The remainder of the Fusiliers had become very much scattered, and in the evening only two officers and fifty men could be collected. Later 170 men were mustered, and these held on to their positions in rain and snow until on the 15th

EAST OF HOOGE, SOUTH OF MENIN ROAD—*continued*.
November they were withdrawn into divisional reserve. Within
the first four months of the War the battalion had been wiped
out twice, losing 1,900 men and over 50 officers.

Nonne Bosschen Sector, 11th November, 1914

ATTACK OF THE PRUSSIAN GUARD

The heaviest bombardment that preceded the onslaught of
the Prussian Guard on the 11th November crashed into the
much-fought sector about the Menin Road west of Gheluvelt.
The 1st (Guards) Brigade under Brigadier-General FitzClarence,
which now consisted of some 800 men of the 1/Scots Guards,
1/Black Watch, and 1/Cameron Highlanders, held the very
meagre trenches from north of the road to the south-west corner
of Polygon Wood. The Wood itself was held by the 1/King's :
450 men with 6 officers holding a mile-long stretch of the line
along the southern edge with no supports or reserve. This line
made a right angle with the 1st Brigade, while the Coldstream
carried it along to the north. This front was a series of holes
spotted along the Wood five or ten yards apart, and holding
each only one or two men.

The whole sector was now in an awful plight, as constant
shelling overhead and a morass of mud underfoot had prevented
the arrival of rations. The men were living chiefly on rum and
biscuits, which with the filthy state of the trenches had begun
to tell on their health. For nearly three weeks they had been
fighting, while each day death took heavy toll among their
comrades.

On the morning of the 11th the columns of gigantic men of the
Prussian Guards [1] came up in assault. They carried their rifles
at the port, the officers sword in hand. Our front-line trench
was very lightly manned, and the greatest weight of the attack
fell on our centre and overwhelmed the Scots Guards, Camerons,
and Black Watch, though their valorous resistance broke up the
coherence of the enemy advance, which, instead of continuing
straight on due north-west, lost direction and divided its front.
There was now, however, a gap in our line into which the Prussians
pushed at great speed, destroying a tiny garrison of cooks and
details of the Scots Guards in FitzClarence Farm, and rushing
two machine guns of this battalion, and of the Camerons, which
emptied their belts at point-blank range before the crews
went under. At Northampton Farm the Scots Guards held

[1] Some of their wounded proved to be too long for our stretchers.

out, and this point was never captured.   To the north of the gap
the 1/King's from their holes in the ground met the 3rd Foot
Guard Regiment with such withering fire that the assault was
stopped.   Here a solid wall of German dead within 70 yards was
mistaken in the half-light for a second attack.   The first battalions of Prussians were now forced to lie down and dig in
south of the King's, who entered in their War Diary that the
battalion found itself " supported on the right by the Prussian
Guard."

.   .   .   .   .   .

Two companies of the Black Watch were entrenched in the
south-west corner of Polygon Wood when the Prussian Guard
attacked.   They were engulfed, and their O.C., 2nd Lieut. M.
McNut, was last seen standing up on the parapet, fighting, revolver
in hand, and holding on to the finish with all his men.   Behind
this trench was a small position strengthened with wire.   This
had been sited and constructed by Major C. Russell-Brown,
23rd Field Company of the Royal Engineers, and was the first
" strong-point " (so called), originating a plan which was afterwards one of the chief elements of defensive warfare.   " D "
Company in support held this position under Lieut. Anderson,
the " strong-point " splitting the attackers into small parties,
which passed on and overwhelmed the companies in reserve,
and managed to get for a time into Verheck Farm, the joint
headquarters of the Black Watch and the Cameron Highlanders.
The two commanding officers, Lieut.-Colonel C. E. Stewart and
Lieut.-Colonel D. McEwan, with Sergeant Redpath (signalling
sergeant to the Black Watch), put up an extraordinarily gallant
defence of the actual Headquarters dugout—a brushwood
lean-to against the farmhouse wall.   Although Colonel Stewart
was wounded in the head at point-blank range by a German,
the three Scotsmen succeeded in repelling the enemy and holding
the primitive Headquarters safe.
Furious fighting continued in Black Watch Corner, and
although the enemy failed to break through the line of guns
behind, and the battalion had broken up the main attack in
this district, the losses were grievous, and only one officer—
Captain Fortune—was unwounded at the end of the day.
The leading units of the Prussian Guard, diverted by the rifle
fire of the British, turned into the shelter of the undefended
Nonne Bosschen, pressed onward, and burst from the western

WEST OF NONNE BOSSCHEN—*continued.*
fringe of the wood.   Here they came face to face with a line
of guns. . . .

. . . . . .

The guns of the 2nd Division Artillery stood in line with
intervals from Bellewaarde to Polygon Wood, the XLI Brigade
R.F.A. being in action east of Westhoek which brought them
behind the 1st Brigade of the 1st Division.[1]   They had been
warned by the fury of bombardment and the severing of all
telephonic communication that something tremendous was
happening on their front.   Their officers in the O.P.s of the Guards
Brigade were cut off, although two corporals, Richardson and
Cook, went out and stayed all through the bombardment trying
to mend the wires.   Major Clark, commanding the 16th Battery,
dashed back with his signallers just as the German artillery began
to lift, and through its fire reached the battery and opened upon
the enemy as they appeared between Polygon Wood and Nonne
Bosschen.   About twenty minutes later Major Rochfort Boyd
arrived from his O Pip near Lone House in the front line.   He
had seen the first charge of the Prussians, " using the bayonet
with a kind of grunting cheer," move upon our front, dividing
to pass the ruins in which he lay.   Realising that he had scarce
time to attempt to get back to his battery before the second
line overwhelmed him, he sprang out and actually came along
with the Germans.   As he was wearing an old-fashioned blue
coat he was unrecognised in the mist, and by gradually " side-
stepping " managed to work his way round the flank of the
front line, and raced to warn the batteries.

The position was growing more and more serious.   Telephonic
communication being cut, Lieut. Lund, Orderly Officer, became
messenger to Headquarters.   On reaching Westhoek he collected
four or five drivers and gunners and men of the Officers' Mess
Staff, issued them with French rifles and ammunition, and
placed them in a sunken lane behind the 16th Battery.   These
men remained in action, firing on the Prussians, till their ammunition was used up, and as the day advanced similar scratch parties
lined the fences, manned farm buildings, and joined rifle fire
with the charges from the guns in driving back the Germans.
The imperturbable nature of the breed was exemplified in the
impossibility of impressing a gunner, even armed with a hand-
gun, of the gravity of the hour.   One man, having collected

[1] Batteries to north and south that brought fire to bear on the Prussians
penetrating the Wood, were the 22nd Battery XXXIV Brigade, and 51st
Battery XXXIX Brigade.

WEST OF NONNE BOSSCHEN—*continued*.

souvenirs in the shape of a German helmet, a second French rifle, and other oddments, carried them from place to place, checking the lot each time, their care being more urgent than the repulse of the Prussian Guard 200 yards away.

About 9.30 Major Clark with the 16th Battery saw hostile rifle fire coming from the Nonne Bosschen in front of him. At this moment Lieut. Murray (Orderly Officer to the XXXIX Brigade R.F.A.) arrived riding an unsaddled horse in great haste to find out the position, and volunteered to reconnoitre for Major Clark. He galloped forward, circling round and reappearing on the other flank, capless, and pursued by rifle bullets, and reported the enemy in force in the Nonne Bosschen. He said he had come in a hurry because his horse, an excitable pulling brute, disliked the bullets, and consequently he had lost his cap, which he must immediately return to find. He galloped off again, and reappeared bringing accurate news of the German positions, and had even found his cap, though he was infuriated because a Boche had removed the badge.

The 5th Field Company R.E. with a small party of the Connaught Rangers held a trench and denied passage to the enemy between Polygon Wood and Nonne Bosschen. The Engineers had left their company cooks—five sappers—behind in bivouac. These men were asked to find out if a house about 400 yards in front harboured any Germans, as shots seemed to be coming from this direction. The five sappers advanced under fire. Arriving within 100 yards, two proceeded to storm the house, while three kept up a covering fire. The garrison bolted, leaving two prisoners in the hands of the cooks.

By this time stronger parties of the enemy came into sight with increasing fire from the Nonne Bosschen, and the break-in of the front menaced a terrible disaster. The XLI Brigade had become, west of the Wood, the British firing line. Every available man who could hold a rifle was collected—drivers, gunners, cooks, headquarters men, two sections of the 5th Field Co., R.E., some few of the Connaught Rangers came in line with the guns; fuses were shortened for only enough elevation to clear the ground immediately in front, and to burst within 300 yards.

So the great Prussian Guard, debouching from the Wood, came on this grim, immobile line of guns, indomitable still, and firing steadily. Doubtless they thought they had reached a strong second line of defence. The picture we see is that of these gigantic men, whose numbers, courage, and military training had pierced the weakest point in our line—we see these picked

WEST OF NONNE BOSSCHEN—*continued*.

troops leading the charge from the Wood into the open, to be flung back by a point-blank fire of guns and rifles, manned by the scratch muster of Britain's last line. They broke and fled back into the Wood.

The magnificent Prussian Guard had been broken and scattered by this thin last line of British resistance. A captured German officer asked a battery commander : " Where are your reserves ? " A hand pointed to the line of guns. Incredulous he asked, " But what is there behind ? " Reply : " Divisional Headquarters."

Is it strange that he cried aloud, " Allmächtiggott " ?

. . . .

The gap forced in the early morning was by now closed everywhere, reinforcements from the 2nd Brigade having been pushed up, but the Nonne Bosschen was still to be cleared of the repulsed parties of the Prussian Guard. The 2/Oxford Light Infantry were in hand and had already been sent up in touch with the 1st Division at Westhoek ; they received the order to counterattack. The battalion now numbered about 350 in all, but they charged the Wood with the extraordinary verve and dash, the disciplined manœuvring, that distinguished the 52nd of old. The pace of their advance through the undergrowth was astonishing, and they drove the Prussian Guards helter-skelter, killing or capturing any who stayed. As the " drive " was pressed through the Wood it reached a hot corner where some Northamptons and Camerons waited in Glencorse Wood. Heralded by a rise of pheasants, the Prussians were beaten out into the open and shot down. The 5th Field Company R.E. joined in charging southwards between the Wood. The Oxfordshires had come through with hardly any losses, and this counter-attack ended the battle.

Nearly a hundred years ago the Prussians coming on the field of Waterloo wheeled in slow time with bands playing in recognition of the prowess of the armies that defeated the Old Guard of France ; and their leader embraced the Regimental Colour of the 52nd. . . .

East of Nonne Bosschen and Glencorse Wood

DEATH OF BRIGADIER-GENERAL CHARLES FITZCLARENCE, V.C.

Here on the 12th November 1914 fell he whose valour and leadership in these battles had gained that very distinctive honour, a name given by the troops—Brigadier-General Charles FitzClarence, V.C., " G.O.C. Menin Road."

EAST OF NONNE BOSSCHEN AND GLENCORSE WOOD—*continued*.

In the middle of a night of storm and torrential rain he led a counter-attack to clear the Prussian Guard from the trenches they occupied after their repulse of yesterday. Heading the remnant of the 2nd Grenadiers and Irish Guards marching in column of fours, he came, went forward alone to reconnoitre, and was shot down by rifle fire. Thus, after the last critical day of the stupendous battle, went forth for ever a great spirit that had inspired victory.

The 1st (Guards) Brigade that had been Brigadier-General FitzClarence's command mustered on the 12th November less than the strength of a half-battalion. It was made up as follows :

Battalions.	Officers.	Other Ranks.
1/Coldstream Guards	None	150
1/Scots Guards	1 Captain	69
1/Black Watch	1 Lieutenant	109
1/Cameron Highlanders	1 Lieut.-Colonel,	
„ „	1 Major, 1 Lieutenant	140
Totals	5	468

Polygon Wood, 1914 [1]

The 1/Bn The King's Regiment came from the fighting about Wieltje, and were put into the fighting line again after a few hours' rest and marched to that south-west corner of Polygon Wood which for sixteen days became their battleground and the supreme test of their endurance. They were ordered to hold the position at all costs, and every officer and man was aware that the costs would not be light, because of the heavy bombardment that was opened upon them from the German batteries at close range on the Gheluvelt Ridge.

Under continuous shelling casualties were suffered hour by hour, until on 3rd November the strength of the battalion had dwindled to 400 men and 4 officers in the line. Rain had fallen heavily and the ground was a quagmire, so that many rifles were choked with mud and could not be cleaned for lack of rifle oil. Sections of the trenches had been destroyed, and in parts the men had to wade knee-deep in water and were chilled to the bone. It was impossible to get any warmth. Fires could not be lit as they would immediately draw German gun fire, and even smoking was forbidden for the same reason. Hot drink was unobtainable, and it was difficult to get up rations owing to the lack of men. Wounded men had to be dragged out of deep slime and there were no dugouts of any kind. There

[1] Epitomised from regimental account, by Sir Philip Gibbs.

POLYGON WOOD—*continued*.

was no illusion in the minds of the officers and men of the King's
Regiment as to their precarious position.   In their weak strength
they were holding a front of nearly a mile.   Their two machine
guns had been put out of action.   Barbed-wire entanglements
and obstacles put up to form some defence were blown to bits.
Our own guns, restricted in ammunition, made but a feeble
reply to the enemy's ceaseless shell fire.   There were no supports
or reserves behind the King's Regiment.   The men had to rely
upon their rifles and bayonets to hold off attack after attack
flung upon their line by the best troops of Germany.

It was upon the 10th November that the enemy gathered
their full strength for the capture of Polygon Wood after days
and nights of heavy bombardments and minor attacks.   Large
bodies of troops were reported moving across the front, and at
5.30 in the evening they attacked the line held by " B " Company,
but could not dislodge it.   At dawn next morning the bombardment increased in fury, many trenches being blown in, and at
9.30 the Prussian Guard was hurled against the battalion front.
It is surely an unforgettable achievement of valour that those
men of the King's Regiment, lacking sleep and food, with dead
and wounded men lying in their ditches, and in such small
numbers, should have repulsed the great attack on their part of
the line.   Although the Prussian Guard succeeded in penetrating
some trenches on the right where the Black Watch and the
Camerons had suffered frightful casualties, the King's Regiment
held the whole of its front unbroken, and beat off all attacks till
the enemy was stopped by the guns west of Nonne Bosschen.

The German Emperor's hopes of a straight walk through to
the coast had been disappointed by that day's history along a
front of which Polygon Wood was but a small point.   But the
1/Battalion of the King's Regiment was one strong link in that
chain of courage which held the British line against great odds.
It was not the end of the ordeal.   The bombardment continued
for four more days.   The attacks were repeated and repulsed
again.   The rain had turned to snow, adding to the physical
misery of the men and revealing the ghastly picture of Polygon
Wood, where many dead lay among the shell-slashed trees.
When at last the King's Regiment was relieved and staggered
back for rest, the surviving officers and men, unshaven, covered
in mud, haggard and spent, were unrecognisable by those comrades who had known them before the battle.   But in their
tired bodies was the spirit of men who had refused to yield an
inch of ground along the road to Ypres.

Gheluvelt Cross-roads [1]

North of the cross-roads east of Gheluvelt is a position of specially proud memory to Yorkshire men. Here the 2/Green Howards held on to their trenches quite immovable for three weeks, under shell fire the whole time, attacked and attacking night and day. From the 22nd October they were defending two fronts where the enemy had forced their way in between them and the Royal Scots Fusiliers. These were days of close and savage fighting under a crescendo of tremendous shell fire ; officers and men showed a wonderful spirit, and as they were blown out of one trench, those who were left moved right and left and never retired. They had a very brief spell of relief on the 29th when they were sent back to rest, but on the same day had to move up again into the fire trenches. The exhausted men, who were comfortably fixed up for the night with kits, blankets, camp kettles, etc., brought up from Ypres, fell in at once and no one grumbled.

On the morning of the 29th the enemy succeeded in breaking through a regiment on their left, and threatened their left rear. The line was forced to fall back under devastating fire for about half a mile—platoons of " A " Company being the last to retire. Colonel King then reorganised the battalion, collected anyone he could lay hands on from other units, formed them up on the road, and led an attack with this scratch force, which not only recaptured the former positions, but later in the day swept forward and occupied some trenches 200 yards in front. This attack was carried out in four lines and the enemy picked up the range directly the first line advanced ; there were many casualties, but the lines went on as if on parade. Colonel's King prompt and gallant action and the magnificent way it was carried out once again " saved the line."

Next day, in an attack of overwhelming numbers of infantry and appalling bombardment, Colonel King was killed among very heavy losses of officers and men. Still the men held on, and no enemy passed the Green Howards, nor did the battalion give a yard. Their strength was now 300, a captain in command.

Château Heronthage [2]

" The 4th D.G.s finished their time in the Ypres Salient in November at Heronthage Château. The stable of the château, and a small trench running through it, was within, at farthest,

[1] From regimental account.
[2] 4th Dragoon Guards, from regimental account by Major-General A. Solly-Flood.

CHÂTEAU HERONTHAGE—*continued*.

12 yards of the enemy's trenches. The stable had been the scene of heavy hand-to-hand fighting a short time previously, the floors were littered with hand grenades, and stalls and men's room above were full of British and German dead, and the smell was overpowering, but it was impossible to remove the bodies.

The troops of ' A ' Squadron occupying the stable made a narrow loophole which commanded a view down the enemy's front trench and a view of his trench system for some distance. One selected marksman alone accounted for forty-two Germans from this point.

Some days after the regiment had been relieved from this position, the stable was found to be untenable owing to its state, and to the terrific trench-mortar bombardment directed on it. It was abandoned and levelled to the ground. It was here that we were introduced to trench-mortar bombs—which we christened the ' Silent Sausage,' and which felled buildings and trees and filled in our miserable trenches. One officer sent word back to say, ' They are throwing oat sacks at us,' and set to work to shoot them in the air with a rifle, but was eventually made to desist by his infuriated squadron leader.

Beyond minor attacks, counter-attacks, small breakages in neighbouring lines, which we helped to regain, in one instance having to get up for the purpose all our squadron cooks, transport men, and other details from the wagon line, as no other reinforcements were available, all of which events followed each other with surprising swiftness, and appeals for artillery support which was never forthcoming (guns being limited to about four rounds per diem), nothing further happened of outstanding note during our occupation of this savoury spot."

An idea of the part played by the 4th Royal Irish Dragoon Guards in the opening months of the War may be gained from the fact that between the date of landing in France and the 1st January 1915 there had been on the regimental books the names of sufficient officers and men to form more than three complete regiments.

> *To arms ! Stand to arms ! Night after fighting day—*
> *Day after fighting night, their vigil keep.*
> *With none to fill their falling ranks they stay*
> *And man the parapet, till under fire they—*
> *God help them ! hold the trenches in their sleep.*[1]

[1] Infantrymen were seen to be asleep when standing to arms under fire.

Near Hooge, 1915 [1]

" Lieut.-Colonel W. T. M. Reeve, C.M.G., had returned to lead the 2/Leinsters in May, having lost his arm in the great battle of November 1914. August found the battalion engaged in that conspicuously successful attack made on Hooge by the 6th Division to regain the trenches lost during a liquid-fire attack. The rôle of consolidation fell to the battalions. The Leinsters lay astride the Menin Road on the edge of the Hooge ruins round the lips of the crater with both flanks in the air. The inside of this vast crater presented a terrible appearance; the enemy had turned it into a honeycomb of dugouts during the period (30th July—9th August) when they held it. Tier upon tier of dugouts made from railway lines of sleepers—yet this cover did not save them from our guns : it became a veritable death-trap. Fully 200 mangled German corpses lay in the crater, and after the Leinsters had completely consolidated the new line they had the task of filling in this crater with lime and earth. Not a blade of grass was visible on this shell-pitted and bleached-up terrain of the Hooge Ridge. All round lay the dead of the 2/Battalion Durham Light Infantry, 18th Brigade, who had carried the position in a brilliant charge.

From dawn till eve of the 12th August a terrible bombardment fell upon the trenches, and 8 officers and 200 other ranks were killed and wounded in the twelve hours.

Situated on the extreme eastern edge of the Salient, we were enfiladed from Bellewaarde Farm on our left flank, from guns behind Hill 60 on our right, as well as from the front.

H.E. sent our parapets and parados spurting skywards to fall and smother the occupants. Soon the trench ceased to provide any shelter whatsoever, and then shrapnel raked our line systematically from right to left.

The situation grew from bad to worse and we were left exposed without a vestige of cover in our ditch. Although it was a bright summer day, the place became quite dark from the shelling, which showed up the shrapnel-bursts flashing every second. The wounded lay at the bottom of the trench with the dead, and many of them were hit for a second time. The evacuation of the stretcher cases was impossible as there was no C.T.

At dusk heavy bombing attacks were launched by the 126th and 132nd Würtembergers on both the battalions' exposed flanks. The enemy advanced in force and surrounded the left flank, but were repulsed after stiff fighting, leaving their dead

[1] From regimental account.

NEAR HOOGE—*continued*.

behind them. The Leinsters did not budge ; in fact a handful of men, led by Captain Alges and Lieut. Marsland, having beaten off the Boches, followed them back to their lines, inflicting losses. Captain Alges and Lieut. Marsland were wounded, the latter mortally, and the corporal was killed.

Lance-Corporal Leonard performed a very gallant act—an enemy bomb landed on an opened box of ' jam tins ' and Mills bombs. The bombs started fizzling and one ' jam tin ' exploded, but, nothing daunted, the corporal rushed at the box and hurled it over the parapet, being severely wounded in the act, but he undoubtedly saved the lives of the occupants of his section of trench."

Hooge

The action at Hooge in August 1915 was remarkable for the trial use of tin hats. These steel shrapnel-helmets were of the greatest use and saved many lives. Their shape was not so martial as the one adopted by the Hun, which suggested the casque of a medieval knight. The British helmet was flat and round and the wearer's head recalled the archers of Crécy, but when worn above the goat-skin tunic in winter the effect was curiously barbaric.

Menin Road, 1917, between Sanctuary Wood and Glencorse Wood

The 18th Division went into trenches before the battle, about Dormy House, Zillebeke Bund, Railway Dugouts, and the areas about Dickebusch, Château Lyard, and the Canal. The " black line " from Shrewsbury Forest running east of Dumbarton Lakes and Inverness Copse to Glencorse Wood was the objective of the 30th Division, and as soon as this was captured the 18th were to " leapfrog " and capture Polygon Wood, now deep in the enemy's land. All these days preceding our attack, the enemy bombardment continued working up in violence, and our telephone wires buried 6 feet underground were the half of them broken, so deeply torn and rent was the ground east of Zillebeke Lake by tons of metal that burrowed and exploded in the ground.

Early in the dawn of the 31st July our hour of retaliation came, as a thousand guns packed along the front roared out in thunder and flame heralding the great battle. Three divisions advanced—the 8th, 30th, and 24th—and the 53rd Brigade assembled, ready and eager for the moment to follow over the

BETWEEN SANCTUARY WOOD AND GLENCORSE WOOD—*continued.*
ground captured on their front and make their own advance ;
but a disastrous error sent the troops ahead of them to Château
Wood, and when the mistaken signal came through saying that
Glencorse Wood was in our hands, the 53rd Brigade rushed into
the face of a strongly prepared enemy, unbroken by any attack,
while our artillery barrage had swept far ahead.

The 6th Royal Berkshire Regiment received no warning of
the mistake, and went to the attack cheering lustily, led by an
officer guide with a yellow flag. As they reached the Menin
Road they were suddenly assailed by an outburst of machine-gun
fire, and the desperate task before them was revealed. Clapham
Junction had to be stormed across the shell-swept stretch from
Sanctuary Wood, and a line of pill-boxes barred the way before
Glencorse Wood could be reached. As a final stroke it was
found that the brigade was not in touch with the 8th Division
on the left. It was a call on the spirit of the 18th Division,
and most splendidly the men responded. Lieut.-Colonel G. B. W.
Hill of the Suffolks was a voice of inspiration, assuring his men
of his confidence that nothing could make them falter before
this check. Lieut.-Colonel B. C. Clay enkindled the Berkshires,
and sheer stubborn valour sent the battalions forward into the
tornado of shells that guarded the approaches to the Wood and
the fire that flamed from the pill-boxes. The Berkshires forced
their way ahead to gain touch with the 8th Division ; sappers,
pioneers, and fatigue parties of the 79th Company R.E. rallied
up to help the open flank. With short rushes from one shell
hole to the next a slow headway was made.

The Menin Road was gained by 9 o'clock by the 8th Suffolk
fighting heedless of loss and slaying two detachments armed with
automatic rifles. The ridge to the south-east was by then ablaze
with machine guns. A private—F. Read—gathered a handful
of men on his own initiative, rushed one very obstructive position,
put the gun out of action, and killed the whole gun team. Lieut.
Wheeler, a conspicuously valiant figure in the attack, was killed
as the ridge was at last gained, and the men drew breath to
charge onward. During this fighting five tanks came up like
prehistoric beasts lumbering in the slime, but the bog clung to
them, and as they heaved in the open four were knocked out by
shells from the enemy. The accuracy of this fire and pre-
dominance of air observation were proved in these days.

The Suffolks swiftly avenged the loss of the tanks by the bold
capture of a German anti-tank gun. Their advance was being
held up by a strong-point some way in front of Jap Avenue,

Between Sanctuary Wood and Glencorse Wood—*continued*.
and a Stokes mortar, brought up to reduce it, proved to have
only fifteen rounds of ammunition.   The anti-tank gun was
swiftly swung round, and sixty rounds were fired into the strong-
point, which was then captured by a rush of twenty men.   By this
time the 6th Royal Berks had seized the cross-roads north-west
of Glencorse Wood, and gained touch with the 8th Division.
The line was consolidated, and headquarters established in the
Menin Road Tunnel.

All day the enemy shelling of the whole battle area was terrific
—no communication could live, and only morse, flashed on a
Lucas lamp, was possible ; Boche aeroplanes sweeping down
tried to extinguish these signals by machine-gunning the signalling
parties.   In this horrible deadly turmoil " one quiet figure
most heroic, most wonderful of all, Dr. Ackroyd, the 6th Berks
M.O., a stooping, grey-haired, bespectacled man, rose to the
supremest heights that day."   He tended the wounded unhurried
and stoically absorbed, in all the flow of cases round Clapham
Junction.   When the reports came in after the battle, his name
appeared with twenty-three separate recommendations for the
Victoria Cross.   He was killed eleven days later without knowing
that the supreme earthly honour had been awarded him.

Later in the afternoon of the 31st the Germans massed for a
counter-attack which was stopped by the Divisional Artillery.
The troops were by now worn out.   They had gained 1,000 yards
of ground, fighting desperately for every yard, and had reached
within 200 yards of Glencorse Wood.

General Jacob said that in the peril of the flank of the Fifth
Army the 53rd Brigade had saved the day.

FitzClarence Farm, 1917

The 11th Royal Fusiliers' first charge on the morning of the
10th August had carried them to FitzClarence Farm, and in
that charge they lost every one of their company officers.   They
were withdrawn from the advance posts and formed a line
300 yards east of Clapham Junction.   Men were few ; the
nearest reserve was in Sanctuary Wood.   Pearcey, the signalling
officer, gathered up servants, runners, and pioneers and came up
from H.Q. in Menin Tunnel.   Some Middlesex men and Northamptonshires helped to fortify the ridge, and Captain E. C. T. Minet,
of the 54th Machine-gun Company, with Captain Shepherd, of
the 6/Northamptonshires, took charge of the line.   A surging
battle, back and forth round the island like fortresses in the
seas of mud, saved the threatened right wing.   Leadership was

FITZCLARENCE FARM—*continued*.

accepted, as leaders fell, by the nearest man ready to take
responsibility, and five of the Fusiliers N.C.O.s were decorated
for the expert fashion in which they took charge, rallying waverers,
collecting the men, holding important points, and captaining the
officerless companies to fresh efforts and magnificent resistance.
One stretcher-bearer—Tom Adams—heroically carrying wounded
men from the fiercest of the battle time after time, added his
meed of encouragement to the waverers, and even collected
stragglers into little posts in the line.

South of Glencorse Wood

The Northamptonshires—cast for a minor part this day—now
found themselves caught into the thick of the fight. A company working up rapidly with the Fusiliers secured forty prisoners
in the dugout south of Glencorse Wood, where their Lewis-gun
teams silenced the machine guns.   Two of the Lewis gunners—
Privates Smith and Farrer—rushed the position with such
suddenness that though they were but two against the nine of
the crew, the position was gained, all the crew who were not
casualties surrendering.

Ritz Street Trench to Zillebeke

On the 11th August Major L. I. C. Paul, of " D " Battery,
LXXXII Brigade R.F.A., lay out wounded in front of Ritz
Street Trench—shot down while taking a subaltern to the
dressing-station. The subaltern, Lieut. Jones, made his way
back with the news. Colonel Austin Thorp picked up a stretcher,
and started out with Lieut. Nichols, calling for volunteers to
attend him. Lieut. Jones led the way to where the group of
abandoned tanks, smashed up in the battle of the 31st, loomed
through the murk. All the way shells dropped about them and
Lieut. Nichols was struck down, but Colonel Thorp and his three
volunteers found Major Paul lying unconscious and wounded to
death, and brought him in. He died next day. The Colonel
carried on, making his way backwards and forwards twice under
the terrific shelling to Zillebeke to bring up the brigade doctor
and more stretcher-bearers for a badly wounded gunner they had
found near Major Paul.

Glimpse Cottage, Hooge, 1917

Captain M. P. Andrews, of the 1/4 Duke of Wellington's, was
in a front-line trench near Glimpse Cottage when a dugout was

GLIMPSE COTTAGE, HOOGE—*continued.*
blown in, burying a number of his men. He set to work at
once to dig them out, and found that among the dead three still
lived, though one was badly wounded. The trench was too
narrow to admit the passage of a stretcher, yet one of the men
was in desperate need of a surgeon's aid. Captain Andrews
climbed out on to the top, helped to lift the stretcher, and then
walked with the bearers across the open, where bullets were
spattering the ground. Before they could reach a communication
trench Captain Andrews was shot in the head, and within a
few minutes he died. " So perished one of the most gallant
gentlemen and conscientious officers who ever served in the
battalion."

Black Watch Corner

The Victoria Cross has often been gained by those who, with
no thought of self and regardless of danger, dare death where
there is a chance of survival. There is a still more majestic
valour where a man lays his life deliberately aside, and goes out
on his way open-eyed and aware of the inevitable end. On the
4th October 1917 the tanks of the " B " Company, 1/Tank
Battalion, went forward to attack the line at Black Watch Corner.
The ground was a honeycomb of shell holes, all landmarks gone,
and direction was easily lost. For three days previously Captain
Clement Robertson had made a reconnaissance of the ground,
under intense shell fire the whole time, and had taped a route
across the Reutelbeek. By the time the attack was launched
all indication of the route had been blasted away by the enemy's
shells and the way between two deep morasses was one of infinite
peril. What was left of a road was in full view of the enemy,
and the advancing tanks were met by a hurricane of shells, rifle
and machine-gun bullets. Captain Robertson placed himself
at the head of his tanks, and walking forward very carefully,
very unhurriedly, led them with the sublimity of patient valour
through the wilderness of death. The tanks reached their
objective and came safely into action as their leader fell.[1]

Hell Fire Corner, 1917

Where many acts of heroism go unrecorded, one has been
put on record by the 42nd Division that took place at that focal
point Hell Fire Corner. The enemy shells set fire to a great
ammunition dump. Amid continued bombardment, and with
the explosive going off in terrific outbursts, the divisional transport
loaded up by the depot and got all the teams and wagons away
in safety.

[1] He was awarded the V.C.

Gheluvelt Cross-roads, 1918

As the Leinster Regiment advanced up through Hooge to Gheluvelt they came upon the little acres of wooden crosses all dated November 1914. Our troops had reached again our foremost advance line when the Salient was formed. The battalion was held up by a strong nest of machine guns and rifles established in the cover of some trucks full of coal. While the Leinsters were seeking to break down the post, some of the Motor Machine-gun Corps came bumping up the road, and, heedless of warning shouts, the leader passed over the cross-roads, and was shot down by the enemy machine guns hidden within a hundred yards. His companion in the side-car jumped out, swung his gun into action, and silenced the enemy. He turned to his wounded comrade lying in the road, and picking him up, placed him in the side-car ; then, starting up, turned and rode back to our lines.

Between Menin Road and Zillebeke Lake, 1918

The line here was held in a series of posts very far apart, and Brigadier-General Johnson, commanding the Divisional Artillery, tells of an uncommon happening when the 29th Division came to hold this front in September 1918. Two N.C.O.s of the ammunition column reconnoitring roads up to our line for the advance lost their way, and approached a pill-box. Corporal Shadgett went in to ask where he was, and found it full of Boches. He had passed through our line all unaware. The corporal drew his—unloaded—revolver, and standing in front of the rifle rack, where all rifles were piled, held the enemy up while he shouted for Bombardier Almond. Then the two gunners marched eight prisoners back to Vlamertinghe.

Menin Road, 1918

In the last great advance the 29th Division passed over the historic ground so valiantly fought for and held in 1914, so valiantly fought over in 1917, and lost in the fearful days of this Spring. The objectives captured on the 28th September included such classic names as Stirling Castle, Glencorse Wood, Polygon Wood, and now with overwhelming shell fire from our side the attackers went forward like a tidal wave and by midday our forces were east of Kruiseecke. Only a notice-board inscribed " Gheluvelt " on the mounds of rubbish showed the site of that village, that place of pride for Britain. Whether by fine feeling of the G.O.C. or by pure coincidence, it happened that this day the 4th Battalion of the Worcesters took Gheluvelt ;

MENIN ROAD—*continued.*
that regiment whose second battalion has immortalised the name.

MESSINES, 1914

On the 31st October 1914 Messines stuck out like a bastion in front of our line along the Ridge. The village was a small one—1,400 inhabitants, a church, a lime-house, and the mill. Just 150 men of the 9th Lancers defended the jut-out east of the village ; on their left the Queen's Bays, on their right two Indian companies of the 57th Rifles. The second line of defence ran plumb through the village, and was held by the 11th Hussars, weary from a great fight the day before. The squadrons of the 5th Dragoon Guards were broken up and thrown in where needed.

Shelling and sniping and sounds of enemy movements increased through the night, presage that something big was afoot, and at a midnight conference it was agreed to relieve the 57th Rifles by the 2/Inniskilling Fusiliers. At 4.30 a.m., just when part of the Inniskillings had manned the trenches on the southern edge of the village, and the Rifles were in the middle of being relieved, the enemy attacked. They sent soldiers in mummer disguise of pugarees ahead of them, and then charged, cheering and blowing horns. They overran the Indians, and right up to the support trench where the 5th Dragoons bayoneted them, and a detachment of the Rifles counter-charged, led by Captain Gordon, who was slain at their head. The 5th Dragoon Guards' barricade was impregnable, and now some reinforcements began to arrive—another squadron of the 5th Dragoon Guards, one of the 10th Hussars, and two of the 4th Dragoon Guards.

In the meanwhile the north-east of the village had been attacked, but the enemy repulsed. As morning broke, and the early mists cleared, a bombardment by heavy guns and trench mortars began to smash up the houses, and machine guns crept close, attacking either side of the bastion where the position of the twelve weak squadrons, with only one battery of horse artillery, was becoming desperate. Still the cavalrymen held on, though their flank trenches had become untenable. By 9 o'clock the 9th Lancers had lost three-quarters of their officers and a third of their men ; and as to retain this out-thrust position meant annihilation, they were withdrawn through the village. The line was now straight and joined up with the Inniskillings in the south and the Queen's Bays in the north. The twelve squadrons had held up the greater part of twelve battalions, the odds at the lowest reckoning being 6 to 1.

MESSINES—*continued*.

After an hour's pause the enemy made a violent attack, bringing a battery of artillery, and engineers to demolish the buildings with charges of explosives. A terrific struggle followed fighting from house to house, the British defending the wide, main street and the Germans bringing up numbers of machine guns. They could not drive the cavalrymen out, and at last at 1 o'clock help came in the form of two depleted battalions from the II Corps, the 2/King's Own Scottish Borderers and 2/King's Own Yorkshire Light Infantry. They charged forward into the storm of shell, and at the same moment the Inniskillings attacked on their right, and the London Scottish were seen to the north. The trenches lost by the Indians were recaptured, and some of the houses in the village. This was the utmost that could be done by our troops, hopelessly outnumbered, overwhelmed by machine-gun fire, and exhausted. The reinforcements, after the rush of their journey ending in the charge, were too weary to do more. But though the Germans had all the advantage of great superiority in numbers—even more of an advantage in night fighting than by day—though their artillery had set the houses held by the British in flames and their machine guns ravaged the streets, yet they could not capture the village.

HORSE

Spur and rowell and ride like hell,
Neck and neck, no matter who fell,
Up the straight, to the rousing swell—
    Ride, ride, ride !

Horn and holloa and all you know,
Steady in hand—for'ard and go !
Ride with the wind, till the wind is slow—
    Ride, ride, ride !

Lance and sabre, and cut and thrust,
Thunder of hooves and whirl of dust,
Rapture of speed and the battle-lust—
    Ride, ride, ride !

 .   .   .   .

Cramp and darkness, and sleepless strain
Afoot to the trench, in the trench remain ;
Hold and endure, and never again
    Ride, ride, ride !

Messines

The London Scottish, on arriving in the Salient on the 30th
October, were sent at once to St. Eloi in reserve to the cavalry,
who were still maintaining their wonderful defence against
6 to 1 odds on the ridges. The battalion was ordered up to the
front of the IV Cavalry Brigade with instructions to advance by
Wytschaete and the Windmill just north of Messines, and to
make an attack south-eastward from this position. But it
proved impossible to pass Wytschaete owing to heavy fire, and
the London Scottish proceeded under some shelter of Enfer Wood
to the west of Messines, and received orders to reinforce the
cavalry holding the road along the heights. By a misunderstanding of the situation the battalion advanced deployed for attack,
and being seen by the enemy were heavily shelled, but reached
the trenches of the 4th Cavalry Brigade ; while the platoon on
the left got into action with German infantry.

Next day they found themselves filling a dangerous gap north
of Wytschaete with the Carabiniers, and the new arrivals proclaimed themselves greatly encouraged by the stalwart bearing
of the veteran troopers. Three of the Carabiniers went into
the open under sweeping rifle fire and brought in a wounded
man ; and the London Scottish considered that they had earned
a V.C. apiece.

The battalion beat off the first attack launched against them
on the ridge that night. The dense mass of the enemy offered
a wide target, though unfortunately the Scots were handicapped
by the recent issue of a new rifle, that proved at the critical
moment of the new soldiers' first battle to be defective. From
evening until 2 a.m. in bright moonlight the enemy surged in
waves against the defenders of the Ridge, only to be stopped
and flung back time after time. At 2 o'clock came a more
violent rush ; the enemy charged with the bayonet over the
centre and left of the advance trench, and, overwhelming it,
crashed between the Scots and the cavalry trenches on their left.
For critical moments the battalion was threatened with destruction should the enemy envelop them from this flank and gain
the height. Colonel Malcolm called for a charge of his small
reserve, and with a frantic struggle our line pressed forward
once more, gaining touch with the troops on the left.

The accounts are of a " prolonged and confused struggle, in
which the irregular line swayed backwards and forwards."
Attack and counter-attack, hand-to-hand fighting, but one
determination of dogged resistance. Communication with other

MESSINES—*continued.*

units was impossible, and all ranks had to act on their own
initiative. Every man stuck to his post until the weight of the
enemy numbers overwhelmed it. Either flank was now threatened and the moment had come to extricate what could be
saved of the battalion. The enemy had suffered severely enough
to allow of Colonel Malcolm disengaging his men, which, gathering
up the wounded, he proceeded to do. With wounded men
supported by comrades in not much better case than themselves,
he withdrew to Wulverghem. The roll was called and about
150 men responded, with the hope that some of the missing
would come in later.

This unprepared battalion, with no machine guns, and with
rifles that were defective, had taken their part in that sparse
heroic line of resistance, and flung back on their bit of the line
the overwhelming tide that threatened else to have broken
through to Ypres.

Messines Area [1]

While two squadrons of the 4th Royal Irish Dragoon Guards
were fighting in the street-battle of Messines, a squadron was
holding a part of the Wytschaete—Messines Road on the 31st
October. " About 4.30 a.m. heavy firing was heard from this
direction, and on visiting our squadron near the windmill it
was found to be heavily engaged ; in a barn they were holding,
our men and the enemy were using alternate loopholes, and if
you stood opposite the wrong one you got shot in the leg. At
the same time columns of heavy infantry could be seen approaching, and information came in that our troops had been driven
out of Wytschaete village. The local situation was quickly
restored, the enemy were ejected from the barn and a squadron
of 18th Hussars which had been in reserve advanced as far as
the windmill, driving back considerable numbers of the enemy,
who were approaching the Wulverghem Road with a view of
cutting off Messines. At about 7 a.m. the enemy renewed his
attack on the windmill in great numbers, and having turned the
flank of the 18th Hussars, drove them back over the Wulverghem
Road. The situation was very serious, but the 18th Hussars
rallied, a troop of the 4th D.G.s was withdrawn from the right
in Messines village, and the machine gun of the regiment was
brought into action to support the counter-attack which was
launched with these few devoted officers and men. By 9 a.m.
the situation was again restored, though at considerable cost,

[1] From regimental account, by Major-General Solly-Flood.

MESSINES AREA—*continued*.

and once more we occupied the windmill and the left flank was
secured and the Wulverghem Road once more opened.   There
was no support or reserves of any sort left in that little
garrison.

A message was now received that if we could not maintain
our positions without reinforcements, we were to retire to the
next position.   There was nothing for it but to vacate the
town which had cost us so dear to hold.   Railston and Powell
had been killed ; Kirkwood, Wright, Davison, and Featherston-
haugh wounded.   It was interesting to learn from a captured
German officer that he could not believe Messines had been held
so long by cavalry.   The Germans imagined that it was held by
a picked corps of machine gunners.   The number of machine
guns with British units was limited to two in those days, so
that we may take it that the rifle shooting of the cavalry was
only excelled by the manipulation of their bolts."

Messines, 1914

The 4th Dragoon Guards had been manning the barricade
that blocked the way west of Messines, and had lost half a troop
before the retirement to Wulverghem.   A young officer, Lieut.
Railston (18th Lancers, I.A.), made a brave effort to save the
life of an old woman who had lost her way, and got between the
lines.   He was killed in the effort.   During this day Sergeant
Woodland was recommended for a V.C. for his gallant stand with
the machine gunners after their officer had been killed.   This
gun was isolated for twenty-four hours, but he kept it in action,
covering the left flank, and maintaining touch with the French
where main German attacks were being launched.   He received
a D.C.M.

Messines, Petit Bois, 1916

In June 1916 work had been begun on the deep galleries that
led ultimately to the great mines under the Messines Ridge,
when, in the Petit Bois, an enemy blow destroyed some 150 feet
of the gallery.   Twelve men were entombed, and the reserve
party laboured under great difficulty for ten days to break out
and make a new gallery.   When at last they got through, they
discovered the bodies of the imprisoned men, who had collected
near the block to listen for sounds of rescue work, and had all
been suffocated, as this point, happening to be the lowest, was a
pit of foul air.   But one man, a miner by trade, had stayed in a
higher part of the gallery, and he was found alive.   He owed his

MESSINES, PETIT BOIS—*continued*.
life to finding half a pint of water in a bottle, which he kept
taking into his mouth and returning to the flask. He feared to
eat the few biscuits that he had through dread of being overcome
by thirst.

Messines, 1917

The Battle of Messines on the 7th June 1917 may be described
as the completely successful example of the " limited attack."
The battle was mounted with the greatest thoroughness, and
the remarkable consummation of the operation was due to the
precision of all the preparations. The outstanding feature of
this most successful battle was the destruction of the enemy
lines by the explosion of a gigantic system of mines. Work
had been carried on for the previous year, and no less than
twenty galleries were driven underground for nearly 8,000 yards
right beneath the German front line ; at their ends monster
mines, containing nearly a million lb. of charges, were laid in
readiness for the British attack.

The second very distinctive feature of this battle is the feeling
of personal touch, of personal confidence in the commander
of the Second Army, that ran strongly through all ranks under
his command. The dominant figure of General Plumer was
known to every man in the line ; his popularity was a force of
infinite value, and the sympathy and understanding with which
he treated his regimental officers led to efficiency and the smooth
working of his plans. He had in a marked degree the talent of
using the best in men, and in Major-General Charles Harington
he found as perfect a response as a man would crave of his
right hand.

The plans for the assault on the Messines Ridge were developed
in meticulous detail and with profound forethought. One of
the most notable features was the management of the preliminary
bombardment. For days before the battle our artillery was
devoted to the breaking up of the enemy defence. Guns of
every calibre were employed to smash up concrete fortifications
and shelters ; to cut wire ; while barrages were dropped behind
his line disorganising communication and shelling billets, and
short hurricane bombardments demoralised the front line. Air
photographs showed the results of these bombardments, and
divisional staffs were consulted as to whether the treatment
had been sufficient or should be repeated. Every division was
required to be satisfied with the preparations.

The infantry were trained on a model that permitted at least

MESSINES—*continued.*

a company to study the position at a time. Means of communication and signalling were carefully thought out, and a message-map devised that had a skeleton form for messages on the reverse side of a map of the German trenches. A final touch of most wise consideration was the arrangement to issue a hot meal at midnight to the troops waiting in the trenches to assault.

These details are stressed because the remarkable success of the attack was due to the precision of all the preparations.

The Messines Ridge displayed at early dawn of the 7th June 1917 one of the most appalling spectacles of the War. Zero hour was 3.10 a.m., and at that moment ten miles of close-packed British guns crashed with one stupendous roar. A flare of light rent the darkness, and as though that flash had torn open a portal of Hell hurling earth afar—fire and flames in crimson towers rushed upward, followed by writhing whorls of inky smoke. The monstrous apparition hung in the sky, overflowing in fire-streams. And beneath this horror earth itself rocked, belching soil, stones, human bodies—a convulsion which has had no parallel from the hands of men.

Nineteen colossal mines had blasted the Ridge, and in a nightmare of gloom and murk the battalions went up to the attack.

Messines, 1917.

In the attack on Messines of the 7th June 1917 there were nine battalions of the Royal Irish Rifles with the 36th (Ulster) Division. The following account of part of the battle has been contributed by the regiment.[1]

Amid a gloom still thick and intensified by a smother of dust, the first wave of the infantry sprang from its trenches and went forward. The second followed at twenty-five yards' interval to avoid the German barrage. The size of the craters to be skirted and the darkness made the keeping of direction a matter of difficulty. It would have been impossible but for the use of compasses by the platoon commanders.

There was no resistance by the enemy in his front or support trenches. Dazed and disorganised by the mines and the tremendous weight of artillery, the few survivors surrendered. Two machine guns only, firing through our barrage, are recorded to have come into action at this stage, on the front of the 109th Brigade. They came into the open when it had passed, on the extreme left flank, and were put out of action, one by a section of rifle grenadiers, the other by a Lewis gun of the 11/Inniskillings.

[1] From regimental account. " Thanks are due for permission to make use of the *History of the 36th Ulster Division.*"

MESSINES—*continued*.

The enemy's barrage was unaccountably light and ragged, even when the violence of our counter-battery fire is considered, and fell upon the British front line. The assaulting troops went straight forward to the Red Line, close upon the barrage, leaving to the "moppers-up" the task of taking prisoners. It was reached at 3.45 a.m. Here there was a halt in the barrage of a quarter of an hour, and here the third and fourth company of each battalion "leap-frogged" the first and second for the assault of the Blue Line.

As in almost every action of the War, the stoutest-hearted German was the German behind the machine gun. The artillerymen, with shell hailing upon their positions, were more anxious to withdraw their batteries than to support their infantry, but the machine gunners lived up to their reputation. As the new waves swept on, dipping now on the right brigade front into the marshy bed of the Steenbeek, guns came into action directly the barrage was past at L'Enfer Wood, Earl Farm, Skip Point, and Scott Farm. At Skip Point, in particular, two guns were handled with boldness, firing till the work was rushed with the bayonet by the 9th Rifles, assisted by a platoon of the 14th which swung in from the left. There was still resistance in this veritable fortress, and some bombing of its dugouts. Upwards of 150 prisoners were taken in it. At Scott Farm an officer was seen standing on top of the work, encouraging his men. He was shot at long range by a sniper, whereat the defence at this point collapsed. There yet remained, however, Jump Point, the strongest position short of the road. By this time the Intelligence Officer of the 109th Brigade was on the high ground beyond Peckham, in touch with his brigadier on the telephone. He reported he saw a yellow flag at Jump Point. Now, the battalion flag of the 14th Rifles was *orange*, a far more significant shade. "I said," writes General Ricardo, "'yellow be damned!' slammed down the 'phone, called the division on the other, and said I wished to report that Jump Point was occupied. Corps was informed accordingly, within a few minutes of schedule time. I was asked by B.G.G.S. Corps next day how we managed our information and communications. I told him, 'by orange flags!'" And so the first flag moved forward from the border of the map at IX Corps Headquarters, which was to mark the progress of the battle, and was stuck into Jump Point.

Messines, 1917.

As the swift advance of the British on the 7th June neared

MESSINES—*continued*.

the German third-line system, the 37/Battalion of the Australian Imperial Force was held by a storm of shell and machine-gun fire.   Captain Robert Grieve alone among the officers was un-wounded, and his company had suffered heavy casualties.   He sighted two hostile machine guns, and attacked them single-handed, racing through the fire that blazed from them, and bombing the two crews to death.   Then he organised what was left of his company, led them on, and gained his objective, securing the position before he fell badly wounded.   He gained the Victoria Cross.

Messines, Despagne Farm, 1917

Messines Ridge having been captured by the British in just one hour and forty minutes, in the battle of June 1917, the Border Regiment was hard at work consolidating the position they had won, and in clearing out strong-points and small pockets of Germans that had been left by the retirement. Corporal H. Carter and Private F. Brown marked down an enemy battery in action ; they ran forward and pointed out its position to a tank that was lumbering along eastwards.   On rolled the tank, boldly escorted by the two men, and, coming near the guns, fired a broadside upon them.   Corporal Carter and Private Brown followed up this opening by charging the guns themselves and, firing two rounds into the dugout, whither the teams had retired, called upon the seven men to surrender, and captured them with the guns and a Helio.   Carter and Brown went on to the next gun-pit ; here the corporal was knocked out by a stick bomb, and Brown, left by himself, took the team of six men prisoners.   He was so elated that he thought he might carry on the good work, and, seeing a strayed charger, tried to mount, but the horse was wounded, and Brown retired to his company, where he was followed by the corporal when he came to.

Messines, Lunn Farm, 1918

" A " Battery, LXXXVIII Brigade R.F.A., was in action just north of Earl Farm in support of the 57th Infantry Brigade, when on the 10th April a powerful drive of the fresh enemy divisions forcing back the line, brought the infantry back to the guns. Captain E. Stuart Dougall (battery commander) immediately ran two guns forward on to the top of the Ridge, that they might clear the crest.   Gas and H.E. shells were con-centrated on our lines ; Captain Dougall rallied the infantry, served out rifles to some of his gunners, and held on with guns

MESSINES, LUNN FARM—*continued*.

and men in line, shooting over the open sights, and checked the enemy advance. One gun was overturned by a direct hit, and the detachment destroyed ; but others took their place and got the gun into action again. Through the long hours Captain Dougall walked about as calmly as though on parade, cheering and inspiring everyone, and assuring the infantry : " So long as you stick to your trenches, I will keep my guns here." As dusk fell, all ammunition was done and orders came to withdraw the battery that had snatched twelve precious hours from the enemy in his headlong advance, and saved a break in the line. The ground behind was torn and pitted with shell holes, and it seemed almost impossible to get the guns across such a country and under intense machine-gun fire. But the guns must be saved and the artillerymen man-handled them for half a mile, and got them away. Four days later Captain Dougall was killed while fighting his guns in defence of Kemmel.

MEUNIER HOUSE. (See POELCAPPELLE.)

MINTY'S FARM. (See STEENBEEK.)

MOATED GRANGE. (See ZILLEBEKE.)

MOLENAARELSTHOEK. (See MENIN ROAD.)

MONT ROUGE, 1918

On the 25th April the Germans, driving towards the Channel Ports and bringing once again a tremendous weight of odds against the British, had concentrated a great force of heavy artillery behind the Wytschaete, Neuve Eglise, and Ravelsburg Ridges, whence from a horseshoe-shaped position they poured shells upon Kemmel, Mont Rouge, and Mont Noir. These heights commanded the passes toward Calais and the coast, and here the sorely pressed British troops had been relieved three days before by a French Corps, fresh from a long rest. The British 11th and 35th Brigades remained in action with the French ; and the 84th Battery R.F.A., with five guns in action some 50 yards behind the crest of Mont Rouge, covered a French regiment of infantry that held Dranoutre. With a battery of French 75's away on the right flank, it was the most forward battery in the area. At 2 a.m. a gruelling bombardment burst suddenly upon the battery position, and continued with full intensity until midday. The 84th Battery, responding to the S.O.S. from the infantry, fought on with increased rate of fire, while one by one the guns were knocked out until only two

MONT ROUGE—*continued.*

remained effective ; the detachments were killed or wounded, and by now only one officer, one sergeant, two corporals, and five men (cooks and batmen) remained to serve the guns. Kemmel Hill and Dranoutre had been captured and the enemy infantry were on the Locre—Bailleul Road, and the allied front line was now in dead ground to the guns of the battery, which received orders to withdraw. Attempts to get up the teams were abandoned after the leading team had been blown up, as the routes under very heavy fire were blocked by overturned wagons and dead horses. Barely 70 rounds apiece were left for the guns, but the batteries continued firing though at a very slow rate.

The French Infantry Reserves were now alongside lining the Ridge, the gaps were closed, and the attack held at Locre. At 5 p.m. the gun limbers with specially picked teams made a fresh attempt to rescue the guns. They came across country through the valley, bouncing over nullahs and shell holes, and galloped up the precipitous side of the hill. Four guns were limbered up —the others were smashed to pieces. Return by the same way was impossible, the hill was too steep ; the road was blocked and shell-swept ; the forward way was the only one open. Over the crest came the guns—directly they appeared a storm of fire burst over them, every German battery within reach opening on them, but too late ; the audacious and unexpected move took the enemy by surprise and the limbers trotted forward, shells falling behind them as they went. They came upon the road near Locre, and swung round toward Reninghelst parallel to and some 300 yards from the firing line. A great tree had been flung across the track by a shell burst, an obstacle completely blocking the way, and 3 feet high at its lowest point. The drivers sat down to it, charged at the gallop, and team after team cleared the leap without a mishap. Behind the Scherpenberg the column passed out of sight of enemy batteries and machine guns, and came back to the wagon line without losing gun or horse. The battery commander had stayed in the position burying the dead and salving what was possible, and he led the remnant of the gun detachment back when night fell.

By 8 o'clock next morning the battery had four guns in action in a fresh position, covering a new part of the line.

MORTELDJE, WEST OF, 1915

The 1/6 West Yorks had endured five months of the wretched conditions in the sector about the Canal bank, north-east of Ypres.

MORTELDJE, WEST OF—*continued*.

On the 19th December this time of endurance culminated in the repulse of the enemy, during the contest of those three or four days when he had expected to overwhelm our troops by the concentration of phosgene cylinder gas. Most fortunately tube helmets had been issued to the troops only a few weeks before this time. The cloud passed over the ground in such heavy waves that it left a deposit of crystals glittering in its wake, and its effect was felt by Canadians on parade twelve miles behind at Bailleul. But warning of the super-attack had been gleaned from recently captured prisoners, and special care was taken to ensure the issue and use of the gas masks, and that they should be in perfect working order.

On the 17th December the Germans bombarded and then sunk into a silence, from which two mornings later there burst a sudden pandemonium, gas being discharged upon our line from shells, cylinders, and bombs of every description. The hissing thick white serpent-coils of the cylinder gas streamed over, while the air was filled with the rocket explosions of the shells, the sky ablaze, the ether thick and cloyed with the deadly fumes.

The men standing to arms were protected by the gas helmets—when they could wear them. Sergeant E. M. Kemode attended wounded when all the stretcher-bearers were killed. He wrote : " I had to take my helmet off. My eyes streamed all the time, and I was coughing, spitting, and drinking rum to keep me going. . . . The whiz-bangs were awful, and an enfilade machine-gun fire swept the top of the trench, so that the wounded had to be dragged along in the mud, using their hands—all leg and body wounds. These lay out all day, but it finished me. . . . The agonies some of the men went through with the gas was utterly hellish, fiendish. I was sick and blinded, and had to be taken away." [1]

The enemy had set a scene of peculiar horror to create a panic among those not overcome by the gas, but when they left their line to attack, they were met, not by trenches of gasping and dying men, but by so withering a storm of bullets and shells that they came no further.

Morteldje (Shrewsbury Trench), 1916 [2]

The Morteldje salient was at the time held by the 16th Infantry Brigade of the 6th Division. On the night of the 19th April the enemy attacked and succeeded in flattening out the whole salient, killing and wounding the majority of the garrison. The

---

[1] *History of the 6th Battalion West Yorkshire Regiment.*
[2] From regimental account.

MORTELDJE (SHREWSBURY TRENCH)—*continued.*
following night unsuccessful counter-attacks were made, except
in one small piece of the line which was held on to with great
difficulty. On the night of the 21st April the 1/King's Shropshire
Light Infantry were ordered up from the Canal bank to retake
the position. The night was pitch dark and torrential rain made
the shell-destroyed ground and tracks practically impassable ;
the men had the greatest difficulty in moving forward at all,
heavily laden with 170 rounds S.A.A., two bombs, four sandbags,
and either a pick or shovel. In some places movement could
only be made by lying flat and pushing through the mud.

Ten p.m. was zero hour ; the barrage came down punctually,
but over such ground in such weather the battalion could not
reach its starting-line in time. Cut off from communication,
the artillery could not be warned of the change in time to delay
the barrage, and the companies therefore had to act upon their
own initiative. The right company, 45 minutes late for the
barrage, attacked at once and reached its objective, losing
three of its four officers. A bombing party under the company
sergeant-major attacked up a trench to the left, and failing to
find the centre attack, held its ground and established posts.
The centre company had no alternative but to move across
country with no tracks to guide them, and reached the starting-
line after overcoming great difficulties at 1 a.m. Just before
2 a.m. touch was gained with the company deploying on their
left and they charged simultaneously. All objectives were
gained, but at a cost of five more officers and a high percentage
of other ranks. The German casualties were very heavy ;
nearly all were killed with the bayonet, our rifles being so clogged
with mud that it was impossible to use them. Two counter-
attacks were beaten off in the early morning. The main German
trench remaining in our hands was, after this action, named
Shropshire Trench, by which name it was known until the end
of the War. The battalion casualties were 8 officers and 163
other ranks. The Colonel was mortally wounded in the last
few minutes of the action and died two days later. These are
the words of the Corps Commander : " I do not think any
battalion was ever set a much more difficult and necessary task,
yet in inky darkness, over shell-destroyed ground, in pouring
rain, the K.S.L.I. went straight to their work, and once more
secured the safety of the left of the British line."

MOUSE-TRAP FARM. (See FREZENBERG.)

MULE TRACK. (See PASSCHENDAELE.)

NEUVE EGLISE, 1914

While the 5th Royal Irish Lancers were billeted at Neuve Eglise in November 1914, during a rest behind the firing line, an officer of the regiment brought a few couple of hounds back after home leave. They were passed into France by an ingenious A.S.C. officer, who explained to the French authorities that they were " pur sang St. Bernards " and required " pour chercher les blessés." They reached the 5th Lancers, and provided some very good sport after Belgian hares, even making some five-mile points. But at the end of six weeks the French represented that hunting was against their military laws, and the pack was sent home.

Neuve Eglise, 1918

For three days and nights from the 11th April 1918 a terrific struggle centred on Neuve Eglise. The 2/Worcesters had come into the line east of the village when the forward rush of the enemy swept up to its outskirts. Attack and counter-attack followed each other, till early in the morning of the second day the enemy broke through on the right, and entering the village struck at the rear of the battalion. But the invading party was annihilated and their machine guns destroyed. The 16/King's Royal Rifle Corps fought stubbornly on the left until all were casualties or prisoners, " B " Company of the Machine-gun Battalion firing until every man was killed. Still the enemy came on in greater numbers, and the Worcesters, fighting for every yard, withdrew into the village. Corporal McBride's first team of machine gunners covered this retirement. As the flanks of our forces were driven in, his machine gun held the pivotal centre; and with two survivors of his team he swung the gun through the traverse, recklessly exposing his own position, but keeping the enemy at bay throughout the night. When dawn came he was surrounded on three sides, and he fell back into Neuve Eglise, carrying his gun, tripod, and belt box. The Glasgow Highlanders attacked from reserve, flinging the enemy out of the village, until a yet more powerful attack drove a wedge between the British battalions.

Throughout another night of fighting, with the bayonet, and rifle fire, a brilliant manœuvre drove the Germans on to the high ground on the right, where they established a machine gun with a party of snipers. Second-Lieut. John Crow, of the Worcesters, attacked with a N.C.O. and seven men, charging with such persistent daring straight up against their fire that the enemy

NEUVE EGLISE—*continued.*
left the high ground and took cover in some houses of the village.
Lieut. Crow followed them—he was a champion rifle shot—and
he picked off the Germans who showed themselves in the doorways.
Then with only two men he rushed upon two machine guns that
were raking the position, knocked out the gunners, and kept off
all counter-attacks, shooting down the lines that came up against
him, until the Boche withdrew. He captured both guns, and
his reckless bravery cheered the men on, so that they held the
post until the evening, when the enemy closed up in force. Lieut.
Crow placed a covering party close to the attackers and his men
got safely away.[1]

During this time, such as remained alive of the 2/Worcesters
were clinging to posts in the village, fighting hand to hand
through the streets ; the Mairie was a centre of the struggle,
and the battle raged round the church, which was intrepidly
defended by Lieut.-Colonel E. L. Stoney, with Padre E. V.
Tanner fighting beside him. The battalion was hopelessly outnumbered, and at last Battalion H.Q. was withdrawn, and a
fresh line established west of the village.

Through the desperate hours the machine gun of Corporal
McBride blazed from the thick of the fight. He was never silenced
for a moment ; when one gun was destroyed, he got hold of
another. From the window of the Mairie he fired into the rear
of the party attacking the church, until a rush was turned upon
the Mairie and bombs flung at the windows. He sprang into
the doorway, and with a rifle, shot the bombers as they threw
their arms up, while the teams drove them back with rifle
grenades at point-blank range. The enemy were held and the
position was uncaptured.

NEY COPSE, 1917

John Moyney, Lance-Sergeant of the Irish Guards, was in
command of fifteen men holding two posts in Ney Copse. The
Würtembergers cut them off, and put a machine-gun post between
them and a bridge over the Broembeek in their rear. The Irishmen held the posts for ninety-six hours. They had very little to
eat, being under orders not to break into their iron rations,
and nothing at all to drink. On the fifth day the Boche attacked
them in force, and not waiting for their arrival, Lance-Sergeant
Moyney and his men rose from their shell hole and attacked

---

[1] Lieut. Crow gained the V.C. He was awarded a peaceful decoration earlier
in the War, when he made a garden of the land near his quarters to grow very
necessary vegetables, and the French presented him with the Diplôme d'Honneur
de l'Encouragement.

NEY COPSE—*continued*.

them ardently with bombs. As greater numbers surrounded them they charged back, cutting their way through the enemy to the river. Here Sergeant Moyney and Private Woodcock held the Germans with rifle and Lewis gun, while the party scrambled and splashed through, where bombs and bullets made a target of the stream. When all were over Private Woodcock crossed, but heard behind him cries of a wounded man in the water. Private Woodcock swung back, picked him up, and carried him to safety in broad daylight over open country Sergeant Moyney was the last to come away.[1]

Rudyard Kipling's inimitable Irishman explains the affair : " 'Twas a bad mix-up from first to last. We ought never to have been that side the dam' river at that time at all. And there's a lot to it that can't be told. . . . And why did Moyney not let the men break into their rations ? Because in a tight place, if you do one thing against orders, ye'll do anything. An' 'twas a dam' tight place that that Moyney man walked them out of.' "[2]

NIEPPE, 1918

In the grim days of April 1918, when every man in the British line was strained to the utmost to hold on until the reinforcing divisions could arrive, the 4th (Guards) Brigade was covering the detraining of the 1st Australian Division. It took up a line from l'Epinette to the Estaires—Strazeele Road on the night of the 11th/12th of April. The enemy in overwhelming numbers, supported by the fire of field and machine gun, attacked with the coming of daybreak, and the 4/Grenadiers and 3/Coldstream drove them back. Then with the 2/Irish Guards in echelon behind their right flank they themselves attacked, charging right into the teeth of machine guns and field guns firing over open sights within 300 yards. They made some ground, and by afternoon the brigade was holding 3,000 yards of front. The enemy attacked again and again, and concentrated intense shell fire, but they were repulsed, though by now the Grenadiers had lost 8 officers and 250 men and in the fierce combat had fired 70,000 rounds of rifle ammunition.

The trains bringing up the Australians were late, and still the brigade stood fast, until next morning the first reinforcing troops had begun to detrain. At dawn the enemy machine guns came up close in a dense fog, and supported by an armoured

---

[1] Both men received the V.C.
[2] *The Irish Guards in the Great War.* Rudyard Kipling.

NIEPPE—*continued.*

car that was pushed to within 10 yards of the post on the Pures-becques Road, attacked again and were again driven back. And so they were driven back along the whole front of the brigade, though in the centre post of the Coldstream there was only one unwounded man : he for twenty minutes single-handed kept the enemy at bay until he was killed. Farther north, the enemy field guns came within point-blank range, getting round the flank of the brigade. The left company of the Grenadiers, under Captain Price, stood back to back and fought it out, while a company of the Irish Guards, sent up to help, were surrounded by the enemy on the way, and only one N.C.O. and six men survived. A corporal of the Grenadier company lived, through the accident of falling into a ditch, to tell the tale of the tragic glorious end. Captain Price fought on until evening, when he had but eighteen men alive, and they now a mile within the German line. Then they charged with the bayonet and drove the enemy back ; charged again, and died fighting.

By now all the officers of the Grenadiers were casualties ; there were six unwounded men in the centre company, twenty in the right ; yet at evening the survivors were still fighting. The right company of the Coldstreamers was surrounded, and when nearly wiped out the few that were left fought their way out, and joined the reinforcement behind.

Thirty officers and 1,244 other ranks were the casualties of the brigade in this immortal fight. These two days' stand enabled the Australians to come up, and the line was not broken through.

NORDWESTHOEK. (See WIELTJE.)

NORTHAMPTON FARM. (See MENIN ROAD.)

NOBLE FARM. (See POELCAPPELLE.)

NONNE BOSSCHEN. (See MENIN ROAD, " Nonne Bosschen Battle "; see also INVERNESS COPSE, and FOREWORD, 1914.)

ONRAET WOOD. (See WYTSCHAETE.)

OOSTTAVERNE RIDGE. (See WARNETON.)

PADDEBEEK. (See PASSCHENDAELE.)

PASSCHENDAELE, 1917

In nightmare dreams, in some visions of Hades conceived by morbid genius, a heavy concentration of horror, dreariness, and woe is brought to bear on our minds, until the strain becomes

PASSCHENDAELE—*continued.*

intolerable. Of such stuff is pictured the battle-ground of
Passchendaele, 1917.

The low ground about Ypres had always been a bog, and
now the constant concussion of monster shells had pitted the
whole surface, so that crater lapped crater, and fœtid water—
foul with every abomination—filled deep pools of unexplored
depth. There was nowhere any solid ground nor dependable
foothold for an advance. So that when a company went over
the top, it was not to attack in the onsweeping lines we picture,
but to seek a path twisting around the lips of shell holes, or to
drag forward foot after foot from the sucking quagmire that held
its victim a mark for shell and bullet. Platoons, stuck in mud
to the waist, were wiped out by machine-gun fire ; wounded
who fell could not rise from the bog ; it will never be known
how many were drowned. It was an added horror that men
could see their comrades caught in the morass, yet could not
get to them, owing to the ground refusing to bear the rescuer's
weight. The atmosphere was heavy with gas, and the ground
became impregnated, so that the fumes hung about for days
after an attack.

This quagmire was fortified against assault by the enemy
during two years of such preparation as his profound military
science could devise. The original cannon-fodder system of the
German Command, counting lives as of little worth, had been
shaken at Verdun and on the Somme, and the British Army
encountered in 1917 a " defence in depth," in which the zone
of morass that was the field of our advance was belted with rows
of reinforced concrete forts—the pill-boxes—which, themselves
impregnable against any but the heaviest shells, commanded
the ground in every direction around, with the murderous fire
of machine guns. The whole of our preparations for the battle
lay exposed under the enemy's scrutiny from the ridges that
surrounded our position, while aeroplanes searched eagle-eyed
from the skies. We could attempt no concealment, and camps
were pitched in the open ; our concentration field was a target,
whereas we had no high level for observation.

The front line was by no means a clearly marked line of
trenches. In the appalling state of the ground no such definite
work could be carried out. The best defence possible in these
conditions was made of shell holes fortified and garrisoned,
irregularly sited and linked to each other. It was always on
the cards that the next shell hole might be manned by Germans,
as the positions were so confused and close together.

PASSCHENDAELE—*continued.*

A " tour " in the trenches meant forty-eight hours spent in a drain of mire and water, where, quite apart from the fact that death or mutilation threatened at any moment, mere existence was wretchedness. This dreary world appeared to be a place cut off from all that is good in life by a circling wall of fire. On three sides the enemy, on one side ourselves, had packed wheel to wheel a monstrous barrier of guns, from whose roaring mouths day and night, night and day, shells raced across the sky, so that the Salient was roofed with ever-flashing, ever-shifting flames.

Ludendorff writes a description of Passchendaele in July 1917 from the view-point of the defenders:

" The horror of the shell-hole area of Verdun was surpassed. It was no longer life at all. It was mere unspeakable suffering. And through this world of mud the attackers [the British] dragged themselves, slowly but steadily, and in dense masses. Caught in the advance zone by our hail of fire they often collapsed, and the lonely man in the shell hole breathed again. Then the mass came on again."

Ludendorff writes later :

" At some points they [his troops] no longer displayed the firmness which I, in common with the local commanders, had hoped for."

Thus the enemy. So it was that life in the trenches, work of transport, or battle fighting were during the autumn of 1917 of equal wretchedness ; and surely courage and endurance were never higher tried nor more greatly displayed.

·   ·   ·   ·   ·   ·

The great difficulty of keeping communications open was met by different methods. Pigeons were invaluable as messengers, although in the weather of the beginning of October they took sometimes as long as twelve hours to fly back, but later the average was only about thirty-five minutes.

The miles of armoured cable buried in the ground before attacks had their weak points in being entirely dependent for repair on human agency ; and an heroic part was played by linesmen who with wire and pliers made their way about in momentary peril of their lives, and mended breaks in the wire. But of all means of communication the most dependable was the runner. These messengers had to be runners indeed, and their task to find a way at utmost speed, and alone, through barrage and dense fighting, demanded a fine quality of courage, resource, and hardihood. That they were the most reliable of all messengers shows how high their standard was.

Passchendaele (Paddebeek Sector), 1917

The short period—some two months—spent by the Naval Division at Ypres was a period of the Salient at its very worst. The long-drawn-out struggle to overcome the deep elastic defence had reached a stage when black despondency had settled as a heavy cloud over the battlefield. The Passchendaele Ridge had to be gained, and only dogged plugging along pushed our line through the marshes. The Naval Division was given the task of crossing the Paddebeek, and capturing the enemy posts beyond, on 26th October, to strengthen the flank of the Canadians. The preliminary bombardment followed by heavy rain had produced the usual honeycomb condition of the ground, and the 1/Royal Marine Battalion and the *Anson* Battalion advanced to the attack winding their way around the rims of the craters, the Marines gaining their objectives as far as Banff House, and a party of the *Anson* taking a group of ruins near Varlet Farm. These posts had been reached by small surviving parties of the attackers, nearly all the company commanders had fallen, and the centre position had not been reached. The conditions were almost impossibly difficult.

The advance in rigid formation became split up into isolated groups, each quite unaware of what had become of the others and as to what was happening, and was met by a fluid defence that, yielding at one point, flowing forward at another, engulfed the forward positions that the advance had captured. However, the *Howe* and 2/Marine Battalions moved forward towards the second objective. The Paddebeek, a little stream now in flood, lay between the British and the position to be won. Up against it went Captain Ligertwood with "A" Company of the Marines, fighting under their own flags. These they had made, while training, from strips of red canvas. Father Davey (Battalion Chaplain) had blessed them, and high above the battle flew the scarlet pennants. Three times their captain was wounded, till, still leading forward, he was again struck down. He rose once more to direct his men before he died. The company held on to the position gained, but in the centre of the line a deadlock had been reached, and there was danger of the enemy cutting our advance posts off from the old front line.

Commander A. Asquith sent up two companies of the *Hood*, in readiness for a hostile counter-attack ; and after a valiant reconnaissance by Lieut. Barclay, R N.V.R., a third company. But the Canadians reported that their left was not in touch ; and a notable achievement of Commander Asquith and Lieut.

PASSCHENDAELE (PADDEBEEK SECTOR)—*continued.*
Garnham, R.F.A., led to the great improvement of the whole
position. These two officers with one rifleman advanced alone
on a reconnaissance which meant " a two-hour walk in full view
of the enemy under heavy fire." They discovered and reinforced
the party of the *Ansons* that were being entrapped near Varlet
Farm ; got in touch and explained the position to the *Howe*
and rest of the *Anson* Battalions, and gained touch with the
Canadians. This turned the fortunes of the day. Our artillery
learned the position of the line to be safeguarded, and the
Canadians were free to carry on their advance. (In the evening
the *Hood* and *Hawke* Battalions moved up and relieved the troops
in the line.) The Marines, who had captured Banff House,
Bray Farm, and Bucks House so valiantly in the morning, had
been forced by lack of ammunition and water to withdraw from
between the closing pincers of the enemy, and these posts were
now captured once again by " C " Company of the *Hawke.* In
the meantime Commander Asquith made another bold reconnaissance to secure the position of the *Hood.* He again reached
the post to which the *Anson* party was clinging, reduced by now
to seven men with their officer, Sub-Lieut. Stevenson, and,
returning, himself led up the relieving platoon.

These confused incidents are typical of the conditions of
mystification, of lack of cohesion, and sense of isolation that
prevailed. One party was cut off for thirty-six hours in front
of the line. Still the five strongly fortified enemy posts had been
captured, and the line advanced some 400 yards. But at a
great cost—14 officers killed, a great many wounded, while in
the ranks the losses of the 188th Brigade were above 500 in each
Battalion. A fine feature of the forty-eight hours during which
the *Hood* Battalion was continuously fighting was the devotion
and gallantry of Surgeon McCracken, who worked unremittingly
among the wounded who lay exposed on the forward slope under
direct fire from the Ridge. He had been with the battalion
from the first days at Gallipoli, and his courage was famous.

The next stage of the battle was still more cruelly fated.
On the 30th the enemy, on the regularity of whose morning hate
we had come to depend, suddenly altered the time, and his
barrage fell disastrously on the 190th Brigade at the very start
of the attack. This was a day of tragic loss. On the left a
company of the Artists Rifles were wiped out when attacking
Source Trench, where the enemy machine guns picked their
targets among men held in the knee-high suck of the mud. The
7/Fusiliers and the 4/Bedfords carried on the futile struggle

PASSCHENDAELE (PADDEBEEK SECTOR)—*continued*.
in the centre.   The 5/King's Shropshire L.I., with equal courage
in intolerable conditions succeeded in forming a defensive flank
between Source Farm and Varlet Farm.   Of the Canadian
Company, that with superb endurance had held to their post,
only one officer and eight men were left at evening time.   And
now an entire change of tactics—a decision to abandon dawn
attacks, and to attack at night after very thorough reconnaissance, brought about a dramatic change.

Sub-Lieut. Brearly and eleven men of the *Nelson* approached
the strongly fortified position in the centre of Source Trench
at 6.10 p.m.   The party split into three ; an N.C.O. and three
men on the left drew the enemy's fire, and Sub-Lieut. Brearly
promptly collected his party and charged from the right.   The
post that in daylight withstood the attack of two battalions fell
to them without a casualty.   The advance of the *Hawke* was
equally successful on the left.

After relief by the *Drake* and *Hood* Battalions, the line went
forward again on the night of the 3rd November, and Sourd
Farm, the only now uncaptured post of any strength, was taken ;
and although the attackers were early observed by the Germans,
they were able under cover of the darkness to make their way
within the enemy's fire, and both battalions reached and secured
the Paddebeek position.

Owing to the method adopted to meet the peculiar nature of
this battle-ground, the line was secured in the second advance
at a cost of only 3 officers and 14 men, and of only 14 officers
and 134 men wounded.   The casualties in the time from October
26th to the 31st had been over 3,000.

Passchendaele (Chinese House), 1917

In the beginning of October 1917 the 1/Royal Dublin Fusiliers
were about to leave the 29th Division, and (for recruiting reasons)
join the 16th (Irish) Division.   The second of the great battles
of Ypres, 1917, opened on the 4th October, and though the 29th
Division was not heavily involved owing to its position on the
left flank of the army, it had a small but difficult duty—to
capture and consolidate three isolated strong-points on and to
the north-west of the railway.   The Dublins appealed to be
allowed to have one more good fight for the 29th before leaving
the Division, and so were entrusted with the important part of
clearing a very strongly fortified block-house known as Chinese
Farm that grimly defied the advance of our forces ; and to gain

contact with the 4th Division where it reached a point 1,000 yards ahead.

The day before the battle Sergeant Ockenden responded to a call from the G.O.C. visiting the battalion, with the promise to be next for a V.C. The Dublins were at their best on that day of farewell gesture. They advanced with an unwavering impulse, and struck forward with steady orderliness, taking their objectives by clockwork, and pushing on to the unpassable torrent of the Broenbeek. And right in front of the whole battalion Sergeant Ockenden fulfilled his promise. He perceived a machine gun that was holding up a platoon, rushed it single-handed and killed all the crew but one, who fled. The sergeant raced after him, ran him down amid the cheers of the Fusiliers, and, under fire all the way, killed him in the open. The same day Ockenden entered a farm, slew four men and took sixteen prisoners. The Dublins had carried all before them, and when the counter-attack came they did not shift a yard.

Passchendaele (The Broenbeek, Condé House), 1917

The 29th Division captured their objectives in the battle of the 9th October, crossing the Broenbeek against a stubborn defence, and advancing in sudden rushes from one shell hole to the next. Condé House was seized with 200 prisoners by the Lancashire and the Royal Fusiliers. At night a flanking party of 30 men was thrown out on the right under Second Lieut. Le Mesurier of the 1/Lancs. Fusiliers. The little band held on through the night ; when the attacking force was relieved they were the last to go back. Only five of that little party survived to reach camp again with their officer, and the battalion turned out to a man and cheered them as they came in.

Passchendaele Sector, 1917

The roads, or what remained of them, were the only reliable line to follow in the Passchendaele Salient, without risk of losing direction entirely ; and for this reason they were the most dangerous from enemy attack. Every yard was registered, and the dead lay unburied along the way, added to as day succeeded day. To avoid the death-walk and strike across country meant a plunge into the death-trap of the mud, and shell pits of deep water. Reliefs carrying the complete rations for a division were known to have been lost in the mud, seeking their way between the shell holes for four days. The engineers and

PASSCHENDAELE SECTOR—*continued*.

pioneer services extended duck-board tracks to all chief centres in the Salient, and infantry when relieved was formed into working parties, so that new and perilous thoroughfares came into being. From Frost House to Tyne Cott ran three miles of route that acquired the name of the Mule Track, whereon men gambled with life and death as transport moved up and down, and shells shattered the road. Lieut.-General Sir A. Hunter Weston, an officer of the R.E., succeeded in producing a " Passchendaele Express." Six little trucks with a small motor-engine crept along at regular times, steadily driven by canny drivers, who dodged the shells so successfully that the train seldom suffered any mishap.

Keerselaerehoek Mound, " Primus Shaft "

This region was a pivot point where troops could be concentrated to meet attacks from the north and east, and here shafts were sunk to underground galleries. Two companies of infantry could be housed in these warrens, sheltered from shell fire, but in extreme discomfort, as they stood always a foot deep in water, kept down to this by hand pumping night and day.

Passchendaele (Vine Cottage), 1917

Vine Cottage was a ruined Belgian farmhouse that masked a pill-box, its 18-inch concrete walls defended by six machine guns. The 3/Battalion of the 1st Central Ontario Regiment found this fortress in their line of attack on the Ridge, and after unsuccessful and costly attempts to capture it, a special attack was planned for the 6th November. The Canadians' advance was hampered by the sticky bog, and although they charged again and again from three sides, hostile machine guns mowed them down and it was impossible to get near enough to bomb the crews. Rain poured down, and the wounded in the fœtid mud were in pitiful case. Suddenly as our men rose in a fresh attack they beheld Corporal Barron—a Scotsman from Banff serving with the Canadians—appear alone on the enemy's flank ; bringing his Lewis gun into action right out in the open, he worked a complete change in the fortunes of the day. He silenced two of the enemy's batteries regardless of their point-blank fire, then, levelling his bayonet, charged the position. The hostile fire slackened, and the Canadians, advancing again, were able to get within their defence and the position was gained. Corporal Collin Barron " with remarkable initiative and skill turned one of the captured

PASSCHENDAELE (VINE COTTAGE)—*continued.*
guns on the retiring enemy." His brilliant action had single-
handed cleared the way for the advance, and he was rewarded
with the Victoria Cross.

Passchendaele, 1917 [1]

The Victoria Cross was awarded to Sergeant Alfred Joseph
Knight, who did extraordinarily good work, and showed exceptional bravery and initiative when his platoon was attacking
an enemy strong-point, and came under very heavy fire from an
enemy machine gun. He rushed through our own barrage,
bayoneted the enemy gunner, and captured the position single-
handed.

Later, twelve of the enemy with a machine gun were encountered in a shell hole. He rushed forward by himself, bayoneted
two, shot a third, and caused the remainder to scatter.

Subsequently, during the attack on a fortified farm, when
entangled up to his waist in mud, and seeing a number of the
enemy firing on our troops, he immediately opened fire on them
without waiting to extricate himself from the mud, killing six.

Again, noticing the company on his right flank being held up
in their attack on another farm, Sergeant Knight collected some
men and took up a position on the flank of this farm, from where
he brought a heavy fire to bear on the farm, as a result of which
the farm was captured.

All the platoon officers of the company had become casualties
before the first objective was reached, and this gallant N.C.O.
took command of all the men of his own platoon and of the
platoons without officers. His energy in consolidating and
reorganising was untiring.

His several single-handed actions showed exceptional bravery,
and saved a great number of casualties in the company. They
were performed under heavy machine-gun fire, and without
regard to personal risk, and were the direct cause of the objectives
being captured.

. . . . . .

The Victoria Cross was awarded to Sergeant John James
Dwyer, who, in charge of a Vickers machine gun, went forward
with the first wave of the brigade.

On reaching the final objective this non-commissioned officer
rushed his gun forward in advance of the captured position in
order to obtain a commanding spot. Whilst advancing he noticed

[1] *London Gazette.*

PASSCHENDAELE—*continued.*

an enemy machine gun firing on the troops on our right flank
and causing casualties. Unhesitatingly he rushed his gun
forward to within thirty yards of the enemy gun and fired point-
blank at it, putting it out of action and killing the gun crew.
He then seized the gun and, totally ignoring the snipers from
the rear of the enemy position, carried it back across the shell-
swept ground to our front line and established both it and his
Vickers gun on the right flank of our brigade.

Sergeant Dwyer commanded these guns with great coolness,
and when the enemy counter-attacked our positions he rendered
great assistance in repulsing them.

On the following day, when the position was heavily shelled,
Sergeant Dwyer took up successive positions. On one occasion
his Vickers gun was blown up by shell fire, but he conducted his
gun team back to headquarters through the enemy barrage,
secured one of the reserve guns, and rushed it back to our position.

During the whole of this attack his contempt of danger, cheerfulness, and courage raised the spirits of all near him.

Passchendaele, 1917

The difficulties of artillery observation were even greater
than in other sectors at Passchendaele. The O. Pip was in the
brewery. One day—the 13th November 1917—an officer,[1]
having reached here by a passage perilous, decided that it would
be preferable to remain, rather than to retire with the other
temporary inhabitants of the brewery when a heavy " strafe "
was opened on the position. The O. Pip was in the cellar of a
half-ruined building, but as there was a vast hole in the roof
and the cellar was lit by candles and cookers, it was amply
displayed to enemy aircraft. The bombardment grew heavier,
the enemy scoring direct hits on the building every few minutes.
And as the O. Pip was shortly smashed into a complete ruin, a
very fine and open view for observation was secured. It was
only when the officer perceived that the whole surrounding area
was in ruins, that his lamp, wire, and rations were gone, that
the wireless station was a tangled mass on which the dead were
lying—indeed it was only when a shell burst inside his cellar,
killing and wounding several of the men, that he decided it was
no longer worth while remaining.

Before 1917 the British ascendancy over the Germans in the
air was established, and reached its high-water mark in the Battle

[1] Of the City of Edinburgh Battery.

PASSCHENDAELE—*continued*.

of the Somme. When the War started, the value of this arm
had not been fully realised, and it was in battle that the Force
grew and came to its own. Over the Salient observation could
only be carried out if it was fought for, and as time passed, the
appalling sight of fighting in the air was watched daily by the
troops held in the mud beneath. The mighty engines, roaring
deeply beneath the snapping rattle of machine guns, would draw
all eyes upwards. It made the spectacle the more thrilling
that it was difficult to see which was friend and which enemy
when, thousands of feet above, a darting, flashing whirl of wings
swept and circled in a tangle of aircraft above the clouds. From
out of the confusion a spark would drop earthward, leaving a
meteor trail across the sky ; and as it fell the blazing mass
showed a machine on fire that finally crashed a flaming wreck
in our lines.

We can turn to the enemy for an unbiassed appreciation of
the daring gallantry of our airmen. A German professor writes :
" The operations were prefaced by innumerable enemy airmen,
who, at the beginning of the preparations for the attack, suddenly
appeared like a swarm of locusts and swamped the front. They
also work on cunningly calculated methods. Their habit is to
work in three layers—one quite high, one in the middle, and the
third quite low. In this way they are almost always able to
menace our airmen from several sides at once. Just as they did
at the beginning of the Somme, the English airmen who fly
lowest showed an immense insolence ; they came down to 200
metres or even less from the ground, and shot at our troops
with their machine guns, which are specially adapted to this
purpose. We, on the other hand, fight them from the ground
with rifle and machine gun."

PETIT BOIS. (See MESSINES.)
PICCADILLY FARM. (See WYTSCHAETE.)
PILCKEM. (See KORTEKEER CABARET, and FOREWORD,
1915.)

POELCAPPELLE

The fortress-like Poelcappelle position had resisted every
attack, presenting a stone wall against which wave after wave
of brigade assault dashed and broke. Bitter disappointment
was added to the burden of life in this disgusting and murderous
stretch of morass and stinking water through which our troops
battled to the ridges. On the 22nd October 1917 the humps
of shattered stones that had been the village, and ground a

POELCAPPELLE—*continued.*

thousand yards beyond, fell to the 53rd Brigade, and even in those days of anonymity the names of the 10/Essex and 8/Norfolk were revealed as the conquerors. The success was achieved by the brilliant scheme of bluff and manœuvring of General Higginson, after the agony of head-on attacks through the abominable battlefield had been suffered in vain.

The 18th Division arrived early in October and took over the line running through the village ; the 55th Brigade opened the attack in deluges of rain, winding forward through the bog like two snakes—Surrey and Buffs on the right, West Kents on the left. A ding-dong fight saw little advance by evening, the rain still fell in torrents, guns and rifles were clogged up with mud, rations could not be got up, and many of the men were without food. The Buffs attacked Gloucester Farm ; Major Nicholson and his surviving officers organised posts in shell holes with the few men they could collect, in which constant levering up was necessary to keep above the slime. His runner, Private Boarer, gained one of the most popular Military Medals of the battalion that day, making six journeys by daylight to Bn. H.Q., and when not carrying messages he turned stretcher-bearer and rescued four men. The 7/Buffs went back to Boesinghe numbering 100 all ranks. The East Surrey were knocked to pieces, and the leading companies were held together under Captain C. E. M. Place, whose wounds were not dressed till hours later. The Berkshire lost their C.O., Colonel Longhurst, and the Adjutant, Rochfort, carried on with one arm blown away for another two hours.

The 53rd Brigade came up to the fresh attempt to capture the obstinate position on the 22nd. The divisional artillery suffered dreadful casualties in the " Gunner's Hell " during the days of preparation. The dipping ground of the Steenbeek held a pack of guns in its slimy depth ; the vanished track of the Poelcappelle Road " between the Devil and the deeps " was one battery position. Superhuman efforts hauled the 18-pounders about, heaving them out of the bog. Batteries were so depleted of N.C.O.s that one had only a corporal and two bombardiers at the guns.

Forty-eight hours' unceasing shelling heralded the great day, and on the night of the 21st the Essex and Norfolks crept forward and dug shallow trenches, a meagre 2 to 3 feet reaching water, which afforded slight protection against the heavy Boche shells. The Norfolks went over the top first and opened splendidly by capturing the Brewery, while the companies to the south bluffed the enemy with a Chinese attack, and drew his attention by

POELCAPPELLE—*continued.*

working dummy figures along their front. The Essex leapt
forward at 7.30 a.m., pushed into the village, captured Nobles
Farm, swept on and seized Meunier House on higher ground
bristling with machine guns, and took Tracas Farm beyond the
line. Such an advance—a thousand yards gained where men
pushed forward through the sucking mud into the teeth of
shell and machine-gun fire—was a triumph of valour and endurance. The Germans attempted a counter-attack beyond a
large sheet of water near Nobles Farm and were met by the
Essex. Two Lewis gunners jumped on to a pill-box at short
range and opened fire. Corporal Tebbitt's gun jammed, but he
remained on top of the pill-box, coolly took the gun to pieces,
vaselined the parts, put it together again and went on firing.
The Germans came no nearer than 70 yards. Next day the
Essex and Norfolks handed over the line that they had so
splendidly captured.

Poelcappelle Area, 1917

The 223rd Brigade and 317th Brigade were the divisional
artillery of the Naval Division. During October and November
1917 they were in the line without relief, covering the advance
first of the 9th Division ; then the operations of the Naval
Division ; and finally the advance of the 1st Division. They
were so short of men that it was an almost impossible achievement
to keep the guns in action, to keep men alive to serve them, but
their fire was never stopped. In " D " Company of the 223rd
only one officer, Lieut. Keeping, R.F.A., with one N.C.O., remained unwounded when the ordeal ended on the 10th November.
But one howitzer still in action alone fired steadily on until the
order came through to cease fire. The brigades were not relieved
until the 6th December. " They had sustained casualties heavier
in proportion than those of the infantry in the worst disaster
of the War."

Poelcappelle (St. Julien Road, the Cockroft), 1917

The Salient, being one vast quagmire that gave through to
water-level at any point, was the worst possible district for the
employ of tanks. Such success as they achieved was rather
due to the herculean labour and gallantry of the crews pent up
within them. The action on the 19th August that takes its
name from the Cockroft was the most entirely successful operation
of these perambulating fortresses in the Salient.

The object was the capture of a group of particularly strong

POELCAPPELLE (ST. JULIEN ROAD)—*continued.*

pill-boxes that, being quite impervious to shell fire, powerfully garrisoned with machine gunners, and surrounded by a zareba of barbed wire, had cost our infantry very dearly in the hopeless attempt to reduce them. Seven tanks set forth through the ruins that had once been St. Julien, and ground and skidded their greasy way along the battered pavé to the Poelcappelle Road, behind the smoke curtain of an infantry barrage. As each tank reached the nearest point to the post allotted to it, it left the comparative firmness of the pavé, plunged away into the bog, and wallowed as far as possible before sticking fast. The first one gained within fifty yards of the Cockroft, the most formidable redoubt ; and though only armed with machine guns, its monstrous appearance out of the swirling smoke must have struck terror to the garrison, for they fled almost at once, and the infantry platoon following the tank was able to occupy the fort with hardly a casualty. The tank was securely gripped in the suck of the mud, and the captain joined the infantry with his crew and Lewis guns. The Maison du Hibou was some way from the road, but the 6-pdr. tank allocated for its capture managed to crawl through the morass to the rear before the mud overcame it, and trained a gun on the entrance. The shock of four rounds of shell, fired at close quarters, drove the garrison out, and the post was taken.

The strongest resistance was met at Triangle Farm, where, with the tank in support, the infantry got into the fortress, and seized it after a hand-to-hand fight with the bayonet. The three remaining pill-boxes—Vancouver, Hillock Farm, and the Gun-pits—offered no resistance at all. This immediate and extra-ordinary success was achieved with a total loss of only 15 men wounded among the infantry, but it had one unfortunate result in encouraging the use of tanks in the Salient. The terrain was impossible. And such a success was never repeated.

East of Poelcappelle, 1917

The 2nd (London) Rifle Brigade when they took over the trenches just east of a few pill-boxes and rubbish heaps, that were all now marking the position that once was Poelcappelle, tell of one or two incidents which paint a vivid picture of the frightful grip of the all-enveloping mud on our struggling forces. " No one who has not seen it, been stuck fast in it, or helped to unstick others, can possibly imagine what it was like." It took hours to cover the shortest distances ; little attempt was made to patrol ; but the runners succeeded with extraordinary

EAST OF POELCAPPELLE—*continued.*
enterprise and agility in getting about at night where no duck-
boards bridged the morass.

It was easy to get lost wandering between posts, and out into
No-man's-land in the dark. On one such occasion an officer
going the rounds with a runner was led by groans to where a
man, three times wounded the day before, was sunk up to the
waist in the sticky clutch of the mud. It was impossible to
move him, but food was given to him, and a promise that help
would come, and next night he was rescued half dead. Such
episodes must account for an untold number of the " missing."
This battalion has a record of four stretcher-bearers who worked
for six hours to get a wounded rifleman into safety, and at the
end of that time had only managed to carry him some fifty yards.

POLYGON WOOD, 1915

A mound known as the Butte de Polygon provided the dugouts for Bn. H.Q. of the 1/3 Monmouths in April 1915. Near by
was Squeaking Pump. The officer-artist who created " Old
Bill " is said to have founded his reputation here. At that
time the Wood still kept its pine trees ; dugouts made by the
French, though very shallow, were so dotted about and roofed
with pine needles that they did not catch the eye of the enemy
aircraft always droning overhead. The French had finished off
this artistic job by carving verses on the trees, and one dugout
was labelled " Villa ma Rose." A French platoon commander
handed over one neat little trench map marked solely with one
dugout—" Your Home "—before hurrying away with his men.

The line in the north having been broken by the gas attack,
German guns had come up on Pilckem Ridge, and enfiladed
our troops where Polygon Wood was our most easterly outpost.
The sector was becoming an isthmus, so that the line was necessarily withdrawn to just east of Hooge Château and Frezenberg,
to the Yser Canal near Boesinghe, shortening the line by 5,000
yards. Polygon Wood, already of everlastingly glorious memory
of 1914, was evacuated on the night of the 3rd May. Each
company of the 2/King's Own, 3/Monmouth, and 1/K.O.Y.L.I.
slipped away while a covering party of an officer and twenty men
sent up " Verey " lights and fired occasional shots from different
parts of the trenches. So successfully was this carried out that
the enemy was still bombarding empty trenches next morning.

**Polygon Wood. (See MENIN ROAD, " Nonne Bosschen
Battle.")**

POMERN REDOUBT. (See INVERNESS COPSE.)

PONT DE NIEPPE, 1918

In April 1918 the Pioneer Battalion of the Northumberland
Fusiliers held the bridgehead on the Bailleul—Armentières
Road. They were at first engaged in making temporary bridges
for the infantry ; a number of rafts made of sheets of cork and
timber frames were joined together to a length of 60 or 80 feet,
and when ready were navigated to their positions in Armentières,
and tucked along the banks under branches and foliage, until
necessity should arise to swing them across the stream, leaving
the permanent bridges free for guns and transport.

On the 7th April Armentières was still inhabited by the
French civilians, whose homes we had for so long defended
against the Germans. But on that date the town was beset by
the scathing bombardment of 30,000 to 40,000 shells of poison gas ;
one hundred of the Pioneers in the town were made casualties
at the start, and the unhappy civilians, who had from the beginning of war clung to their homes, now fled while a heavy bombardment burst upon the town and the roads. Our men did what
they could to get them away, and passed them back to the
French police. The Boche were attacking in force and advancing
rapidly, and in the sector north of the town five German divisions
bore down upon five British brigades. A 15-inch howitzer in
front of the Lys was destroyed by its commanding officer, as
there was no time to get up the tractors to move it. Through
the worst zones the runners, fleet-footed and intrepid, found a
way to carry the messages, but a shell hit Bn. H.Q. and most
of the runners assembled were killed. The Pioneers held the
bridges until all our troops were over, then blew them to pieces
at the enemy's feet, and the fine old Pont de Nieppe was exploded
late that night. Next day the battalion made a stand at
Erquinghem Bridgehead, the 11th Platoon holding up the
enemy and beating down a machine-gun barrage by rifle fire.
When the time came to retire they cut the bridge in two, darting
back through the one only small gap in the wire behind them,
under close machine-gun fire from front and either side. Only
half the platoon got away, and many were wounded.

The remaining bridges were destroyed by the Pioneers with
felling axes, while the enemy on a ridge within 300 yards brought
a number of machine guns and snipers to bear on them. The
covering parties kept this fire down until the bridges fell in two
and floated away.

Near the church four men were hacking at the last one, and
three took cover from the fearful intensity of the machine-gun

PONT DE NIEPPE—*continued.*
fire ; but one man, Private Wainman, stuck to his post, and
succeeded alone in cutting the bridge apart. When all civilians
and the main bodies were away, the covering parties received
the order to withdraw, and with a final burst of fire they took
their way to Nieppe.

POTIJZE, Between Château and Verlorenhoek

On the 13th May 1915 the 8th Cavalry Brigade received
orders to counter-attack and recapture a front-line trench on
Frezenberg Ridge. The Essex Yeomanry had orders to come up
on the right of the 10th Hussars in front of Potijze, under command of their C.O., Lieut.-Colonel Shearman. The Essex
advanced from their trenches in echelon of squadrons to come
alongside the Hussars, ready for the attack. Major Roddick
led them out, a pipe between his teeth, his stick in his hand,
as they filed from their trenches. The men dashed forward
cheering and shouting and reached the Hussars when—at the
exact moment of their arrival—a little bunch of Germans bolted
from a trench 200 yards ahead across the open. A wild shout of
" Tally-ho ! Tally-ho ! Yonder they go ! " burst from the Essex.
Nothing could hold the two regiments, and up the hill, like hounds
in full cry, they went. They surged over the crest, and, ahead
of time, ran into our bombardment. The trench was captured,
the Germans retiring after a final burst of fire at close range,
and Major Roddick was killed at the head of his men. This
trench was ankle-deep in mud, but the battalions promptly
comforted themselves with cigars, cigarettes, and rations left by
the enemy. The lull, however, was short, and soon violent
and accurate fire began to crash into the trench. The line
was a single one and unsupported, and strong parties of the
enemy came round threatening the right. Lieut.-Colonel Shearman was shot down and killed. The bombardment grew in
intensity, but for two hours the men in the trench endured.
Rifles were jamming in the liquid mud, and the position was
becoming untenable. " B " Squadron of the Essex had manned
an irregular line of shell holes, a few men in each, where the
O.C., Captain Ruggles-Brise, has described the drumming of
incessant machine-gun fire as reminding him " of the song of a
sewing machine." In his shell hole were seven men, and as the
rifles jammed and the magazines would not work, four who were
already wounded sat in the slop of the drizzling rain in the bottom
and acted as loaders. But though they tried to clean up the
rifles as they loaded, only single shots could be fired. Sergeant

POTIJZE, BETWEEN CHÂTEAU AND VERLORENHOEK—*continued*.
Deakin was shot through the temple and died as he stood,
and in these crowded quarters his body stiffened in the attitude
of firing at the enemy. Towards evening the squadron in the
forward trench received orders from the 10th Hussars to file
out and retire from the line they had captured, and which had
now become impossible to hold. Lieut.-Colonel Deacon was
never heard of again. Captain Ruggles-Brise, in too exposed a
position to move, hung on till nightfall, when the squadron quietly
slipped away. The stand that the 8th Brigade had made " did
more than anything else to stop the front here from going
entirely " ; the Germans had been held back long enough to
allow of an unbroken line being established during the night.

The 10th Hussars had been reduced to 4 officers and 98 other
ranks.

Potijze, 1915 [1]

The 1/North Staffords were holding the front-line trenches in
advance of Potijze. The line ran down to the Ypres—Roulers
Railway, and up the hill to Railway Wood, a re-entrant forming
a very pronounced salient that was held by a garrison of one
platoon. The Germans had sapped up to within 30 yards of
the apex, and established a small post.

The night of the 4th/5th July had passed peacefully enough,
nor had any incident of note occurred during the early morning
of the 4th. The men had " stood down," day-sentries had been
posted, and the usual routine of trench warfare followed in the
ordinary way. It was between 8 and 9 a.m., and Lieut. W. G. F.
Smith, the officer on duty in " C " Company, was making his
rounds preparatory to being relieved for breakfast, when he heard
a salvo of " whizz-bangs " fall over to the right in the direction
of the salient, followed almost at once by the unmistakable
crash of bombs. He immediately called upon Private Bray, a
bomber who happened to be in the trench near him, to follow,
and hastily picking up some bombs, set off to investigate. In
a few moments he discovered that a party of Germans, under
cover of the salvo, had rushed the salient, surprised the sentries,
killed or driven out the garrison, and were now exploiting their
success northwards towards " C " Company. The position was
critical. It was obvious that no counter-attack could be expected
for some little time from the regiment on the right, and the
Germans, by virtue of surprise, had obtained that active initiative
which is so supremely important in all bombing contests. Lieut.

[1] From regimental contribution.

POTIJZE—*continued.*

Smith did not hesitate. Sending back a man to raise the alarm, he and Private Bray started to counter-attack on their own. Both of them were expert bombers, and, attacking determinedly, they soon held the Germans, whom they had no difficulty in outranging. The Germans, whose success had been so far easily gained, were disturbed by this resolute opposition, and grew flurried. Some of their bombs were thrown too soon, with the result that they lay for a few seconds before exploding, and presently, as the British bombs began to burst among them, the Germans flung theirs without attempting to pull the igniting string. Private Bray, who was running short of bombs, quickly turned this carelessness to his advantage, and, picking up the unignited bombs which fell near him, threw them back—this time properly ignited—at the enemy. On one occasion at least Private Bray, picking up an ignited bomb, flung it back before it had had time to burst. Treatment of this nature was not in accordance with the Germans' plan, and the raiding party began to withdraw, pursued by one officer and one man. Before, however, they had gone far, C.S.M. Stapleton arrived with a bombing party, and the retreat became a rout.

It was then discovered that the parapet of the salient had been so severely damaged by the enemy's shell fire that the trench was almost untenable. Lieut. Smith accordingly seized the opportunity to organise a working party to repair the breach. While, however, he was directing the work, the enemy suddenly opened a heavy fire from their advanced post, and he was shot through the head. Private Bray then went "berserk," and standing in the breach over his officer's body, he hurled bombs into the enemy post with such effect that all fire ceased from it, though not before the German snipers had put two bullets through his service dress cap. The breach was then repaired, and the trench handed over to its garrison.

Potijze, 1915 [1]

On 29th May the Faughs were holding trenches east of Potijze Château, when the enemy made another gas attack. The battalion showed conspicuous gallantry in spite of the pain caused by the gas, and as the Germans advanced to the attack they met with such resistance that they never succeeded in developing their attack on the battalion front. On the other hand, the machine guns, and especially Captain Bull's company, materially assisted the troops farther south by enfilading the

[1] From regimental contribution.

POTIJZE—*continued.*

German attacks. On this day the enemy employed lachrymatory shells, which made the eyes very painful.

There were many instances of gallantry. Private G. Wilson, a gallant machine gunner, when the rest of the gun team were knocked out, fought his gun single-handed, and when the emplacement was blown in, moved his gun to a fresh position and again brought it into action.

On the night of the 25th May the battalion had to mourn the loss of a particularly fine young officer, 2nd Lieut. C. E. Cooke, who was shot dead whilst out with a covering party. He had been wounded before, and many times mentioned for gallant conduct. He was known to his men as " the Sandbag King," and when he was buried, as was necessary in continuous fighting, in the mud where he fell, every man in his platoon knelt down and shook him by the hand.

These were hard times, the hardships only being equalled by the cheerfulness with which the soldiers endured them. In addition to being constantly under fire, the troops were in the open for weeks together without shelter, and as an instance of minor privations the men were warned not to drink running water, as it had been proved that the enemy had poisoned the streams with arsenic.

Among the many fine soldiers lost in this prolonged battle was Sergeant Patrick Collier, who was shot through the head at a point in the Salient where the trenches were only a few yards apart. When his officer found him mortally wounded at his post, he was trying to raise himself, and when spoken to, replied, " It's all right, sor ; I'm only waiting for the ninth second." He had been a boxer, and fancied himself in the ring. Sergeant Collier has been described as " the straightest and most respected non-commissioned officer of his battalion."

Another instance is that of two men who were great friends. One of them was killed by a shell, and an officer found his companion sitting on the fire-step crying bitterly. He knew it was useless to offer consolation. The next shell reunited the comrades. Such men were typical of the rank and file of the Royal Irish Fusiliers.

POTSDAM, 1917

On the 20th Sept. the 27th (Lowland) Brigade swept forward to attack the Germans in the sector towards Zonnebeke, the strong pill-box defence checking the impetus of the advance. Potsdam was a massive fortification rendered the more im-

POTSDAM—*continued.*

pregnable by a pill-box near to it. The left assaulting company of the 12/Royal Scots came into a range of machine-gun fire so fierce that it threatened to break up the whole attack. The men flung themselves down into the cover of the craters, and for a brief moment the advance was paralysed. Captain H. Reynolds, a man of wonderful gallantry, gathered up a half-dozen men near him, and, darting from shell hole to shell hole, got below the enemy's field of fire and right up to the walls of the stronghold. Captain Reynolds lobbed a grenade up to a loophole, but the Germans stuffed it up with a pack, and the gun from the midst went on firing. With utter carelessness of self, with magnificent daring, Captain Reynolds grasped the ledge, drew himself up, and with all his strength squeezed a phosphorus bomb into the loophole. His tunic was torn to pieces by the storm of bullets, but as by a miracle, his body was untouched. The bomb exploded, burst into flames, and to escape suffocation the garrison retired at the rear into the hands of the six waiting Scots. Three Germans were killed, seven surrendered. Captain Reynolds with two men ran on to Potsdam, which surrendered to an attack of the Royal Scots in front, and some South Africans detached from their unit in the north. The fortress was surrounded and 70 prisoners with 2 machine guns were captured. Captain Reynolds was awarded the V.C.

RAILWAY WOOD.   (See POTIJZE.)
RAYMOND FARM.   (See LEDEGHEM.)
REUTEL RIDGE.   (See MENIN ROAD.)
RITZ STREET TRENCH.   (See INVERNESS COPSE.)

ST. ELOI, 1915

The 3/ and 4/Battalions of the K.R.R.C. arrived in France from India and took over the disconnected and water-logged trenches from the French near St. Eloi in February 1915. The 4th Brigade after three days in these ditches had 500 men temporarily but completely crippled with trench feet. The 3/Battalion was the first to distinguish itself by a brilliant attack with the bayonet, capturing some trenches that the enemy had rushed from another brigade the evening before. Here Captain (and Adjutant) Franks, with Rifleman Shee, swept through some trenches and almost single-handed cleared the enemy out, capturing twenty prisoners The 4/Battalion opened their campaign with a notable sortie, attacking a section of new German trenches, where the Boche had come to within

ST. ELOI—*continued*.

10 yards of our line in an open sap. The battalion proceeded
to occupy a trench known as Number 21, from which they
launched the attack. " D " Company with a party of twelve
bombers filed off, the whole place being lighted by a brilliant
moon, and they came quickly under the deadly fire of a machine
gun trained on the opening from the trench. Our field guns
were sending beautifully timed shells into the main enemy
parapet, but the boom and rattle of gun, rifle, and machine gun
increased from the enemy side. " B " and " D " Companies
now followed up the attack across 100 yards of open, and found
the entrance to the trench by the gruesome markers of two dead
corporals propped up like sentinels on either side. The trench
was a ghoulish place, full of corpses of every regiment, lying
and crouching in every attitude, some still grasping swords
that stuck up from the mud—the man-trap of a nightmare.
In places this ghastly crowd left no room for passage, and the
riflemen climbed out and crawled along by the parapet, scrambling
in again when they could. They reached an angle where they
came up with the first company. Just beyond this corner the
trench was blocked by a barricade, a veritable fort of sandbags
and wire ; in front of it lay a heap of thirty of our dead and
wounded who had faced the ambush. No one could live round
that corner ; no one could leave the trench to flank the barricade
—it was covered by machine guns and rifles at 80 yards' range
that waited for any man to appear. Nearly the whole of " D "
Company had been wiped out. The gallant attack was brought
to a standstill. The 3/Battalion next came up in support, and
the 4/ retired behind the breastwork, leaving one company in
the captured trench. They were bombed and bombed again,
till their captain, with a bullet through the chest and arm and
twice wounded by bombs, found himself with only four men left
alive and unwounded. Then the survivors crawled back. The
casualties among the 300 who had gone into action were 113,
all the bomb throwers and their officer being killed.

St. Eloi, 1915 [1]

In the Christmas of 1914 due south of Ypres, at the neck of
the Salient stood the battered little village of St. Eloi. Being
in a commanding position on a slight ridge, it had been the
scene of much bitter fighting for its possession during the first
battle of Ypres.

Sometimes it was in the enemy's hands, sometimes in ours,

[1] From regimental contribution.

ST. ELOI—*continued.*

but more often it was midway between the contending parties in No-man's-land, when its skeleton houses lent themselves admirably to the keen scouts of both sides at night.

The particularly hard winter, the colossal shell fire, and the numerous overflowing " tanks " had turned the terrain into nothing better than a morass. The so-called British trenches were only disconnected waterlogged rifle pits, and they afforded no protection whatsoever. There was no parapet, no parados, and dugouts were unknown. There was no trench paraphernalia such as duck-boards, "Verey" lights, trench pumps or periscopes. Steel sniping plates had been provided and were stuck up on the so-called parapets, but they were perforated like sieves by the enemy snipers who lay concealed in a well-built trench just 100 yards away on the ridge.

The Leinsters came into the line south-east of St. Eloi at Christmas-time. Their right flank rested up against the famous Mound of Death and their left flank ran back towards Triangle Wood.

The cold was intense and a biting sleet drove in their faces as they traversed through a sea of mud. Some of the men, laden with boxes of ammunition and rations, became bogged up to their waists in the mire and had to be hauled out by main force.

Dawn found the 100th Foot, which only three months previously were going round in shorts and shirt-sleeves on the plains at Fyzabad, standing over their knees in a muddy slime exposed to a snow storm in their sodden great-coats.

Could the sudden climate changes have been greater, from the scorching plains of an Indian summer to the trenches in the waterlogged flats of Flanders in mid-winter ? And to cope with these hardships the men had nothing more than their pre-War or peace-time marching order.

During this period evening snipers were particularly hostile, taking full advantage of their opponents' weak position. Not a minute passed but there was not the slat of a bullet in the rotten parapet, the ping of a ricochet off the steel sniping plates, frequently mingled with a stifled yell from a great Leinster who would suddenly collapse and sink to the bottom of the trench to be completely engulfed in liquid mud. The cold, the wet, the slime and filth of trench life in the Ypres Salient during this period were such as to make an impression never to be obliterated from the minds of those who suffered and survived.

This condition lasted for just over a month, the 1st Leinster

St. Eloi—*continued*.

Regiment marching back and forth to the trenches round about
St. Eloi.

On the 14th February there was a sudden interruption of this
routine by an attack on the part of the Bavarians.

After an artillery bombardment lasting for six hours, the Germans advanced at 2 p.m. in their hordes against the 100th Foot.

In spite of having been plastered by shells of all calibres,
the Leinsters were in fine fettle and jumped up on their muddy
parapets and stood ready to meet the enemy with their bayonets
and " with sorra a twist of th' ould barbed wire between us, the
b—— Jarmans, and the devil himself." The regiment on our
left retired, leaving the Leinsters' left-flank company in the air,
and it was immediately set on by the enemy as the weak spot.
Though this company put up a fine show, they were completely
overwhelmed by sheer weight of numbers and had to retire.

One of the battle Vickers guns which had been in an advanced
position effected a fine withdrawal, and Private Courtney,
although hit in five places, snatched his spare-parts bag from in
front of the very noses of the Boches and retired.

On the 14th March the 1/Leinsters were resting in Dicke-
busche when they received sudden orders to fall in for the line,
to counter-attack and recover some ground lost by hostile under-
mining, including the Mound. In admirable fashion the 100th
deployed east of Voormezeele and advanced to the attack.
The country was difficult for night advancing, intersected as it
was with ditches. The highly trained battalion managed to get
up to within 50 yards of their objective under the cover of the
darkness, and then with a wild cheer rushed the Boches with fixed
bayonets. Angry and isolated scraps went on throughout the dark
hours, but the dawn saw an end to the pig-sticking. The casualties suffered by the battalion during these operations were 16 officers killed and wounded and 257 other ranks killed and wounded.

But there was much honour for the 1/Battalion. The Prince of
Wales's Leinster Regiment received a mention in the C.-in-C.'s dispatches for their gallantry in their first action in European warfare.

This happy document was dated 17th March, the most suitable
day for Irish soldiers, being St. Patrick's Day.

St. Eloi Craters, 1915 [1]

The St. Eloi craters having been lost, the 1/North Staffordshires were sent into the line on the 29th October with instructions
that they were to be recaptured. " D " Company was given

---

[1] From regimental contribution.

ST. ELOI CRATERS—*continued.*
the honour of retaking the trenches. These three craters lay in No-man's-land—the lines here being about 95 yards apart—and commanded a fairly large sector of ground. It was necessary to know the strength of the party in occupation and details of their defence ; Lieut. D. G. Chew crawled out to the nearest lip of each crater in broad daylight on the 30th October, and discovered that during the day a solitary German sentry was the only occupant in each one. That the craters were strongly held at night time, a reconnaissance the previous evening had already proved. At dusk Lieut. Chew led out the attacking party, and occupied the craters without opposition. One party of diggers immediately set to work to establish the position on the lip and dig communication trenches, while Lewis guns were placed on either flank, and a party of bombers awaited the arrival of the enemy. The work of consolidation was half completed before the enemy entered the craters. As soon as they arrived they were met with a shower of bombs which inflicted on them heavy casualties, causing them to retire. Three-quarters of an hour passed in hard work under heavy rifle and machine-gun fire, and then the enemy made a determined attack to regain the craters. They were met with Lewis-gun fire, rifle fire, grenades, and trench mortars, which smashed up their attack with heavy losses. Lieut. Chew killed one German with a very light pistol fired point-blank. Two more determined attacks were launched during the night, but they met with the same fate, which was due to the leadership of Lieut. Chew and C.S.M. Gould. Lieut. Chew earned an M.C. for this night's work, " when by his promptness and dash in reorganising and leading the men near him, he was mainly instrumental in repelling three German attacks. Although wounded in the face, he refused to leave his post till daylight, and then returned immediately his wound was dressed."

After a night spent in wiring the front during a running bombing fight, the consolidation of the position was completed, and it was inspected by the Brigade and Divisional Commanders, who congratulated the battalion on taking and consolidating the position so quickly with very small casualties.

ST. JEAN. (See KEERSELAERE, also FOREWORD, 1915.)

ST. JULIEN, 1915.[1] (See also KITCHENER WOOD.)

About 5 p.m. on the 22nd April 1915 the shelling abruptly ceased and a strange and ominous sight was witnessed. On

[1] Contributed by Lieut.-General Sir Herbert Uniacke.

ST. JULIEN—*continued.*

either side of Langemarck something which looked like spurts of whitish smoke began to appear at set intervals on the ground in front of the German trenches. Clouds formed by these jets, gathering in volume, eddied and swirled until they united into one continuous low cloud-bank of a peculiar greenish hue and yellow above where it caught the rays of the sinking sun. On-lookers saw this bank of cloud, drifting before a light breeze, begin to move towards the French lines. It was the first use of poison gas in war. That its use was forbidden mattered little to the Germans, for they violated practically every rule contained in the Conventions and Declarations respecting the laws and customs of war ; and they showed their knowledge of guilt in the case of gas by keeping all mention of it out of bulletins, papers, and books for several years. But its success was un-doubted ; " the French troops, staring over the top of their parapet at the curious screen which ensured them a temporary relief from fire, were observed suddenly to throw up their hands, to clutch at their throats, and to fall to the ground in the agonies of asphyxiation. Many lay where they had fallen, while their comrades, absolutely helpless against this diabolical agency, rushed madly out of the mephitic mist and made for the rear, overrunning the lines of trenches behind them. Many of them never halted until they had reached Ypres, while others rushed westwards and put the Canal between themselves and the enemy. The Germans meanwhile advanced and took possession of the successive lines of trenches, tenanted only by the dead garrisons, whose blackened faces, contorted figures, and lips fringed with the blood and foam from their bursting lungs, showed the agonies in which they had died." [1] By 7 p.m. there was no formed body of French troops east of the Canal, though many brave individuals and groups remained and attached themselves to British units in the ensuing fighting.

St. Julien, April 1915

On the 23rd April the 2/Royal Dublin Fusiliers were sent at half an hour's notice up from Bailleul to join the reinforcements that were being rushed into the gap between Bixschoote and Langemarck, where the French troops had been overwhelmed by the first gas wave. Orders were for a counter-attack on St. Julien. As the Dublins charged over the difficult and un-reconnoitred ground, through tangles of barbed wire and a maze of trenches, they were met by machine-gun and rifle fire, and

[1] From *The British Campaign in France*, by A. Conan Doyle.

ST. JULIEN—*continued.*
pounded by shells from the great howitzers in the rear. The
men were falling right and left. An officer present writes:
" One unforgettable incident remains in the writer's memory :
one company which had lost all its officers, and which had been
ordered to retire, was doing so in disorder, when the small untidy
figure of Colonel Loveband, clad in an ancient British warm and
carrying a blackthorn stick, approached quietly across the open,
making as he walked the ' lie-down ' signal with his stick. The
effect was instantaneous, and for hundreds of yards along the
front the men dropped and used their entrenching tools." [1]

. . . . . .

Two companies of the 3/Canadian Battalion under Major
A. J. E. Kirkpatrick held the enemy, between Kitchener Wood
and St. Julien, on the 24th April 1915. They had not received
the orders for the retirement of the Canadian left wing, and so
fought on, the ground behind them being open to creeping
machine-gun and rifle fire. That evening only 43 men mustered
of the two companies, nearly all wounded, and 2 being totally
blind. But they had held the enemy for precious hours.

St. Julien (near), 1915

Lance-Corporal Frederick Fisher of the 13/Canadian Battalion
was in command of a machine gun and four men, when the
Canadians were called upon to stand fast on the left flank of our
army, beyond which the Turcos and Zouaves, flying before the
fresh horror of the gas, had left a four-mile gap. Every gun was
in action to help the valiant defence, and a battery of 18-pounders,
commanded by Major W. King, stayed, firing point-blank charges
into the enemy as they came within a couple of hundred yards.
But guns, pointed at the enemy like rifles, cannot be so easily
withdrawn, and it was a desperate struggle for the detachments
and supporting infantry to man-handle them into safety at the
last possible moment. Corporal Fisher saw the imminent
danger, and rushed his machine gun in front of the battery. He
remained right out in the open, mowing down the advancing
Germans till all his crew had fallen, been replaced, and again
wiped out. Belts of ammunition were rapidly served up to him,
and he fought on unwaveringly, until the guns behind him had
been dragged out. Corporal Fisher went forward to meet the
enemy and kept on firing, slowing their advance, until, with his
finger still on the trigger, he was shot dead. He was awarded a
posthumous V.C.

[1] Crown and Company: *2nd Battalion Royal Dublin Fusiliers,* by H. C. Wylly.

St. Julien, 1915 [1]

On the 25th April the 1/Battalion Royal Warwickshire Regiment formed part of a force marched up from Ypres at midnight to deliver a counter-attack in an endeavour to retake St. Julien. The urgency of the crisis had not admitted of efficient artillery support being arranged or even of thorough previous reconnaissance. The attack was launched at 4.30 a.m., the Royal Warwicks being on the left of the line and, fighting with the greatest intrepidity, pushed its way to within 70 yards of the German trenches ; but, under the murderous machine-gun fire, it could get no farther. Lieut. Gowett charged at the head of his platoon right up to the German trenches, but every man save one was killed in this gallant action, Lieut. Gowett himself falling on the very parapet. After two hours' desperate fighting the battalion was compelled to fall back to a line of trenches which was then consolidated and held. The battalion suffered terrible losses in this furious struggle. Seven officers were killed ; nine others wounded or missing. The casualties in other ranks were over 500.

St. Julien, South-West of, 1915 [2]

The advance of the Lahore Division on the 26th April was a particularly fine one, over nearly a mile of open ground under a murderous shell fire. The leading troops had almost reached the front line of German trenches and were making good progress when suddenly before them rose the ominous greenish-yellow fumes of a thick gas cloud. A steady north-east breeze was blowing, and in a moment the troops were engulfed in the deadly reek. It was impossible for the unprotected men to get forward. Many of them died where they stood. The suffocating cloud passed slowly over, but the condition in which the stupefied survivors were left by the poisonous fumes made any immediate further advance out of the question. So the whole line was brought to a halt, and those still living dug themselves in where they lay. General Smith-Dorrien in his subsequent report, after pointing out that adequate artillery preparation was in the circumstances impossible, describes the attack as being made " up an open slope in the face of overwhelming shell, rifle, and machine-gun fire, and clouds of poison gas . . . but it prevented the German advance and ensured the safety of Ypres." Taking all things into consideration, few episodes of the fighting round Ypres show greater collective gallantry than the attack of the Lahore Division, and though the cost was terrible, no men

[1] From regimental account.
[2] Contributed by Lieut.-General Sir Herbert Uniacke.

St. Julien, South-West of—*continued.*

died that day with greater glory—" yet many died and there
was much glory." No more fitting tribute could have been
laid by India on the altar of the British Empire when at the
hour of destiny her armed manhood arrived to aid in holding
the sagging line against a mighty enemy. And no pathos more
poignant than the fate of these soldiers from the rolling plains
of the Five Rivers and the hills beneath the Safêd Koh, who of
their own free will crossed the ocean to die for the British Raj
in the mists of a strange land.

SANCTUARY WOOD, 1915 [1]

The 16th Lancers were holding trenches that ran from the
bottom of the valley up a slight hill, and then along the top, in
what was afterwards known as Sanctuary Wood. They consisted of a front line and a support line about 20 yards behind,
joined by short lengths of trench, with one communication
trench on the left flank, where " D " Squadron joined a French
Territorial Division. The regiment had its three squadrons in
line, each having one troop in support.

At about 6 a.m. on the 21st February the Germans exploded
three mines at short intervals on the left of " D " Squadron.
They immediately attacked and drove the remnants of " D "
Squadron along the trench and over the hill. The mines buried
Lieut. Ryan, who was dug out alive later by the Germans and
taken prisoner, and about ten men. The remainder suffered
severely in the retirement. Major Neave rallied some of the
men and with the help of his own squadron held up the Germans
coming down the trench long enough to enable Captain Tempest-
Hicks to get a machine gun on to the parapet. The fire from
this gun drove the enemy to ground and prevented him continuing his advance across the open. One of the men lay under
the parapet, just in front of the gun, and shot down several
Germans who were trying to work down the trench covered by
bombers. Meanwhile Major Neave was mortally wounded and
Captain Evans wounded. The support troops of " A " and " C "
Squadrons were ordered to make a counter-attack, which they
did across the open, getting into the loop trench, both the troop
leaders, Lieuts. Beech and King, being killed. Major Shannon,
who had now taken over command, got a barricade built in the
trenches and the loop-line consolidated. The Germans made no
further attacks.

From regimental contribution.

SANCTUARY WOOD—*continued.*

The 1/Leinsters were billeted in May 1915 in Sanctuary Wood in some log huts erected by the French. As a place of " rest " these were found very wanting, and the French with their sense of language had named them " Demi-repos." When they were built a " half-rest " might have been obtainable, but they were within a few hundred yards of the trenches when the first battalion came to them for the second time. " The huts were sodden with wet, swarming with vermin, and owing to their proximity to the enemy, fires were not permitted by day. Hot meals therefore could only be obtained at night, and as everyone was working during the hours of darkness, even a decent wash was an impossibility. One brave officer did attempt to have a bath in a shell hole, but the Germans immediately sent some heavy stuff over and enjoyed some good practice while the bather dressed in record time."

Sanctuary Wood. (See also **MENIN ROAD.**)

SHRAPNEL CORNER. (See **ZILLEBEKE.**)

SHREWSBURY FOREST TO BULGAR WOOD, 1914

A movement of battalions was taking place on the afternoon of 31st October to conform the line with the withdrawn position to the north on the Menin Road, when the enemy attacked where, on the left of the Royal Sussex, there was a gap. General Bulfin swung the battalion with the Northamptons round to form a flank in front of Shrewsbury Forest running north from Groenenburg Farm. The confusion of the moment made the position serious, and the left of his force began to be pressed back. Ordering the Northamptons to hold on at all costs, he sent the Gordon Highlanders (200 strong) and half the Sussex to prepare a position behind them, and brought the Oxfordshires up in line on his right.

At 3 p.m. a warning was issued by General Capper that the position might become untenable, and outlining a line of retirement. The whole situation seemed hopeless : Germans were streaming into the wood ; the crash and boom of gun fire was appalling. Undaunted, General Bulfin decided on one last counter-attack. He gave the exhausted Sussex and Northamptons his orders—when they heard reinforcements cheering behind them they were to open with one minute rapid fire. " Give the enemy the mad minute," then all together, charge with the bayonet. Up came the reinforcement—eighty men in all (including transport and cooks) of the 2/Gordon Highlanders under their tall leader—Captain J. R. Stansfield. General Bulfin

SHREWSBURY FOREST TO BULGAR WOOD—*continued.*
instructed them and gave the signal. Yelling with fierce cries,
they charged forward ; a fury of fire burst from the Sussex and
Northamptons. Amid the terrific noise the three battalions
leaped forward and into the enemy with the bayonet. The
Germans were utterly astonished, and broke before the onslaught
of an imaginary mass of machine guns and fresh troops. Right
and left the British joined in the wild charge. The Oxfordshires
on the right, the Royal Dragoons on the left—the 10th Hussars
and the Northumberland Hussars arrived and joined in support.

The effect of this brilliant manœuvre was astounding. The
enemy fled in a rout, leaving their dead in heaps. Right up to
the north the influence spread ; the men were so carried away
with excitement that they could not be halted till they had gone
a good half-mile.

As a result most of the ground lost in the morning was regained,
and the line re-formed again.

Shrewsbury Forest. (See **MENIN ROAD**, " **Nonne Bosschen**
Battle.")
SHREWSBURY TRENCH. (See **MORTELDJE.**)
SKIP POINT. (See also **MESSINES.**)
SOURCE TRENCH. (See **PADDEBEKE.**)

SPANBROEKMOLEN, 1915

In the beginning of March 1915 Lieut. Cyril Martin of the 56th
Company R.E. led a party of six bombers against a German
trench, drove out the enemy and strengthened the trench,
reversing the parapet. He had been wounded in the morning,
but carried on regardless, and succeeded in holding the trench
with his little party against the repeated attack of numbers
in great force, until after two hours the order came to retire.
For this achievement, which held up enemy reinforcements at a
critical time, he received the Victoria Cross.

Spanbroekmolen, 1917

One of the great mines prepared by a year's excavation for
the Battle of Messines was at Spanbroekmolen on the front held
by the Ulster Division. Not long before the day of the battle,
enemy shells destroyed the passage to the charge ; so that up
to the last moment it was uncertain whether this mine would
be fired. The 171st Tunnelling Company burrowed night and
day, frantically digging a fresh gallery, and on the day before
the action announced the work was done, and it was " almost
certain " that the mine would explode. The infantry were
warned not to wait if it failed to go up. It fired, 15 seconds

SPANBROEKMOLEN—*continued.*

late ; and though the concussion flung some men, already moving forward in No-man's-land, to the ground, there were no casualties.

SPOILBANK, 1915

On the 14th February 1915 the 2/East Surrey were rushed up from Kruisstraat to Spoilbank. The men had been out all night digging support trenches, and some, with feet too swollen to pull on their boots, marched in their socks, refusing to fall out, as they would " get along somehow." Arrived at Spoilbank, they were ordered to recapture two trenches west of Triangle Wood, that the Germans had snatched from another regiment. The battalion went up at half its strength, five platoons being already in adjoining trenches, and the numbers also being reduced by many casualties. " A " Company led the attack, weakened to two lines. As they came under the hostile fire, officers and men were rapidly shot down, but the advance never wavered until a turnip field so clogged their passage that the attackers, striving to drag their way knee-deep in mud, were killed almost to a man. Only a few gained to within 80 yards of the enemy before they fell. The leading platoons of " C " Company, undaunted, followed up in short rushes till they reached an abandoned enemy trench, all the officers and the sergeant-major having been killed or wounded. Here the survivors stayed, as the company ahead had been wiped out, and there was no possibility of so few carrying the position. And the pith of the story is this. The trench attacked was flanked by trenches still held by British troops, and so it was necessary to order the East Surrey to advance *without firing.* The companies had gone up into the storm of enemy bullets with tied hands, and had been destroyed while unable to hit back. Two officers and 25 men stood to arms that evening.

STEENBEEK, 1917

One day orders were received by two batteries of the 4th Divisional Artillery that a barrage was to be fired next morning, and instructions would be sent later. During the night the whole area of their positions was plastered by a sudden and furious bombardment. " The officers' dugouts were hit almost at once and all the officers killed or wounded. Men fell where they stood or died in their shelters. It was raining and dark and almost impossible to see in the gas masks that had to be worn, and more than one man, removing his mask to see if his comrade was still living, was overcome by gas and so succumbed. As casualties occurred they were cleared, and more men fell in this

STEENBEEK—*continued.*

act. By the morning there were hardly a half-dozen men in
the two batteries who could stand up. In the 134th Battery
R.F.A. all that were left were Acting Bdr. Fisher and Gunner
Houchin. These two men had cleared away the wounded,
sorted out the ammunition, and squared up the position to the
best of their ability. At dawn they were alone in their glory,
except for the dead ; they were the battery—they had inherited
its traditions and meant to be worthy of their regiment—they
would carry out their portion of the barrage as far as two men
with one gun could do so."

They took the barrage orders, set their sights, and at the
appointed hour opened fire. The news had reached the wagon
lines ; an officer and a few gunners hurried up to the gun line
and it was not until the battery came into being once more that
the indomitable Fisher gave in and was carried away, gassed.

Steenbeek, 1917

The first advance of the 51st Division moved straight ahead on
the 31st July, so good had been the preparatory training, and in
the first half-hour fortified places, including Minty's Farm and
Kitchener House, fell into the hands of the 6/Gordons. "C"
Company passed through and at 8.30 dug in in two lines, 250 yards
south-west of the Steenbeek. While working on this position they
were observed by enemy aircraft flying low. Captain Hutcheson
(Company Commander) waited till the planes had gone home to
report, and then shifted his two lines—one 100 yards forward,
one 100 yards back. His foresight was justified when the
enemy started violently to bombard the evacuated ground.
(This company, when withdrawn after two days, had only lost
two killed and ten wounded.)

While the men were at work on their defences two Boche
machine guns from across the river started to fire upon them
from close range. Private George Macintosh took a revolver
and some bombs, and went off on his own initiative alone to stop
the mischief. He ran from one bit of shelter to the next, and
across the river, not yet swollen by the rain as later in the day.
Having got safely forward some 200 yards, he scouted round
the emplacement, rushed in on the machine gunners flinging his
bombs, killed two and wounded one of the Boches, and seizing
the machine guns carried them back to his trench. The splendid
courage and the lightning swiftness with which he acted gained
for his company the time to consolidate their position, and for
himself the Victoria Cross. Rain drenched the battlefield that

STEENBEEK—*continued.*

afternoon, and by the time the battalion was withdrawn on the
2nd August the state of the trenches was deplorable, but nothing
daunted the high hearts of the men. They had had no sleep
for sixty hours after the opening of the battle ; but when on
their way back one man fell over his head in a shell hole full of
water and came out " quacking," the battalion took it up and
marched the fourteen miles back to camp, quacking all the way.

MARCHING SONGS

Listen to the rhythm of their marching song—
                    *Left—left—*Tramp.
Can you beat the ballad that is swinging them along ?—
                    *Left—left—*Tramp.
Do they sing of battles gory,
Do they vaunt a hero's glory,
Do they tell their noble story ?—
                    *Left—left—*Tramp.

Listen ! they are chanting a refrain for tears—
                    *Left—left—*Tramp.
They demand that earth shall witness their unutterable fears—
                    *Left—left—*Tramp.
They bemoan a maiden flighty,
Till they swell a chorus mighty,
Crying " Send us home to Blighty "—
                    *Left—left—*Tramp.

Singing of their terrors, and their loves, and woe—
                    *Left—left—*Tramp—
Up into the battle irresistibly they go—
                    *Left—left—*Tramp
And they'll march the way unheeding,
Till their feet are bare and bleeding,
And no power on earth will stay them
Short of power enough to slay them,
While the air will throb for ever
With the lilt of their endeavour—
                    *Left—left—*Tramp.

Steenbeek.   (See BOESINGHE.)

STOUT WOOD.   (See MENIN ROAD.)

TOWER HAMLET SPUR, 1917

In September 1917 the 26/ and 32/Battalions of the Royal
Fusiliers had a very hot time in an attack on the Tower Hamlet

TOWER HAMLET SPUR—*continued.*
Spur. To reach the jumping-off point the duck-board track was too narrow for the relieving troops to pass each other, and men making way stepped off into the quagmire, and had the greatest difficulty in getting out again. The two battalions went over the top so swiftly on the barrage that as the enemy curtain of shells dropped it fell behind them ; they advanced into savage machine-gun fire. They gained their objective, but the 32nd had lost more than half its strength, and nearly all the officers were casualties. Worse still, the 26th was almost wiped out ; in less than ten minutes only one officer was unwounded of the nineteen who had gone forward. Lieuts. Firth and Jones held on with such men as were left ; Lieut. Jones, wounded in the chest, and with the drums of both ears burst by an exploding shell, did not report his wounds until two days later. Late in the afternoon the 20/Durham L.I. came up. The line was held, although at one time broken on the left, where the enemy were thrown back by the men of the support line, who turned and met them with a burst of rifle fire, fighting back to back with the men in the front. At the end of three days, food and ammunition ran out, and Private Sturgis volunteered to get through for supplies. He got through, being blown up on the way, and fainted on reaching Battalion Headquarters. Directly he came round he led a party forward with food and ammunition, and ran right into the enemy barrage. The party were somewhat daunted, but Sturgis drove them on at the point of his rifle and they brought their succour to the front line. The battalion was withdrawn at the end of five days. They had lost 363 men, including 23 officers—the greatest casualties that they had so far endured in one operation.

TRACAS FARM. (See POELCAPPELLE.)
TRIANGLE FARM. (See POELCAPPELLE.)
TYNE COT. (See PASSCHENDAELE.)
VANCOUVER. (See POELCAPPELLE—ST. JULIEN ROAD.)
VARLET FARM. (See PASSCHENDAELE.)

VELDHOEK
The 1/East Surrey record that on the 29th October 1917 their stretcher-bearer parties were allowed to carry their load of wounded undisturbed along the Menin Road within 400 yards of the 49th Regiment of the German 15th Division. That this should be worthy of entry in the War Diary of a battalion has its own significance.

Veldhoek. (See MENIN ROAD, "Nonne Bosschen Battle.")

VERBRANDENMOLEN, 1915

The 5th Leicestershire Regiment in June 1915 came into the line east of Verbrandenmolen. On the 19th our troops exploded an enormous mine and captured Hooge Château and part of the village ; this brought a swift retaliation in shell and rifle bombardment of that sector, and the tunnelling company and artillery east of Verbrandenmolen were called upon to divert the enemy by springing a mine in company with an artillery strafe. Accordingly 1,500 pounds of ammonal were packed in the gallery beneath the enemy redoubt opposite, and a smaller mine also laid which was exploded on the evening of the 23rd to attract the enemy into the redoubt. The artillery at the same time played for half an hour upon the position. An hour or two later came the riposte. A dull roar and the sound of tumbling clods brought Captain Griffiths and the officers from their collapsing dugout, climbing along the blocked tunnels to find the front line had been blown to pieces, and a large crater in the place where our listening post had been ; into this crater trench-mortars and rifles were firing their hardest. The garrison of the trench, except for a few wounded men, had disappeared—engulfed in the fallen debris. For 80 yards there was no longer a front line. The battalion now came racing to the rescue. Colonel Martin of the 4/Battalion, finding a small disused trench running towards the crater, sent parties up this cut, to bridge the gap and fortify the crater lip with sandbags. Every available man, any orderlies, and batmen collected and started to dig out the buried men in the listening post, but many were missing, and a day or two later the body of Sergeant S. Bunn was found buried at his post, the flare pistol he had been about to fire grasped in his hand.

A few days later the battalion tunnellers with Lieut. Emmerson were at work underground when they came upon a German gallery. Private H. A. Starback broke in at once and found all in readiness ; the charge laid, the wires leading back to the enemy lines. Without any regard to the imminent danger of being heard—in which case the enemy would have blown up the mine at once—Starback set to work cutting the leads. This done, the engineers could safely take out the half-ton of westphalite that lay ready under our position. Two nights later it must have been a very surprised enemy officer who pressed the

VERBRANDENMOLEN—*continued*.
button in vain ; his attempt was betrayed to us by a sudden
violent outburst of rifle fire, that equally suddenly ceased.

Verbrandenmolen, East of, 1916–17

The 47th Division came up into the Salient from the Somme
in October 1916 and took charge of the front between two
Australian Divisions in what was known as the Bluff and Hill 60
Sectors.   The tunnellers had been at work here for a twelvemonth,
and the great mine under Hill 60 was ready and waiting for
" the Day " still nine months in the future.   This mine was
guarded as the great and secret treasure of the division, and its
charge was in the hands of two separate systems—the infantry in
the high-level and on the surface, and the tunnellers in the low-
level workings.   The plans for an immediate operation to explode
the mine and attack and capture the Hill were all prepared, in
case counter-mining by the enemy should interfere prematurely
with the big scheme.

Here, as everywhere in the Salient, our gun positions were
known to, and overlooked by, the enemy on the ridges.   Brisbane
Dump, Dolls' House, Trois Rois, Lankhof Farm, had been
occupied by our batteries in succession on and off since 1914,
and were constantly knocked to pieces when the enemy felt in
the mood for " hate."   It was only remarkable that they were
ever in existence.

VERLORENHOEK RIDGE, 1915

Farther to the east on the right of the Lahore Division another
fine advance had been made by a brigade of the 50th (Northumbrian) Territorial Division on the 26th April.   The officer commanding the battery of artillery in action in the vicinity thus
described it at the time[1]: " The Northumbrians had only just
arrived from England.   They were rushed up to the front to
assist in the defence of Ypres.   I don't suppose any of the men
of this gallant Territorial Division had ever been under fire
before.   The first shell that fell among them will be stamped
for ever on my memory.   As their leading lines topped the
Verlorenhoek Ridge some 2,000 yards behind our battery position,
they came into view of the German artillery observers, who
opened on them with heavy and light artillery.   At a steady
pace with perfect intervals they advanced.   It flashed through
one's mind as to how these untried troops would stand their
first baptism of fire.   Would they face the great ordeal without

[1] From *The British Campaign in France*, by A. Conan Doyle.

VERLORENHOEK RIDGE—*continued.*

flinching ? Looking at them with powerful glasses at this short range, the sight was truly inspiring. Not a man altered his pace or his direction, except those who were left lying on the ground. As steadily as the oldest veterans they continued their advance without a falter. The dead and wounded were left for the stretcher-bearers. How often during this battle had we seen the Germans bolting from our artillery fire, and the German is a brave soldier. It made one proud indeed to see our young Territorial troops go through their first ordeal with a courage, a steadiness, and a perfect discipline which could not be surpassed. It encouraged one at a time of great strain to feel that such men could not be defeated."

Between Verlorenhoek and Hooge, 1915 [1]

" The Blues took their part in the counter-attack that recaptured the gap made by the Germans in their gas attack between Verlorenhoek and Hooge, to the south of the 10th Royal Hussars. On the evening of the 12th May the 3rd Cavalry Division received orders to take over the trenches on this line. At the moment the 8th Brigade was in reserve. The 6th and 7th Brigades carried out the relief from dead-tired infantry, who reported that the Germans had been spending the day ' registering ' and that next day their successors in the line would be ' for it.' Their prophecy proved completely correct.

At four in the morning the enemy started an intensive bombardment on the front line, and also, for the first time in the War, on the back areas as well. To this our guns could give no adequate reply. The enemy appeared in no hurry to attack us. On two occasions the bombardment ceased, and the 7th Brigade opened rifle fire (the Germans were only fifty yards away) ; but when it was apparent that there were still troops left alive, it began again. The trenches, such as they had been, were at the top of a long gradual sloping rise, backwards to Divisional Headquarters at Potijze. No troops could expect to get across this alive, so when part of the 7th Brigade were driven out of their trenches, they did not retire, but moved slightly back to the right flank to the trenches occupied by the Royals (6th Brigade). There was no line behind except the G.H.Q. line, which was incomplete and ran about half a mile in rear. Here the 8th Brigade were standing in reserve. The Germans, having driven this gap, did not advance, but intensified their bombard-

[1] From regimental contribution.

BETWEEN VERLORENHOEK AND HOOGE—*continued.*
ment on either flank and on the G.H.Q. line. At 10 o'clock
orders came for the 8th Brigade to attack after a preliminary
bombardment, and at 12.45 the regiment moved into a preparative
position in rear of the wood immediately north-east of the Witte
Poort Farm. This was in rear of the 6th Brigade H.Q. and was
necessitated by the impossibility of a frontal attack. All those
features which made war so unpleasant a pastime were conspicuously in evidence. Our preliminary bombardment was
practically nullified by the extreme shortage of ammunition and
the overwhelming superiority of the German artillery. The
mud was appalling, and the men could not keep their rifles free
of it. It was raining incessantly, and the advance, from the
men's point of view, was not made any easier by an order issued
that every man was to carry into action a spade as well as a
rifle with bayonet fixed ; for at this period of the War the illusion
still existed that in greater speed lay greater safety. The
counter-attack was launched at 2.30, and with so much success
that not only were the trenches regained, but, passing beyond,
the Blues drove the Germans out of their former front line as
well. But the cost was very heavy. Five officers were killed :
Captain G. V. S. Bowlby, Captain the Hon. C. Phillips, Lieuts.
Lord Spencer Compton, W. T. Davson, G. Pullen. Six were
wounded : Captain A. W. Foster, Captain M. Wemyss, Lieuts.
Lord A. Leveson-Gower, Viscount Wendover (afterwards died
in hospital), J. Murray Smith, G. Ward Price. Only three came
safely through the action. Of other ranks, 277 went into action ;
of these 97 were casualties, and 15 missing. Captain Phillips
died most gallantly, encouraging the men with view-halloes until
he got into the German positions, when he bayoneted two Germans
and shot a third before being shot himself by the fourth man
in the section. Lord A. Leveson-Gower was found in a shell
hole, shot through the thigh, the sole survivor of his troop,
seated on a diminutive unwounded German, smoking an
immense cigar.

This attack was carried out, and succeeded in filling a gap
through which the enemy were waiting to pour ; when behind
the regiment, G.H.Q. line was the only remaining line of defence.
And this line was incomplete, held only by H.Q. and staff men
and a few strayed remnants of infantry. There were no supports
available, as everyone well knew. The regiment remained in
the position hanging on under these conditions and heavily shelled
for many hours, until darkness fell and reliefs eventually took
over."

Verlorenhoek Area, 1917 [1]

On the 25th June the 12/Battalion H.L.I. took over the front
line immediately east of Ypres, with orders to make themselves
offensive to the enemy, prior to the big attack, and the ground
was scrutinised with a view to discovering the best method to
adopt.

Patrols went out nightly to try to get some information as
to obstacles and conditions. It was not an easy task. Having
slipped into and scrambled out of half a dozen shell holes, all
sense of direction was lost and it was very often a matter of luck
where the bedraggled patrol fetched up and if it got any useful
information. After poring over aeroplane photos and maps
and studying the ground through glasses, Lieut.-Colonel St.
John decided to recommend a daylight raid as offering the best
chance of success.

The battalion came out of the line and went into training,
and on the 22nd July were back in their position.

Two days later the two raiding companies moved up with
the front line. It was an anxious time with so many men in
the front and support trenches. Would the enemy discover the
concentration ! Would one o'clock never come ! Ladders had
been placed opposite gaps in our line. Men of the first parties
are standing by them. The men are all lightly equipped in
skeleton order and only carrying 50 rounds of ammunition.
There is only a second or two to go. A general movement takes
place. The officers move along to their positions. Belts are
tightened. At last our artillery barrage crashes down. The
raiders are off. From behind the barrage looks good. It is
really excellent. What is happening ? It is extraordinary how
slowly the time goes. Everything seems to be going well. The
enemy is evidently surprised. His artillery has not opened out
yet. " Front line taken, little opposition." The first message
relieves the tension. Some prisoners appear. They don't look
to be disheartened at being captured. Only seven minutes have
gone. Messages come in and the raid is progressing well. The
leading groups followed the barrage right to the enemy reserve
line without a pause, keeping very close to it—from 35 to 50 yards
away. The enemy had no time to put up a fight. The next
group stopped at the support line and the last group at the
front line. After rounding up the prisoners, the wire and trenches
were examined and dugouts bombed. The withdrawal then
commenced. Forty hectic minutes and the raid was over. It
was a great success, and there were only 21 casualties, of which

[1] From regimental account.

VERLORENHOEK AREA—*continued.*
I was killed and 17 only slightly wounded. Some 80 prisoners
of the 19th Fus. Regiment captured, including 2 officers, and
valuable information obtained. It was one of the biggest, if
not the biggest, daylight raid carried out up to that time, two
companies, consisting of 10 officers and 186 men, taking part.
It may not be out of place to quote one of the messages received :
" The Brigade Commander wishes to send you heartiest con-
gratulations on your splendid success to-day, in which all ranks
of the brigade will join with him."

Verlorenhoek. (See GRAVENSTAFEL and POTIJZE.)

WARNETON, 1914 [1]
" On the 17th October the 3rd K.O. Hussars relieved the 4th
Hussars and some of the 12th Lancers, who were holding part
of the line of the 2nd Cavalry Division in front of Warneton.
The front was held by the regiments extended for 2 miles south
of the Messines—Garde Dieu Road, facing south-east. ' J '
Battery R.H.A. came quickly into action on the bank of the
Wanbeek north-east of Gapaard ; the machine-gun section at
the Gapaard cross-roads ; while the squadron advanced, and
fighting developed about Warneton. The line was held in small
isolated posts dotted along the front and open everywhere to
enfilade fire. Entrenching was done with any implements that
could be obtained in the neighbourhood, and the horses were led
back and concealed. By the 20th the whole front of the regiment
was hotly engaged, and a storm of shells crashed into the line
and into the villages of Garde Dieu and Gapaard throughout
the day. The position was desperate, fighting everywhere, and
at last at four o'clock in the afternoon, in spite of the dogged
determination and gallantry of the firing line, it became clear
that this scantily posted line could not be held. There was no
haste, however ; the regiment held, and disputing foot by foot
every yard of ground did the dismounted men fall back to
their horses. An officer had been sent to select the next
position to retire upon. To the Oosttaverne Ridge the battery
and its escorting squadron fell back. The flank squadrons on
the Ridge, and the centre and headquarters, slowly withdrew.
The retirement was carried out in capital order and the regiment
collected just north of the Ridge, while ' B ' Squadron was

---

[1] From regimental account.

WARNETON—*continued*.

ordered by General Gough to occupy the farm in the valley north-west of Gapaard, and which was in its line of retreat.

For some seven hours the three weak squadrons of the 3rd, supported later in the day by one equally weak squadron of Carabiniers, a total of some 400 rifles, certainly no more, had held off a determined attack of what was estimated to be three battalions of German infantry.

The whole of the 5th Cavalry Brigade was now up and hard at work entrenching astride the Gapaard—Oosttaverne Road in touch with the 3rd Cavalry Brigade, which had also been attacked and driven back on the left of the regiment. At about 6 p.m. the 3rd was ordered to extend this line towards Messines, until touch was obtained with the composite regiment. It was already dark, and there was no certainty of the position of these troops, but the regiment advanced by compass bearing towards Messines, within a mile of the position reached by the enemy. ' After all these years how that short ride comes back to one. A pitch-dark night ; the Colonel with a candle lantern under his cloak which kept blowing out ; his led charger, and escorted by a couple of men ; intent himself upon his compass bearings. The head of the regiment some five or ten yards behind him, horses stumbling along in half-sections—mud up to their hocks ; and every man knowing that two hours since the regiment had disengaged a strong line of German infantry a short mile away on the left.' A farm and windmill were reached and occupied ; and held by heavy fighting throughout the next day. Major Combe, commanding the right squadron, was severely wounded early in the fight, but gallantly continued in his command, fought his squadron throughout the day, and brought it out of action. By the time he was ordered off his horse at 5 o'clock in the afternoon he was barely able to keep his seat in the saddle. But the Hussars had gained touch with the Composite Regiment and the line was once more complete. To quote the Press Bureau : ' The Cavalry has fought whether mounted or in the trenches, to the admiration of the whole Army.' "

WELLINGTON FARM. (See ST. JULIEN.)

WESTHOEK, 1917 [1]

"On the 1st August the 8/Prince of Wales Volunteers were ordered to move up to Westhoek Ridge in relief of the South Devons. During the relief the enemy attacked immediately

[1] From regimental account.

WESTHOEK—*continued.*

north of the Ypres—Roulers Railway, pushing back the exhausted Middlesex ; ' D ' Company of the South Lancs counter-attacked and regained this position. The rest of the battalion completed the relief of the Devons and held on until the 7th August ; they were then relieved, but were sent back suddenly after four days, owing to the heavy casualties suffered by the battalion that had taken over the position. During the whole time the most appalling conditions were experienced—incessant torrential rain and a sea of mud ; the battalion held the ground won intact, and even pushed forward. The conduct of C.S.M. Lewis, D.C.M., M.M., and of Sergeant Durham, M.M., during this period was worthy of the highest praise. They remained on duty without rest for days together, assisting Captain Chambers, who had no company officers, and on the night of the 5th, along with Captain Bryden, M.C., and the O.C. Company carried out a reconnaissance of the Ypres—Roulers Railway as far as the entrance to the village of Zonnebeke. Then between the two lines a heavy machine-gun fire from a post of the Leinster Regiment was opened on the party. This was followed at once by a heavy fire from the enemy, and for a considerable period the party were unable to move. At last, seeing no chance of escape if they remained, it was decided to risk the shooting and try to clear the railway embankment to cover by a sudden rush. This was done successfully, and on the other side of the railway a line of enemy concrete gun emplacements was discovered, unoccupied but piled with enemy dead. This discovery enabled posts to be advanced and making the position of the enemy in Zonnebeke very precarious.

During this period, as well as holding the line intact against counter-attacks, over 150 wounded men who had been hit on the 31st July were rescued and safely evacuated by the two front companies, an extraordinary effort when the state of the ground, weather conditions, and the incessant heavy shelling and fire of the enemy were considered. The stretcher-bearers in some cases were hardly able to get along for the mud, and it often took as long as two hours to reach the regiment and post 500 yards away."

The command of Lieut.-Colonel (acting Brigadier-General) Clifford Coffin, R.E., was held up while attacking on the 31st October 1917. Making a forward line in shell holes, they established a position under the blast of machine-gun and rifle fire from front and flank. Brigadier-General Coffin went forward to inspect his posts and, entirely regardless of the bullet-swept zone, walked quietly and cheerfully from one shell hole to another,

WESTHOEK—*continued.*

advising and encouraging the men. He influenced them to
such good effect that, in spite of the extremity of the peril, the
line was held. His courage and example alone prevented the
troops from being driven back. He was awarded the V.C.

Westhoek. (See MENIN ROAD.)

WIELTJE, 1914 [1]

On the 20th October the 1/Kings had arrived at Ypres from
the Aisne area, and on the following day marched out beyond
Wieltje, but did not come into action, although heavy fighting
was in progress. On the 24th October orders were received to
support the 22nd Infantry Brigade, whose line was reported to
be broken by the enemy in the direction of Polygon Wood, and
from that date the King's Regiment was heavily engaged and
suffered many casualties. During an attack on Nordwesthoek
village "A" Company came under sharp fire from loopholed houses
and Lieut. Denny, of " D " Company, fell mortally wounded,
while later in the day Colonel Bannatyne, commanding the
battalion, was shot through the heart by a German sniper. On
the following day the attack continued, and two officers—Captain
Batten and Lieut. Wallace—were killed, among other losses.

On the 26th October two companies lost all their officers in a
further attack upon the village and upon the enemy's trenches
along the Becelaere Road, which were captured under heavy
fire with great gallantry by non-commissioned officers and men.
The Germans endeavoured to regain their ground at the point
of the bayonet, but were flung back with heavy losses and the
1/Battalion of the King's Regiment held its position until relieved
by the Highland Light Infantry in the evening of the 28th
October. It then received a cheering message from the Divisional
Commander, General Monro, saying, " Your Regiment has done
magnificently."

Wieltje (Mouse-trap Farm) (also called Shell-trap) [2]

The 2/Lancashire Fusiliers took over a position in the neighbourhood of Shell-trap Farm on the morning of the 1st May.
Next day the Germans bombarded with incendiary shells that
set every farm and building ablaze, till one after another all were
burnt out, including the temporary dressing-station of the
battalion. " The afternoon was quiet and beautifully fine, and

[1] Regimental account epitomised by Sir Philip Gibbs.
[2] From regimental contribution.

WIELTJE (MOUSE-TRAP FARM)—*continued.*
then everything seemed to start at once. We had just started
tea when one of the sentries shouted to us to look at the German
trenches. We looked, and saw gas coming out in great jets, like
water out of a hose, and shooting straight up in the air, at intervals
of about thirty yards all along the German parapet. The warning
was at once given, and respirators, which then consisted only
of a strip of flannel soaked in a prepared solution, were donned.
The men stood to and started firing rapidly into the oncoming
gas, which had sunk low down and looked like a yellowy-green
sea of waves. We got the full force of the gas, and as the
respirators were not much use, many of the men were soon down,
suffocating from the fumes. Those who were able stood valiantly
to their guns in spite of the awful difficulty they had of breathing,
which the slightest exertion doubled." At the end of the trench
Private John Lynn stood to his machine gun, and faced the
poison fumes without a respirator. For an hour and a half he
fired upon the enemy, driving them back ; then, coughing his
heart out and gasping for breath, he hoisted the gun right up on
to the parapet, and, invisible to the enemy in the swirling cloud,
poured out a stream of lead that swept the ground in front and
flung the attackers back. He saved the trench and he saved
his comrades, for there was no further assault that day. They
found him lying, suffocated, near to death. " This is the last
carry," he gasped as they lifted him ; but from his dugout he
heard the threat of another attack and struggled to go back to
his gun. He died in twenty-four hours in great suffering, and
his sacrifice was honoured with the Cross " for valour."

East of Mouse-trap Farm

The depleted battalions holding the forward slopes of Frezenberg Ridge had been annihilated by overwhelming shell fire
on the 8th May 1915, and a gap two miles long was torn open
in the line desperately defending Ypres. At the north of this
gap the 2/Northumberland Fusiliers stood like a rock, while
the storm beat against front and flank. Lieut.-Colonel Enderly,
hearing that a counter-attack had been begun, resolved to hold
on at all costs. He flung out a short defensive flank, that made
and manned a small parapet. Here the battalion stood indomitably until night fell, when the enemy appeared from the rear,
and opened machine-gun and rifle fire upon the wounded and
stretcher parties. Soon afterwards a tremendous concentrated
bombardment burst upon the front ; a sudden rocket signal
followed and the guns suddenly ceased fire ; then the German

EAST OF MOUSE-TRAP FARM—*continued*.

infantry dashed forward. But still the 2/Battalion was invincible, and with casualties of 15 officers, including the C.O., and 482 other ranks, they could not be overwhelmed. " A " Company still held out under Captain A. C. Hart, until he was killed while he covered the flank of his men with a revolver, and shot a German officer who called on him to surrender. Only 116 of the battalion survived, but the Germans abandoned all attempts to overcome their magnificent resistance.

Mouse-trap Farm [1]

" On the 13th May 1915 the 1/Battalion East Lancashires were holding the breastworks and trenches to the right of Shell-trap Farm in front of Wieltje. At dawn, i.e. 4 a.m., a very heavy bombardment of our line began and went on all day until dusk at 7 p.m. It was one continual roar and bursting of shells that came from our front, and also from our left rear from the direction of Pilckem. Jack Johnsons and heavy howitzer shrapnel came in convoys of four ; at times twelve 6-inch shells a minute were bursting along a 50-yards' length of trench and made the ground fairly shake. We had no heavy guns to reply with and had to take our gruelling in silence, while the Germans watched the performance in great glee from their trenches. At 6 a.m. there was a lull for fifteen minutes, and then the bombardment began again fiercer than before ; a minenwerfer also joined in and planted its shells in the breastworks, causing great gaps to open. At 7.30 the first infantry attack came ; opposite our trenches it was repulsed at once by our rifle and machine-gun fire before they had advanced many yards. Opposite the breastworks one party of thirty Germans got up to our wire and lay down to snipe. 2nd Lieut. Salt had watched their movements, and as soon as the shelling lifted from his breastwork on to the support line, he attended to those Germans and not one moved again.

At 9 a.m. another attack was launched against the breastworks. A German bombing party got into the advanced breastwork and with their bombs killed Lieut. Knight and many men. We had no bombs to fight them with and so were at a great disadvantage.

They then advanced against the remaining two breastworks, and in gallantly defending the right one Major Rutter and Lieut. Canton were both sniped through the head, while at the left one Lieut. Salt suddenly found himself being sniped from

[1] From regimental contribution, by Lieut.-Colonel G. H. Lawrence, C.M.G.

MOUSE-TRAP FARM—*continued*.
Shell-trap Farm into which the Germans had got and this fire caused heavy casualties in the two nearest breastworks. He put some men into the shell holes facing the farm to keep down the sniping, and Lance-Corporal Thorne and Private Cowburn advanced to the bridge over the moat and, although both were wounded, they stuck to their posts and prevented the enemy crossing the moat.

Lieut. Salt kept back the bombing party by firing over the traverses at them. He was shot through the top of his head, but pluckily held on, and when the German officer exposed his head and shouted to him to surrender in English, his reply was to shoot him dead. The support company now came up, and the Germans vanished to their lines and did not attempt any more attacks, but kept up the shelling till dusk. Lieut. Salt, on being reinforced, collected his platoon, and all that was left of it was one sergeant in a fit, two wounded lance-corporals, and four privates, of whom two were wounded. The men stood the bombardment very well, and Captain Dyer relates how in the middle of it he came on a group of five men ' arguing the point ' fiercely, and on inquiring what it was was told a loaf was missing from their rations ! "

> These were a people of uncouth words,
> The shibboleth and slang of herds.
> A curse or a jest expressed their need,
> Strange blasphemies evoked their creed,
> With ribald comments that deprecate
> Deep motives inarticulate.
> Emotion wore a mummer's mask
> That mouthed no drama, did not ask
> Heroics, if we but admit
> The blighter tried to do his bit.
>
> They construed words above all price,
> Valour and love and sacrifice.

Mouse-trap Farm, 1915

On the 13th May 1915, a day of cold winds and dismal rain, the 2/Battalion Essex Regiment were temporarily attached to the 11th Infantry Brigade. At 4 a.m. the Germans started their attack. The cavalry holding the line suffered terribly, and by 7 a.m. it was evident that there had been a retirement and the Infantry Garrison of Shell-trap Farm, a vital point in the line,

had been driven out by the enemy. The O.C. of the Essex at
once ordered one of his companies to counter-attack. Dashing
forward through the hostile fire, the men were held up for a
time by the moat surrounding the farm ; but one of the regimental
machine guns was rushed up, and under cover of its fire the company flung themselves, cheering, across the moat, and with an
irresistible charge drove the Germans out.

It now became clear that our trenches running from the Farm
to the Fortuin—Wieltje Road had been partially vacated, and
the Essex were ordered to restore the situation. At 8.30 a.m.
the attack, carried out by the three remaining companies, started,
being marked by the greatest boldness and determination ; as
the Essex passed the Rifle Brigade, the men of the latter jumped
up in their trenches and cheered them to the echo, a truly inspiring
spectacle. Advancing in quick time, swept by high explosive
and shrapnel, the companies topped a slight ridge where machine-
gun fire opened on them. Pressing on resolutely without a check
they arrived within about 300 yards of the trenches, when with
a roar the whole attack broke simultaneously into a double and
charged home.

Mouse-trap Farm, 1915

The 2/Royal Dublin Fusiliers held a line from 150 yards south-
east of Shell-trap Farm southward, with one company in reserve
in trenches north of Potijze Wood. On the night of the 23rd May
Colonel Loveband had a presentiment that gas was threatening ;
he gave a personal warning to company officers, and saw that
the ten vermoral sprayers were in working order. In the early
hours of the morning a red light shot up from the enemy lines.
Heralded by a roar as of a great explosion, the green cloud of
gas swept over the trenches. The doctor—Captain Russell—
looking after the men got a whiff of gas before his respirator was
fixed. Men could be seen pouring out of Shell-trap Farm, and
soon the enemy were in, and started enfilading the Dublins with
machine guns, while heavy shells crashed into the trench, seconded
frightfully by gas shells. The colonel sent messages as to the
gravity of the situation to the 10th Infantry Brigade, but it was
an almost impossible task to get into touch. Every orderly
sent back was hit, yet volunteers for the job did not fail. Colonel
Loveband was shot through the heart early in the attack. A
gap was made on the left of the battalion by retiring troops ;
some of the Dublins began to fall back, but stopped as they saw
their own officers standing intrepidly. Russell was wounded,

MOUSE-TRAP FARM—*continued*.

but kept on tending the men as gas and wounds claimed more and more victims. An officer—Lieut. Tarletan—" mad with gas and badly wounded," crawled from the firing line with a message which he managed to deliver, though almost speechless. His chief anxiety was centred on the loss of his " Verey " pistol, and he was very distressed until it was found safe in his haversack. These were then rare and precious. The Dublins with the 9/Argyll and Sutherland Highlanders held on, expecting supports. The urgency of the hour is reflected in the messages that came through.

Shanks—machine-gun officer—sent : " Enemy are strongly entrenching themselves between Shell-trap Farm and ' D ' Company's trenches. We are extremely weak. Reinforcements urgently needed. . . ."

Maclear sent : " Very many of our men are surrounded. We must have reinforcements." Just before the enemy got into " D " Company's trench Maclear dashed forward leading a party with bombs, and was killed.

2nd Lieut. Kempston, " B " Company, sent : " For God's sake send us some help ; we are nearly done."

A message went back to 10th Infantry Brigade at 12.45 p.m. : " Reinforce or all is lost."

The hours passed, every officer but one was killed or wounded or frantic with gas. Little was ever heard of " C " Company in front of Shell-trap Farm, machine-gunned from the lost trenches on their right, but at noon they were seen still fighting. By evening there were no Dublins in front of Battalion Headquarters, and since 2.30 there had been no fighting ; there had been no surrender and the line was held until all the Dublins were killed at their post.

" Please withdraw your headquarters and all men in the retrenchment if any are still there and report at Brigade H.Q. west of the Canal." This message was received at 9.30 by the one officer left alive, Captain Leahy ; and with his full strength, 20 other ranks, he withdrew—the full strength remaining of a battalion of 17 officers and 651 men who had stood to arms that morning.

Wieltje, South of (St. Julien Road), 1915

The first Victoria Cross awarded to a Territorial in the Great War was the one gained by Lieut. Woolley, of the Queen Victoria's Rifles, on Hill 60. The first Territorial ranker to win the Cross was Lance-Sergeant D. W. Belcher, of the London Rifle Brigade, who

MOUSE-TRAP FARM—*continued*.

had been previously in the Q.V.R. He was in charge of an advance
breastwork, which was continually being blown in, and on the
morning of the 13th May 1915 the troops near him were withdrawn
during a very violent and continuous bombardment. Lance-
Sergeant Belcher had a handful of men with him, and he chose
to remain, holding his position with great skill and gallantry
throughout the day. The enemy were within a couple of hundred
yards, and each time he saw them collecting for an attack he
opened upon them with rapid fire. As the *Gazette* records, the
sergeant's heroic stand " prevented the enemy breaking through
on the Wieltje Road and averted an attack on the flank of one
of our divisions."

Wieltje, 1917 [1]

" Wieltje dugouts ! Who that saw it will forget that abominable mine with its ' town major,' its thirteen entrances, the water
that flowed down its passages and poured down its walls, its
smells, its sickly atmosphere, its huge population of men—and
of rats ? From behind sack-curtained doorways the coughing
and groaning of men in uneasy slumber mingled with the click
of typewriters."

Wieltje. (See KEERSELAERE.)

WINCHESTER FARM. (See ST. JULIEN.)

WIPERS

There be men who will tell you now
That we wasted our lives—and how
        The fight we fought,
        And the deeds men wrought,
Were for nought but a devil's war.
They say that the way we stuck
For years in the mud and muck
        To hold the line
        Is no story fine,
But a Hell to forget—no more.

I'm not the one to deny
We have cursed for a reason why ;
        But there's one I know
        I would not forgo,
And this was a war of men.

        [1] *History of the 36th Ulster Division.*

WIPERS—*continued.*

I learnt what a pal was worth
When nothing was left on earth ;
If I'm down on my luck,
His cheer and his pluck
Will save me now—as then.

So we count this a peerless name
And this is the right we claim—
Who have stood the test
From torment to jest
And men have declared us true—
The password is ours to give
As long as our day shall live ;
Wherever men meet,
In desert or street,
" Wipers " shall pass us through.

WULVERGHEM, 1914

I suppose nothing demands a higher type of courage than stretcher-bearing. To carry a wounded man steadily over rough ground under fire, when a stumble or jar might be fatal, is all in the day's work of the stretcher-bearers, and not at all " conspicuous bravery." It is magnificent.

T. E. Edward Rendle had a chance to do something out of the common. He was a stretcher-bearer of the Band of the Duke of Connaught's Light Infantry, and was for eight days in the trenches at Wulverghem, removing the wounded who were being buried by the parapets, crashing under heavy shells. He was frequently warned to " come down," but carried on calmly until one of his officers, Lieut. Colebrooke, was wounded beyond a section of the trench which, having been blown in by the bombardment, was filled up, and had to be crossed in the open. Rendle with another officer, Lieut. Wingate, crawled over to him and bound up a severed artery. The uncovered space lay behind them, and Lieut. Colebrooke had to be got back somehow. Rendle with his bare hands scraped up a narrow trough while the enemy fired whenever he raised his head, until at last he could worm his way through, carrying the officer on his back.

Rendle received the V.C.

Wulverghem, Christmas 1914

An extraordinary truce was honoured by the opposing armies during the first Christmas of the War. All along the line the

WULVERGHEM—*continued.*

soldiers fraternised in No-man's-land, burying the dead, exchanging newspapers, and actually souvenirs of badges and buttons. The Leinsters, in one part of the line, describe the enemy as chanting in perfect time : " Play the game ! Play the game ! If you don't shoot, we won't."

The Germans had been grossly deceived as to their successes : many believed that Calais and even London had been captured. A British officer at Wulverghem was asked to describe the fall of London, and to say whether it had been destroyed by Zeppelins. This truce was never repeated.

Wulverghem, 1914

Death was stalking through the field
Where never a man was seen.
Trenches in front, dugouts behind
And the field of death between.
Dank and wet was the dreary day,
Starving cold were the men at bay.

Sudden, a sturdy figure rose,
A dixie in either hand—
Stared across at the distant line,
Stared at the death-swept land.
" A damned unhealthy spot," said he,
" But if I don't go, mates'll get no tea."

Steady and slow he plodded off.
Death came raging round,
With blast of shell, and scything shot
That tore and razed the ground.
We held our breath to see him killed.
His only care that nought be spilled.

He reached the line, and up and down
He carried heat and cheer
'Till no man lacked—then turned and faced
Again that way of fear.
The God of Battles spread his shield
And Death drew beaten from the field.

Wulverghem. (See DRANOUTRE.)
WYTSCHAETE, 1914

On the 31st October, while vainly trying to storm Messines, the Germans sent two divisions to try to capture Wytschaete,

Wytschaete—*continued.*

a larger town that had contained 3,500 inhabitants, lime-works and factories. The 2nd Cavalry Division was strained out from the town to the Comines Canal, just 3,250 rifles to hold 3½ miles, with three batteries of horse guns, and strengthened during the day by six batteries of French 75s. Even reckoning the German division at two-thirds of their full strength, the odds attacking our dismounted troopers were at least 5 to 1. The usual heavy shelling blew in the trenches, and many men were buried, but infantry attacks were stopped by our guns. At midday one of our few brigades—the 4th Cavalry Brigade—was diverted with the London Scottish to help the defenders of Messines. This weakening of the line was compensated for by the arrival of two squadrons of the 1st Life Guards and later by a French Cuirassier and an infantry brigade, who at night took over the left of our line, and the 4th Cavalry Brigade was withdrawn into reserve. Throughout the 31st the whole line from the Canal to Messines had been held intact, except for the flattening of the salient east of Messines. But the losses of the 2nd Cavalry Division in four days had been a third of their number, leaving a strength of about 1,200.

On the 1st November Wytschaete was occupied by the Composite Household Cavalry, a regiment of 415 fighting strength from the 4th Cavalry Brigade; against them were launched at midnight nine battalions of the 6th Bavarian Reserve Division, bringing odds of 4 to 1 to storm through and seize the town. Farther south a general attack developed in lines, ten German companies against about 600 men. The fire of the 400 cavalrymen was steady and for a time actually held the Germans off, but sheer weight of numbers told at last, as it must in night fighting, and at dawn the 400 were forced back to the southwestern exit of the village. With the coming of daylight all possible reinforcement was gathered from near and far, small though it could be. The 12th Lancers reached the hillock on the north of the village. Two battalions from the II Corps that had marched up to Kemmel—the 1/Lincolnshires 800 strong and the 1/Northumberland Fusiliers only 350—though weary to death with fighting and marching were under way within fifteen minutes of receiving the order. The 3rd Hussars came in support. Two companies of the advance guard of the French 32nd Division arrived down the Vierstraat Road. Immediate attacks were made upon the enemy in the village, but failed in the confusion and dim light against heavy rifle fire from every house.

WYTSCHAETE—*continued.*

During the night the weighty general attack along the open ridge had rushed between the isolated posts that were our line and large numbers of the enemy attacked from every side. But the Ridge was held against the overwhelming tide, and the flow turned back—breaking in one place against a squadron of the Carabiniers, standing like a rock. A reserve company of the London Scottish made a timely charge, and the British on the right never moved from their trenches, only falling back a little on their left to the line of the Wytschaete—Messines Road. As dawn came, yet greater numbers flowed between the isolated posts, and the positions on the middle of the ridge were surrounded. Then the defenders came from their trenches, and, not waiting to be captured, hacked their way through, and fought back until they re-formed at Spanbroekmolen. The Lincolnshires were by now in a fold of ground 200 yards east of Wytschaete, and seeing the cavalry and London Scottish fighting their way back from the ridge—Lieut.-Colonel W. E. V. Smith in command, already wounded—held on to cover their withdrawal. Battered by German artillery, and under heavy fire from infantry from flanks and rear, the battalion succeeded in its object of diverting the enemy ; but though they had only been fighting here for a few hours, the Lincolnshires and Northumberland Fusiliers had lost 30 per cent. of their strength. The attention of the Germans was thus concentrated on these doings to the west, and at about 8 a.m. the 12th Lancers on the north of Wytschaete with a squadron of the 28th Hussars made a sudden attack and broke right into the town. So staggered were the enemy hordes at this unbelievable success of a few squadrons, that they were unable to repulse, and before they recovered breath to attack again, the head of the French 32nd Division advanced once more, and in one sweep Wytschaete was recaptured and cleared of the enemy.

Wytschaete, 1914 [1]

On the night of 31st October, when the Germans launched a fresh attack with two fresh corps against seven miles of front which was held by only seven weak cavalry brigades, a very serious penetration occurred, and the enemy got into Wytschaete and Messines. The French troops coming up to reinforce the sector were still several miles away, and unless the situation were dealt with at once, nothing could prevent a German advance through to Kemmel Hill. The only available reinforcements

[1] From regimental account.

WYTSCHAETE—*continued*.
were the 12th Lancers, who had been relieved about 8 p.m. that same evening, owing to their heavy losses during the previous forty-eight hours ; and two very weak and tired infantry battalions—the 1/Lincolns and 1/Northumberland Fusiliers, who had been placed at disposal of G.O.C. Cavalry Corps.

The two infantry battalions attacked by the Kemmel— Wytschaete Road, and the 12th Lancers along the Groote— Vierstraat Road, and in spite of their exhausted state attacked with the greatest spirit and vigour. There was no time for any reconnaissance. No artillery support was available or possible, and the troops simply charged straight for the village. It was a very dark night, though burning Wytschaete afforded a certain amount of light as the troops approached it. The outskirts were full of hedges and fences, besides the big woods, and the advance of the two infantry battalions would have been a difficult one even without opposition. The infantry attacked about 2 a.m. ; the 12th Lancers, who had farther to go, and received the order later, about 2.30 a.m. The Northumberland Fusiliers on the right made slow progress ; the Lincolns, after very severe fighting, managed almost to clear the Bois de Wytschaete and pushed the Germans back to the edge of the village. The 12th Lancers deployed at the south-west corner of the Grand Bois, and coming in on the flank of the German attack met with little opposition and gained the Ridge due north from the village, on which the windmill stands. Although they were hopelessly outnumbered, and without support on either flank, their sudden appearance and the vigour of the attack demoralised the Germans, who up till then had fought very stoutly. The two infantry battalions at once pushed forward ; the whole village was quickly cleared, the enemy fleeing in great disorder. A line was established well east of the village, and held till the arrival of French reinforcements about 10 a.m.

Wytschaete Cross-roads, 1914 [1]

After the fall of Messines the enemy continued to press their attack in numbers and covered it with the heaviest concentration of artillery yet experienced. The 4th Dragoon Guards occupied a line of detached trenches on the right of the French with whom we joined up at Wytschaete Cross-roads. This was a vital spot, and the machine-gun detachment was told off to cover it. Intense artillery fire was maintained on all positions from early morning, followed up at intervals by infantry assaults. The

[1] From regimental contribution, by Major-General A. Solly Flood.

Wytschaete Cross-roads—*continued.*

French on our left were shelled out of their trenches. Our trenches were blown in and many officers and men buried. But our machine guns under Sergeant Woodland held ; the officer was killed ; and a troop of " B " squadron under Thwaites, despite many casualties, also held. The enemy failed to get the cross-roads.

With the Queen's Own Oxford Hussars, which regiment was sent up during the day and had been held in support, we all went forward in the dusk of evening to eject the enemy who were in portions of our shattered trenches, and in this manner relieved our M.G. detachment and the remains of Thwaites's gallant troop, many of whom had to be dug out.

We lost Elmslie and Ramsay killed, and Thwaites and Chance were wounded.

After its last of many dips into the Messines Sector the regiment was promised forty-eight hours' rest and was moved on the 11th November back to Meteren in the pouring wet, its last elements getting into billets about 10 p.m.

By 1 a.m. the same night we were on the march again, and in the grey dawn of the early morning we found ourselves marching through Ypres in thick snow.

Piccadilly Farm, near Wytschaete, 1918

On the 28th September the 1/5 Battalion King's Own Scottish Borderers (T.F.) advanced on Piccadilly Farm. Corporal Louis McGuffie single-handed entered several enemy dugouts, taking many prisoners. He proceeded to go from dugout to dugout alone, collecting prisoners, and forced an officer to surrender with twenty-five men. While the battalion was consolidating its position, Corporal McGuffie saw some of the enemy slipping away, and dashing after them he brought them back. He also was instrumental in the rescue of some British soldiers who were being led off as prisoners. He was killed by a shell later, and his great gallantry was rewarded with the Victoria Cross.

Wytschaete, 1918 [1]

" On the 11th April 1918 the 64th Infantry Brigade, of which the 1/Battalion East Yorkshire Regiment formed part, was attached to the 9th Division for the defence of the Wytschaete—Messines—Kemmel Ridge against the onslaught of the Germans. The battalion was disposed on a front of about 1,000 yards with three companies in the front line. ' A ' Company, under

[1] From regimental contribution.

WYTSCHAETE—*continued*.

Captain Robinson, M.C., held the exposed and dangerous right ;
' B ' Company was in the centre under Captain Ball, M.C. ;
while ' C ' Company was on the left under Captain Sleath.
' C ' Company, under 2nd Lieut. A. D. Robinson, was concentrated to lend support to any part of the somewhat extended
line.   Battalion H.Q. was established on the north-west boundary
of Grand Bois.   The days preceding the 25th April were spent
in improving the defences, which consisted of disjointed trenches
and shell holes ; it was obvious that ere long the enemy would
attempt to dislodge the British from this remaining portion of
the Ridge : the only line of defence behind the position was
China Trench, about 1,000 yards due east.   The strength of
the battalion was some 500 with full complement of officers ;
Lieut.-Colonel J. H. Coles was in command.

The night of the 24th was suspiciously quiet.   Before dawn
next day the enemy shelled the front line heavily with gas and
other projectiles, and the re-entrant between Onraet Farm and
Grand Bois was soon filled with gas.   The valley behind was
next treated in the same way, and by 5 o'clock the bombardment
of the battle area was as intense as had been that of the 21st
March.   The German infantry now advanced in mass formation
against the battalion front, and soon the right flank was in the
air.   At Battalion H.Q. all was anxiety, the heavy shell fire
soon severed all communication ; the heavy, leaden cables
connecting with Onraet Farm, which were buried 8 feet in the
ground, were pierced.   Sergeant Tierney and Lance-Corporal
Hardy, with their gallant signallers, made several attempts to
mend this cable line and the field lines to the companies until
after 6 a.m. no telephone communication was possible.   Runners
were sent to the companies, but none returned, and eventually
only the C.O.'s and Adjutant's runners were left at Battalion H.Q.

2nd Lieut. Tatlow tried to get forward to find out what was
happening to the companies, but the shell fire and rain of machine-
gun bullets were so continuous that progress was impossible.
However, from the eastern edge of Grand Bois he saw the turning
of the right flank of ' A ' Company, but the smoke enveloping
Onraet Wood prevented any observation of that part of the
line.   Meanwhile ' C ' Company, after a desperate fight, was
captured ; ' B ' Company was rolled back on to Onraet Wood ;
' D ' Company was drawn into the fight and were attacked
from left flank and rear.   The shelling had ceased, but the
smoke and gas clouds made it difficult to see what was happening
even a few yards away.   The enemy tried to pour through a

WYTSCHAETE—*continued.*

gap in the wire opposite the southern end of Onraet Wood : a sergeant of ' A ' Company knelt on the top and fired ' rapid ' on the enemy and checked their advance through the gap.   About 6.30 a.m. the enemy had pushed through to Onraet Wood, while every yard was fiercely contested.   With still no news from the companies Lieut.-Colonel Coles was anxiously discussing the situation with the very small party left at Battalion H.Q. when in rushed Sergeant Culliney with the news that the enemy were coming over the hill from Wytschaete.   All ranks were quickly rushed out into a line ; Culliney rejoined his men of the police, who had been posted on the road to stop stragglers ; about twenty men under the Adjutant manned a line from Battalion H.Q. to the road ; another twenty were stretched out north of Battalion H.Q. under 2nd Lieut. Tatlow, who placed his snipers on the roof.

The situation had become desperate : the C.O. sent off a pigeon message to Brigade H.Q. for help, and then walked up and down the line and encouraged all ranks to stick to the position as long as possible.   No one could say what was the fate of the companies.   Some strong patrols of Germans were trickling forward 200 to 300 yards to our front.   There were two fights in progress, one against the companies, the other against Battalion H.Q., which no doubt the Germans thought was another line of defence.   Sniping and steady rifle fire kept them for some time from advancing in strength.   By 7.30 the forward firing was no longer heard.   ' B ' and ' C ' Companies were *hors de combat,* their ammunition expended, and they had suffered heavy casualties.   The same fate had befallen ' D ' Company, though 2nd Lieut. Robinson managed to escape after capture.   At 8.30 ' A ' Company were rushed and, being out of ammunition, were captured after a resolute fight.   The enemy pushed forward : still no succour came !   No messages of any kind !   Battalion H.Q. was cut off from everyone and very near to being surrounded. Soon the little party was fired on from Bois Quarante and it was evident that both flanks had given way, and shortly a determined effort was made to rush the group from front and left.

Lieut.-Colonel Coles perceived that it was useless to retain the position, especially as under the fierceness of hostile machine-gun fire to raise one's head meant certain death.   An orderly withdrawal back to China Trench was commanded.   During a few seconds' pause in the storm of bullets Lieut.-Colonel Coles left with his runner, shouted to Tatlow to follow in a moment or two, and then the Adjutant's party.   For a second or two the

WYTSCHAETE—*continued.*

withdrawal escaped notice, but the enemy soon became aware
of it, and a further hail of bullets and a rapid advance of the
enemy broke the orderly retreat of the little groups into a most
exciting rush from shell hole to shell hole with mobile machine
guns on three sides within 200 or 300 yards. Lieut.-Colonel
Coles was shot through the head : he died painlessly and instantly.
Tatlow was wounded again and all his party became casualties.
The remnants of ' D ' party rushed across country, joining the
others, and they were now chased by rifle patrols until the
shelter of China Trench was reached. The Adjutant's party
had completed a shell-hole rush about 30 yards at a time for
nearly 1,200 yards as the crow flies, but covering a much greater
distance in finding cover from the hail of rifle and machine-gun
bullets. When all were in, only the two officers with Lance-
Corporal Banks and some six men were the survivors of the fight,
joined later by some twenty more slightly wounded men who
had avoided capture."

Wytschaete (South of), Grand Bois—Onreat Wood—Zero Wood, 1918

The German onrush had surged through where, between
Armentières and Neuve Chapelle, their attack had—disastrously
—opened just one day before the Portuguese Divisions were due
for relief. Within twenty-four hours the Germans had come
with little opposition to within two miles of Bailleul. Ploegsteert
and Messines, hotly contested, were outflanked and fell ; the two
last ridges that guarded the plains to the west were threatened.
On April 17th the enemy attacked Kemmel Hill and were
repulsed, and during the next few days French troops took
over the Kemmel sector from our troops. The British right
flank now rested on the Messines—Kemmel Road. On the
24th the 6/West Yorks took over 1,000 yards of front south-
east of Grand Bois to Zero Wood, the relief being made in bright
moonlight during a gas-shell bombardment. This position
crowned the heights that dominated the Kemmel defences and
the plain west of Ypres ; and should it be seized only the Veirstraat Ridge would remain as the final barrier. The Wytschaete-
beek grooved a deep valley between the Petit and Grand Bois,
and through this valley early on the 25th April marched the
Germans, after the most tremendous bombardment that this
district had so far endured. The battalions in the front line
were isolated by the devastating hail of shell, but put up so resolute

WYTSCHAETE (SOUTH OF)—*continued*.

a defence that the enemy advance was broken up, lost impetus, and Veirstraat was saved. Everywhere along the front line groups fought on, scorning to retire, long after the battalion was surrounded ; and, inspiring confidence right through the ranks, held on for twelve hours, delaying the enemy onrush for that critical time. The three front companies never came back to tell the tale of their Thermopylæ. One after another they were overwhelmed, not only by machine-gun fire, but by small field guns that were brought up and fired point-blank into the shell holes they manned, while aeroplanes swept low, emptying their belts upon them. At 6.45 news came that a company of the 1/6 W. Yorkshires were fighting a gallant and hopeless rearguard action, and Captain Sanders, V.C., was seen on top of a pill-box wounded and valiantly rallying his men, firing his revolver point-blank until he fell. Battalion headquarters was early cut off, and few of the staff survived the stand they made. The C.O., Lieut.-Colonel Wistance, was killed. Captain H. E. Robinson, M.O., turned runner when his aid post was blown to pieces ; he was shot through the head while carrying a message. Regimental Sergeant-Major H. Barker died in the midst of the enemy, fighting till the last. But their aim was realised ; for some hours the enemy was completely checked, and the battalion kept their hold on the Grand Bois until 7.30 that evening. They lost 18 officers and 557 men that day.

YPRES

Ypres was a city of beauty. Its heart of beauty, the Cloth Hall, carried the insignia of the royal days of mediæval craftsmanship. In 1914, when this city lured all unwittingly the German Kaiser, war closed in and the terrified inhabitants fled. But the enemy being stayed, the people came back, and until the spring of the following year they carried on their affairs, billeted our soldiers, and though on the very edge of the battleground, the city lived.

In April 1915 it was destroyed by fire. For thirty days it was bombarded monstrously, for thirty days it flamed. Except where the black impenetrable smoke of shells blinded the battlefield, the flare of the burning city was the torch by which they fought who defended it from capture. And all the while the unhappy people were fleeing. Pictures of women and children struck down in the streets ; pictures of soldiers carrying them into shelter and dressing their wounds ; pictures of little carts loaded with all a family's goods surrounded by the family, and

YPRES—*continued*.

all destroyed by one shell; pictures of rending and crashing masonry entombing those beneath, of destruction and fire—this was Ypres in the very lovely spring days of April 1915.

Thereafter the place was abandoned to warfare. Above-ground the walls and stones were daily battered to more indistinguishable ruin ; within the ramparts and cellars, armies lived. No traverse of place or street could at any time be made unhazarded by the obliterating crash of shell or the whining massacre of bullets. Times when columns passed through, and troops marched on as fate allowed. Times when figures flitted across the open, halted behind meagre shelter, slipped from stone to stone through ghoulish alley-ways, across ghost-ridden spaces.

Blind-man's-buff in death's playground, where the hunted were the blind.

Ypres, 1914

The 3rd Cavalry Brigade marched into Ypres on the 13th October—the first British troops to enter the town. They watered and fed in the Grande Place, which at that time still stood perfect in its ancient beauty. No shells had fallen on the town, and the looting of all the wine and jewellery shops by Uhlan patrols three days before was so far the first sign of war. The brigade marched down the Menin Road the following day, and as they passed Hooge Château the Baron and his wife came out and gave General Makins all the information that he had as to German movements.

Ypres, 1915 [1]

The 6/Duke of Cornwall's Light Infantry returned from fierce fighting near Hooge, and while in reserve were billeted in the town in August 1915. The greater number were in the rampart dugouts, but one company chose to occupy the cloisters of St. Mary's. Very unwisely a trench cooker was left smoking in the open near by, and this attracted the notice of a German scout, as his 'plane dipped over the town. A day or two later heavy gun fire opened from the direction of Houthulst Forest, and as the enemy had the exact range, shells—chiefly from the Austrian 7·2-inch howitzers—fell in a continuous stream among the houses. For five hours there was no lull, and in the south-west corner of the cloisters forty-four men of the D.C.L.I. were entombed under a huge mass of stone debris. The Town Major of Ypres organised a rescue party, which included some men of the 11/King's Liverpool Regiment (Pioneers), and tried to dig

[1] From account of an officer of the regiment.

YPRES—*continued*.

out the men who were buried. Wedged in the masonry and fully exposed throughout was a corporal, who at last was reached by the rescuers. His first request was for a cigarette, and as his arms were pinned one was put between his lips, and he remained contentedly smoking until he was released. During the gallant attempt at rescue the Adjutant of the D.C.L.I. and Major Barnett were killed. Some of the imprisoned men were saved, but when the war was over the bodies of forty British soldiers were found in a cellar beneath ; evidence showed that they had been caught on the 11th August, the same date that a platoon of Cornishmen failed to answer the roll-call.

Ypres—the Work of the R.A.M.C.

" In Arduis Fidelis "[1]

West of Ypres in April 1915 lay a country district, bright with the varied hues of young grass and early crops, and wild-flowers raising their delicate, dew-tipped heads to the genial sunshine. The fresh beauty of the scene tempted men to hope for an early termination of the War, and to dream, perhaps, of a London season, the quiet of a nestling hamlet, the joy of a favourite trouting stream, or the exhilaration of the fresh breezes over the yellow gorse and smooth putting-greens of the best of all golf-links. But on the eastern side of the town a tornado of bursting shells crashed on the trenches and fields, the roads and villages of the Salient. It was from an inferno of burning houses and shattered trenches that medical officers and their men had to rescue the sick, wounded, and dying.

Brave acts, self-sacrifice, and initiative were common to all units engaged in the second battle of Ypres, when the organised line held by the French and British troops was temporarily broken by conditions previously unknown in warfare. The heroic deeds of the medical personnel in front-line medical units are best commemorated by describing everyday incidents in the evacuation of the wounded during the last few days of April and the early days of May 1915.

The whole of the medical arrangements were completely disorganised by the concentration of the terrific shelling which was rapidly razing Ypres to the ground. Because the town had become so dangerous, there was a general evacuation, and the G.O.C. of the V Corps ordered all the medical units there to move back. When the German gas attack was launched on the 22nd April there was only one main dressing station fully established and ready to receive casualties.

[1] Regimental contribution by Major F. J. Mitchell, R.A.M.C.

YPRES—*continued.*

The treacherous and altogether unexpected discharge of asphyxiating gases was directed at 5 p.m. against the French division holding the line on the left of the Canadians. As the guns shelled the position, a vast cloud of greenish-yellow gas rose from the German trenches and drifted slowly against our allies and our own line. The heavy vapour crawled into every hole and corner. It filled trenches and dugouts. This cloud of chlorine-smelling gas, carrying certain death, drifted over the Canadians. Many of the troops in the support trenches, reserve lines, and in billets behind the lines, after the agony of fighting for breath, were suffocated. The main route of evacuation became congested by " mixed mobs of Europeans, Algerians, and Turcos, officers and men reeling in one writhing crowd, rending their clothes, coughing and vomiting blood and falling by the roadside as they came." In this crowd, pushing and fighting their way to the rear, were the last remaining local inhabitants of the surrounding villages. Against this ever-increasing mass, dispatch riders on horses and motor-bicycles and army wagons were vainly endeavouring to make headway. When the line was broken, confusion reigned supreme. The diary of one medical officer records the suddenness of the confusion. He had that afternoon taken advantage of a quiet spell to visit a sick officer. On his return he found the road blocked by a stream of French soldiers and transport against which he strove in vain to make headway. He then tried to get round by another road, only to meet a similar stream, and amongst them some of his own men, from whom he learned that they had been ordered to retire. Next day another party which had been left in Ypres rejoined the unit, reporting that their dressing station had been heavily shelled and was in flames. In such a holocaust and in face of such a débâcle had the medical service to alleviate the tortures of the maimed and suffocated, and carry them, to the number of 30,000, from the very jaws of Death. How was it done, and what were the feelings of those who did it ?

Normally the wounded are dressed and brought to the regimental aid posts by the regimental stretcher-bearers, who apply the first field dressing. The field ambulance personnel evacuate them to the nearest advanced dressing station on stretchers carried by the bearers, or in wagons and cars if it is possible to bring these vehicles so near the line. From the advanced dressing station the wounded are passed to the main dressing station, and so to the casualty clearing station, where they are treated

YPRES—*continued.*

and classified before being sent to the base or to rest camps.
But in the confusion which followed the gas attack, the medical
officers in regimental aid posts and advanced dressing stations
had to meet the situation and organise their resources as best
they could.   They had to act alone, each on his own initiative,
and usually in complete ignorance of what was happening round
him.   Thus the advanced dressing stations established themselves
where they could, moving from point to point as the enemy
shells found them, and keeping in touch with the troops nearest
them, to whichever division they might belong.   A small overflow dressing station became practically a main dressing station
through which over 4,000 men were passed, and as the days
went on and the medical officer in charge organised the supply
of dressings to the regimental medical officers of the division he
served, the unit found itself acting also as a medical stores depot.
    What this effort cost them, only those who made it know.
The combatant officer was trained in service conditions before
going abroad ; he was familiar with the work, and in most of
his duties he was accompanied by his brother officers and by the
men he had trained.   In action, all the natural impulses of the
fighting animal were roused, and when men " see red " they
become for the time reckless of danger and all bodily injury.
The officers and men of the medical service never know the joy
of battle.   They must face danger in cold blood, and amid the
ghastly wreckage of a battlefield they must relieve the suffering
and prevent the human destruction which war in calculated
cruelty aims at accomplishing.   And so heroism shines through
the brief narrative of the *Gazette* of the 23rd June 1915, which
records the acts which won for Captain Scrimger of the Canadian
Army Medical Corps the Victoria Cross.
    " During the very heavy fighting between 22nd and 25th
April, Captain Scrimger displayed continuously day and night
the greatest devotion to his duty among the wounded at the
front.   On the afternoon of 25th April 1915, in the neighbourhood
of Ypres, when in charge of an advanced dressing station in
some farm buildings which were being heavily shelled by the
enemy, he directed under heavy fire the removal of the wounded,
and he himself carried a severely wounded officer out of a stable
in search of a place of greater safety.   When he was unable
alone to carry this officer further, he remained with him under
fire till help could be obtained."
    Many of the medical officers had been sent from home straight
into the battle, so great was the need for them.   For the regular

YPRES—*continued*.

officer the ordeal was terrible, but it was almost unendurable
for the middle-aged general practitioner, who had left his wife
and family, or for a rising young specialist who had changed
his morning coat for a uniform and within a month found himself
transferred, at night, into that hell which was the Salient. Yet
they endured it. They found themselves in unknown country,
faced with unimaginable dangers, knowing little or nothing of
Army methods or what was required of them ; and yet, with
no thought of gaining honour or reward, they gave the best
that was in them to the service of the wounded. Captain Marshall
Allen, a clever and enterprising assistant surgeon of the maternity
hospital in Dublin, was sent thus to join a regiment in the middle
of the night. Undaunted, he collected his cases from the open
fields, sorted them out during a battle so fierce that he did not
know whether he was in German or British lines, and for thirty-
six hours on end dressed the wounded. Twelve men had frac-
tured thigh bones, which he set in splints he had himself shaped
with an old axe from the wood of broken doors and windows
found near his aid post ; and so well had he done his work that
these cases were passed on to the casualty clearing station
untouched.

The courage of a regimental medical officer was no less severely
tested when he accompanied his regiment to the front   On
those roads, with shells falling on all sides, no body of men
could hope to reach the trenches without loss, and though men
fell the regiment went on, leaving the medical officer to care for
and evacuate the wounded and bury the dead. When the
40th Pathans came under shell fire for the first time, a shell
burst in the centre company, and Captain Hodge, of the Indian
Medical Service, had to remain behind with twenty-two dead
and wounded. The regiment had lately arrived in France and
were rushed up to fill the gap in the fighting line created by the
first gas attack. Captain Hodge was thus abandoned in a
strange land, cut off from the regiment he knew. The feeling
of being left alone in these circumstances, when everything about
the resources of the area had still to be learned, was unnerving
even when the usual arrangements for the evacuation of casualties
were working smoothly ; when all around was ruin and disorder,
the strangeness and horror of his situation were appalling enough
to make the strongest quail, and only a sense of duty and the
great traditions of his calling could enable Captain Hodge to
surmount the difficulties which faced him.

The second stage in the evacuation of wounded was carried

YPRES—*continued.*

out by field ambulance personnel. Parties of stretcher-bearers under a medical officer were sent out at intervals to clear the wounded from the regimental aid posts. At this time there were no wheeled stretcher-carriers or comparatively safe, well-organised communication trenches. All the severely wounded had to be carried a distance of from two to three miles across country, or dragged along ditches, usually in the dark, under heavy shell and machine-gun fire. The stretcher-bearers never flinched, and always endeavoured not only to carry their wounded in comfort but also to protect them from further injury. In the battle, when the line changed from day to day, from hour to hour, the location of aid posts was no easy task, and even if the stretcher-bearer parties were supplied with guides, guides often lost their way and the party had to stumble over areas where death lurked. How few realise what this tension meant, when every unit in the firing line was calling for more and more bearers to evacuate their wounded! Again and again the bearers, after returning with their wounded, were sent out into the darkness to the trench or aid post where the need was greatest. The following simple extract from the war diary of a field ambulance illustrates how dangerous this duty was and how courageously it was faced.

" The bearer division were again under heavy shell, rifle, and machine-gun fire. They were delayed 1¼ hours by the ignorance of a guide, and at 3 a.m. were forced to take shelter in dugouts. All wounded were evacuated, the bearers returning at 10.30 a.m. The bearer division acted with great courage, returning several times to collect the wounded, the casualties amongst the bearers being 11 out of a total of 70. Special praise is given to Private Jacob, Privates Jenson and Thickner who were wounded, and Lance-Corporal Herrington, Private Ford for special daring in evacuating the wounded."

Those in the advanced dressing stations had a nerve-racking time in great peril. They were shelled from position to position, until ultimately the stations which had been opened on the Ypres—Brielen Road, at Hampshire Farm, Wieltje, and Potijze, were concentrated in the cellars of St. Jean, a village which was rapidly being shattered by shell and consumed by fire. The scenes in these dressing stations were awful, and for all medical officers in charge there was no more harrowing experience than the heavy shelling of a station, surrounded as they were by fatigued, badly wounded, and helpless men. The thought of defenceless and suffering patients being battered to death,

YPRES—*continued.*

suffocated under falling debris, or buried under stones and earth
became almost overpowering. Then there was the horror of
poisonous gases. Again and again the deadly clouds drifted
over the trenches and even reached the dressing stations, obliging
everyone to work with pads tied over their noses and mouths to
prevent the inhalation of the foul fumes. Men were brought in,
livid and moribund, with a yellow froth pouring from their
mouths ; or " choking, making agonising efforts to breathe,
clutching at their throats and tearing open their clothes," fighting
for breath, only to die some hours later. And in those first days
no one knew what treatment, if any, could relieve their agony.
In many of the war diaries of the units which supplied the
personnel of these dressing stations, records are available showing
the cool and thoughtful work of the medical officers and men in
ministering to their patients and arranging for their comfort and
evacuation while the dressing stations were being heavily shelled.

The advanced dressing station was not the final resting-place
of the wounded man. He had to be evacuated through a main
dressing station, organised by a field ambulance, to a casualty
clearing station. That journey in many other parts of the line
on the Western Front was undertaken in comparative peace and
safety, but not from the Ypres Salient in the days of the second
battle. Intermittently throughout the day slightly wounded
men worked back from point to point, and those more seriously
injured clambered painfully on to lorries, empty supply and
ammunition wagons, or any other vehicles on their way to the
rear. The main body of seriously wounded were, however,
evacuated by divisional convoys composed of stretcher-bearers,
ambulance wagons, and motor ambulance cars. These convoys
set out towards dusk, and perchance had an easy time for a
short part of their way, but sooner or later they came under heavy
artillery or machine-gun fire. What could have been more
appalling than that nightly walk, under heavy fire, through
burning villages—the death-trap of many—or across that single
bridge by which the main convoys entered the Salient ? It was
a danger-point always, strewn with upturned wagons and guns,
slaughtered horses, and dead and dying soldiers. Could there
have been anything more gruesome to a non-combatant than
those pitiful sentinels ? There was not the stimulus of revenge.
He was not to get to grips with the enemy. There was only
the professional and human thought of retrieving and helping
the men who had fought so heroically against overwhelming
odds. The simple narrative of two incidents taken haphazard

YPRES—*continued.*

from the official diaries reveals the steady courage which every evacuating party showed in a peril intensified by ghastly horror.

" On this date one of our motor ambulances was proceeding over the Menin Bridge with several bearers returning to Poperinghe when a shell burst in rear of it. The bearers, seeing that an ammunition wagon team and drivers had been hit, stopped the ambulance, got out and found the team of six horses and several men lying in the road. The horses were shot by an artillery officer who was passing, and the bearers dressed the injured men under shell fire, and placed all but one of them in the ambulance and sent them on to Poperinghe. Private Stephens then made his way across the bridge, which was being heavily shelled, into a house previously used by a medical unit, searched for and found some morphia and a hypodermic syringe, then returned to the remaining wounded man, who was dying in great agony from an abdominal wound from which his intestines extruded, and gave him a dose of morphia. The three bearers then carried him into the shelter of a neighbouring house and stood by for some time until he died.

" The whole work was performed under heavy fire from high-explosive shells which were bursting within a few yards, as was their subsequent progress back through Ypres. The names of the bearers are Private P. M. Stephens, Private W. F. Matthews, and Private Piper."

" Received instructions to send a party of men to Ypres. . . . Sergeant Jenkins, Lance-Corporal Hadlow, and four men detailed with two Ford cars. On arrival the party found the place cleared. They were subjected to heavy shell fire, the two motors were damaged, and one driver of 81st Field Ambulance wounded and missing. Three civilians were recovered from the fallen debris. Sergeant Jenkins, Lance-Corporal Hadlow, and Driver Sawyer, A.S.C., M.T., and men displayed great courage in carrying out their duty, only leaving when the district had been thoroughly searched. Lance-Corporal Hadlow was dressing a case in a cellar when he was shut in by falling debris. He completed the dressing, dug himself out, and removed his patient."

The actual driving or the shelling and damaging of a motor-car may seem small things in the awful destruction of this battle. Yet it is sometimes in the small events that cool and enduring bravery is most needed, as the following extract proves.

" It was on the night of the 25th April a convoy was sent up from Vlamertinghe to above St. Jean to sweep the field of wounded. The motors stopped in St. Jean to load some wounded

YPRES—*continued.*

when a shell exploded, blowing up our ambulance wagon, wounding Major Duval and Captain McGibbon and Privates Fortnum, Brisbois, Demeule, Labelle, Davis, and Selborne. Three privates and one driver died. The second shell dropped also on the remains of the ambulance wagon and set it on fire."

No men spent themselves more ungrudgingly than the drivers of the ambulance cars, whether men of the R.A.S.C. attached to the medical units or drivers of the British Red Cross Society. The devotion of the British Red Cross drivers was all the more striking in that they were serving a voluntary association and had no assurance of pensions for themselves or their families if they were maimed or killed. The risks they took were great. The cars went right up to the advanced posts, even to within 300 yards of the enemy ; and for a time, owing to the bending back of the line after the 22nd April, they were actually clearing wounded along a road parallel with the firing line and coming within 500 yards of it. Cars and drivers were not numerous enough to organise reliefs, so that the drivers had to work every night and often through the day, besides keeping their cars in running order. Though between the 22nd April and the 13th May forty-three of the cars were damaged, only three were abandoned. The foreman of the workshop unit was killed in an attempt to recover one damaged car, and another car was " abandoned " only because it had been destroyed by further shells before the workshop personnel had succeeded in removing it.

The nervous strain on the drivers was extreme and the personal danger great. They drove without lights, finding their way as best they could in the darkness or by the sudden glare of bursting shells and " Verey " lights. They never knew where the road had been broken by a great shell hole, strewn with debris, or blocked by fallen trees. They were so utterly exhausted that sometimes they fell asleep even while driving ; and yet, shaken and exhausted as they were, they never failed to respond to the demands made on them. They were nerved to endure up to the very limits of human strength by the thought of the men they served, whose heroism they emulated, and of whom, in the weeks between the 22nd April and the 13th May, over 30,000 wounded were brought by their efforts from the shell-ploughed fields of the Salient.

One of the terrible features of the Salient was that the wounded were never safe from bursting shells. Even so far back as the main dressing stations or the casualty clearing stations they were not out of danger, and as one refuge after another was shelled

YPRES—*continued.*

they had to be hastily removed, sometimes to the open fields. What suffering of body and mind—and not of the wounded only—lies behind the laconic statements of the war diaries kept by all officers commanding field ambulances !

" Hospital hit many times. One large shell bored right through the house. Had just removed patients from room or thirty at least would have been killed. At 3 a.m. 30th [April] began to evacuate and loaded our own cars in midst of showers of shrapnel which burst too high to injure many. Two of our motor drivers wounded at gate of hospital. No further accident till the seventy patients were loaded and away. Then we all lay down in house and slept till morning, when shelling ceased."

" 27th.—At 4.30 p.m. shrapnel burst over the village followed by 5·4 high-explosive shells. Wounded carried out into the fields and personnel not actually needed sent also. Shells came very near, a dispatch rider being seriously wounded a few yards away. Two wounded killed next door. Houses on main street badly shattered. One whole family killed. 28th.—Enemy again shelled village. Patients cleared to neighbouring farm without accident."

So from open fields, battered trenches, burning villages, and ruined houses the officers and men, Regulars, Temporaries, and Territorials, forming part of or attached to the British, Canadian, or Indian Medical Services, collected the suffering casualties in this poisoned area under a hail of bullets and shells. They brought them slowly but with every possible care across dangerous and harrowing areas, back to the hospitals where clever surgeons by operation and gentle and sympathetic women by nursing were to save their lives. Worthily did all members of the medical personnel play their part in assisting to sustain the *moral* of the troops while they were engaging the enemy at this critical time, and once more they achieved the honour of acting up to their corps motto : " In arduis fidelis."

YPRES, 1917.[1] The Asylum

" On the night 13th/14th July 1917, ten lorry loads of 60-pdr. shell, in charge of a sergeant and of Corporal Wadsworth, A.S.C., were drawn up, prior to off-loading on the main Ypres—Vlamertinghe Road a few yards west of the Asylum and facing towards Ypres. Owing to traffic congestion the vehicles were halted in close order. Immediately behind them was a convoy of

---

[1] From a regimental account.

YPRES—*continued*.

lorries of the XIX Corps Siege Park laden with 9·2-inch high-explosive ammunition for delivery to a howitzer battery close in rear of the 1st/2nd London Heavy Battery. These latter vehicles had no connection with the 60-pdr. ammunition convoy and were manned by Corps Siege Park personnel. After the lorries had delivered their 60-pdr. shell and had moved off, an enemy shell scored a direct hit on the leading lorry of the remaining seven and set fire to the petrol tank as well as blowing up the load of ammunition. The explosion and the flare from the burning petrol gave the position away completely and a brisk fire was opened on the convoy, so that in a few moments one more 60-pdr. lorry was in flames as well as some ten to twelve 9·2-inch ammunition vehicles. Between the two lots of burning vehicles stood five lorries, laden with 60-pdr. high-explosive ammunition and intact up to this moment. Several men were killed and wounded, and the survivors accordingly were ordered to take cover in some dugouts a few yards west of the convoy. Corporal Wadsworth, however, decided to attempt to save the five unburnt lorries and at the same time to minimise the risk of death and injury to the personnel of such batteries as were situated close to the scene of the fire. He therefore left his cover and crawled past twelve burning lorries, laden with 9·2-inch ammunition, to the rearmost of the five intact vehicles. This machine he started up and slowly manœuvred, single-handed, out of the line of closed-up vehicles, eventually driving it westwards in reverse gear past the burning vehicles in rear, and into a position of safety some 150 yards clear of the convoy. He then returned for the next vehicle which was unharmed, and repeated the same performance no less than three times, saving four lorries laden with 60-pdr. high-explosive shell. Returning for the fifth and last undamaged vehicle of his convoy, he was caught in the open by the explosion of one of the intervening lorries of 9·2-inch ammunition and blown off the roadway down the embankment on the south side of the road. Here he was found unconscious some two and a half hours later. Corporal Wadsworth's gallant act saved four lorries, four hundred rounds of 60-pdr. ammunition, as well as the near-by batteries."

ZANDWOORDE, 1914

The Germans had captured Kruiseecke on the 26th October, the acute salient at that point being cut off, and, owing to the perilous situation of the 20th Brigade, the cavalry on their right

were called upon to help cover their retreat. General Byng
had too few squadrons holding the wide front to do more than
spare one regiment to make a demonstration and divert the
enemy. The Blues in reserve in Klein Zillebeke Wood were
chosen for this and galloped forward along the line due east to
Zandwoorde. Officers in a trench observed that it was a curious
course to select for a point-to-point, where a head might not
be raised without drawing fire. One squadron dismounted on
the Ridge, and as a volley of rifle fire burst from them, the
other two galloped on eastward, prolonging the line, menacing
the German flank. They had achieved their object, as the
enemy turned towards them with heavy fire, and as night fell
they were withdrawn, having diverted attack from the 20th
Brigade. This affair is the only movement of cavalry reported
in the enemy official diary that day.

Zandwoorde, 30th October 1914

For over an hour a mass of artillery—some 260 heavy guns—
plastered the slopes of Zandwoorde, pouring fire into the narrow
trenches of the 1st and 2nd Life Guards on the forward slope.
The parapets were blown in, and many men buried, but the
three or four hundred cavalrymen held on, even while an overwhelming infantry assault followed the bombardment, and an
order came to retire to the support trench. One squadron of
each regiment and the Machine-gun Corps of the Blues were cut off.

No one can know, but we can picture, what happened then,
and it is the enemy who give us the key to that picture. They
tell us that when the battalions of his XV Corps at last reached
the high ground they came where " two whole British squadrons
with their machine guns lay, dead and wounded, completely
annihilated in one meadow on the battlefield."

Zandwoorde, North of, 1914

When news came that the cavalry had been shelled off Zandwoorde Ridge, the 105th Battery had a section in the open and
the 106th one in the Woods, south of Heronthage Château ; they
turned upon the enemy who appeared on the summit of the
Ridge with two batteries in action on the northern side. The
British battery commander justly observed : " They had very
little ammunition, but plenty of time to look for targets." And
they dropped their few shells with such accuracy that the German
detachments were seen escaping, and they remained away for
over an hour. Then heavy concealed howitzers opened on the

ZANDWOORDE, NORTH OF—*continued.*
English section, so they set fire to a windmill, making an im-
promptu smoke screen, and withdrew under its cover.

Zandwoorde, 1914

When Zandwoorde was overwhelmed on 30th October the
first troops to the north—the Royal Welch Fusiliers—were
outflanked. For three hours they endured a terrible hail of fire
into their trenches in full view of the enemy. As the Germans
came over the Ridge, they took possession of a farm to the right
rear of the battalion and opened fire at 30 yards' range, coming
round to the rear, but keeping at a distance in front. At this
moment a German battery on high ground got the range with
shrapnel, and flailed the line from end to end. The Welshmen,
with ammunition failing, rifles jamming, fought staunchly on
until they were utterly overwhelmed. Lieut. Dooner, boldly
carrying a message across the open, was shot down. Colonel
Cadogan, commanding the battalion, saw him fall, and ran out
to help him. As he stooped to raise him, the Colonel was killed.
Only eighty-six survivors mustered that evening.

ZILLEBEKE, 31st October 1914

Here the 1/Battalion of the Irish Guards met the storm that
broke on the 31st October. Under a tremendous bombardment,
with trenches blown to pieces, the line came near the breaking-
point. The battalion held on in the Wood for thirty-six hours,
without food, every man fighting every yard of ground. Their
staunchness saved the right flank, and during the week the
casualties were 613 all round, the remnants being made into
two shrunken companies. Rudyard Kipling recounts how " years
later a man remembering that fight said, ' 'Twas like a football
scrum. Everyone was somebody, ye'll understand. If he
dropped, there was no one to take his place. Great day ; an'
we not so frightened as when it came to the fighting by machinery
on the Somme afterwards.' " [1]

Zillebeke Woods, 1914 [2]

The 4th Dragoon Guards, coming straight up from the magnificent defence of Messines and the Wytschaete Cross-roads,
came late into the front-line trenches in Zillebeke Wood by
midnight the 13/14th November. The enemy's trenches were

---

[1] *The Irish Guards in the Great War*, Rudyard Kipling.
[2] From regimental contribution, by Major-General Solly-Flood.

ZILLEBEKE WOODS—*continued*.

at a distance varying from 20 to 30 yards. The Wood was in a horrible state, many trees were cut down by shells, and a mass of branches and strands of barbed wire separated the opposing trenches. In the many assaults, on both sides, men caught in the wire had been shot and their bodies were left suspended on the wire, which was strung from tree to tree.

To make matters worse, the weather at the time was intensely cold, the coldest part of the winter of 1914–15, heavy falls of snow alternately with sharp frosts. Fighting was continuous, cooking of food or drying of boots impossible, and the men were too wet and cold to sleep.

Much useful work was done by patrols who crawled at night through the debris and reconnoitred the enemy's lines. Sergeant Thomas, of " C " Squadron, on the night of the 13th penetrated into the German trenches, a portion of which had been abandoned, and found them piled with dead. He returned with this and other valuable information, also with sufficient pairs of boots taken from the freshly killed Germans to equip his troop. There was considerable good-humoured jealousy expressed in forcible language by the men according as the boots, when they were distributed and fell to their share, were still warm and pliable from their late wearer or were cold and stiff from a long-dead enemy. This was our first reinforcement in footwear since leaving England.

Zillebeke, 1915

When the 3rd Cavalry Division were entrenched in front of Zillebeke in February 1915, our line was so near that of the Germans that the breadth of No-man's-land varied from 80 yards on the right to only 10 yards on the left of the line—so close that a German tossed a matchbox into the trenches held by the Blues in which was a note : " We are a battalion of an Alsace regiment. Don't shoot us and we won't shoot you. Vive la France ! but Germany comes first." The line held by the Essex Yeomanry was distinguished by a peculiar tree—a tree as others of the mutilated stumps that were all that remained of Zillebeke Wood as far as the enemy could see. But this tree was a bit of the earliest camouflage—in truth a 20-foot length of drain pipe fitted with mirrors and covered with bark—a gigantic and very useful periscope. It remained for weeks a great success, until imitation led to a somewhat surprising sudden growth of trees in the district which brought enemy marksmen into activity against them.

Zillebeke, 1916

A great demand was made on the heroism of men by whom unknown acts of valour were performed in the dreary duty of bringing up ammunition and material along shell-swept roads through the hours of darkness. Howsoever severe the bombardment, they never failed to arrive when they were needed—all honour to the driver and his horses. One night the ammunition wagons of D/102 had gone through the desolating nightmare of the shell-swept road, striving to reach the battery near Zillebeke. Many drivers and horses were down. Captain W. Pasteur, already wounded, kept the teams working until he was hit by a shell and both his legs were shattered. With wonderful fortitude he kept on directing the last wagons until he died.

Zillebeke Lake, 1917

An ingenious captain in a battery that was in the line on the shores of Zillebeke Lake acquired an old punt. When the enemy strafed his position he would pack as many gunners into the craft as its ancient sides would hold, and paddle out into the middle of the lake, where they remained in comparative safety until the fire died down.

On the 2nd August 1917, " B " Battery of the 83rd Brigade R.F.A. had for officers' mess a hole in the shore of Zillebeke Lake covered by tarpaulin. Shells dropped daily in the water and all around the battery. On this day the O.C., Major Cyril Palmer, and three young officers were sitting in their mess when a 5·9 fell right upon it. The subalterns were killed on the spot, and the major, dreadfully wounded, died next day. Only a little pet kitten crept out unhurt from the holocaust. The guns and the new mess were hit three times again until permission was obtained to move the battery, when it took seven hours to haul one 18-pdr. through the morass for 250 yards. Zillebeke !

Zillebeke, 1917

The 18th Division came up from the Somme high-hearted in the knowledge of the splendid part they had played in the fierce and stubborn battles in that region. They took their place in the lines about Zillebeke. They came to a horrible realisation of something more awful, more foul, than they yet had dreamed. The battle was due for the 31st July, and in the early days of the month the Division took over. E'er ever the great attack was launched, the appalling nature of the sector, at the mercy

ZILLEBEKE—*continued.*

of the enemy whose monster guns dominated them from the ridges, was brought most bitterly home to every man of them. The Divisional Artillery met the storm first. The 82nd and 83rd Brigades, brought by Brigadier-General Sidney Metcalfe to a polished pitch of efficacy, boasted that their eight batteries of field guns were commanded by seven regular officers of eight years' service—the eighth officer being a born gunner. By August's end only two of these eight were alive and unwounded. The battery positions, in the open north of Zillebeke Lake, were dug in a two-foot crust of earth above water, elephant iron was the only cover, the ground was soaked with mustard gas by nightly bombardments, and during the day regular "area strafes" swept and blasted the sector with shell of every calibre. In spite of all, the gunners did well the job in hand, making ready for the battle. D/82, losing four out of its six 4·5 howitzers in one wire-cutting day, was specially mentioned by the C.-in-C.

"On the occasion referred to not more than fifty rounds had been fired at the German wire when a hostile 50–cm. battery opened a steady and accurate fire in enfilade. Each time the British batteries opened, salvos of 15–cm. shells raked the position. Four of its six guns were put out of action and two ammunition dumps were blown up, but the remaining two guns continued in action until the last of the 400 rounds had been fired. A few days later when our infantry advanced over the sector this battery had shelled, the enemy's wire was found to have been completely cut."[1]

Journeys up to the line, hauling up ammunition and supplies through the nightmare hours of darkness, were part of the dreary mission of these days of preparation. The way ended from Shrapnel Corner in wooden tracks through the morass. A traffic way was made by Colonel Simmons, Divisional C.R.E., known as the famous A.T.N. track; passing south of the lake outside all map routes and marked by white three-foot posts, it led from Reninghelst to Clapham Junction. The road provided the enemy with a carefully registered target whereon every hit scored. Its length was crammed with a slow procession of transport often blocked for hours while the wreckage of splintered wagons, while bodies of men and horses were cleared from the way. "Many a man learned Christianity while waiting at Shrapnel Corner," said a Padre. When the day of the great attack arrived at last on the 31st July it came as a relief to all after the agonising preparation.

[1] Sir D. Haig's Dispatch, 25/12/'17.

South of Zillebeke,[1] 1917

" C " Battery, 162nd Brigade R.F.A., was in action south of Zillebeke from the 13th September to the 22nd October, 1917, during the fighting for the Passchendaele Ridge. Between these dates the battery was under unceasing heavy shell fire, having no less than nineteen guns destroyed or put out of action by direct hits. The battery at all times displayed great gallantry, never failing to respond to calls for their fire, whatever the conditions. On one occasion after it had become necessary to clear the battery position temporarily owing to intense concentrated fire of German 8-inch batteries right on to it—two guns being completely destroyed—the S.O.S. was received from the infantry. Led by their officers, the men manned the remaining guns and fired till the order " Stop " was received, the hostile shelling increasing in violence as time went on. One officer and ten other ranks were killed and several wounded on this occasion.

Again, on the 4th October in precisely similar circumstances the detachments manned the guns instantly on the S.O.S. being given, after the position had had to be cleared. While firing in response to the call, one gun was destroyed and twelve other ranks killed and wounded by shell fire.

Between the 13th September and the 17th October 1917, four officers and sixteen other ranks were killed and two officers and eighty other ranks wounded in the battery. It was not until at last they had insufficient men to maintain the guns in action that the battery reported it could not carry on as efficiently as was to be desired. Orders were in consequence given that the battery was to be withdrawn from action, and it accordingly returned to its wagon lines, four N.C.O.s and six gunners being all that was left.

Zillebeke Lake, 1918.   The Moated Grange

An identification was required from the enemy to clear up the situation near Zillebeke Lake on 8th July 1918. 2nd Lieut. R. B. Wright, of the 6/West Yorks, volunteered for the work, and at once made a most daring reconnaissance. In broad daylight he crawled out into No-man's-land, and wriggled his way through long grass until, 500 yards from our line, he could see a post that he suspected to be held by the enemy. Sounds of movement could be heard in dugouts 60 yards off ; however, regardless of the risk, Lieut. Wright crept forward in the noontide

[1] From R.A. notes contributed by Lieut.-Gen. Sir Herbert Uniacke.

ZILLEBEKE LAKE, THE MOATED GRANGE—*continued*.

brightness, snaked under the wire round the suspected trench, and jumped in. It was untenanted, but obviously only recently abandoned. Back he crawled, and asked for seven volunteers to go in daylight, hold the post, and lie in wait for the Germans' return at night. An immediate response gave him his party, nearly all boys eighteen years of age. They crept back to the post, arrived safely, and from thence proceeded and surrounded a shelter full of sleeping Germans. Lieut. Wright went in, and the Germans—there were nine—surrendered. The patrol started to herd them back to our line. Just then the enemy perceived them, and two or three strong parties rushed out from their line ; one of the prisoners drew a concealed revolver, there was a fierce fight, and the little patrol was utterly outnumbered. Lieut. Wright was shot through the head and killed, but his boys succeeded in getting two of the prisoners away, killing the rest. And three of these boys stayed with the body of their fallen officer, out in No-man's-land, near the enemy lines in broad daylight ; and when they could come in several hours later, they brought their charge with them.

Zillebeke. (See MENIN ROAD.)

ZONNEBEKE, 1914

Among the gorgeous acts of fighting heroism—great deeds carried with racing blood—one comes here to one of these acts of stern and constrained valour when a non-combatant endures the terror of shot and shell.

"For conspicuous bravery and devotion to duty," Lieut. A. M. Leake gained a bar to the Victoria Cross already won in South Africa. Tending the wounded under fire ; carrying wounded men into safety. For him no relief of tension in fierce rush and vehement thrust, but hands kept gentle and steady. For him no battle-cries, but a quiet and encouraging voice. He stands for an order of courage that flamed through our armies, and in priest and surgeon was pre-eminent in our countrymen.

Zonnebeke, 1915

Captain L. G. Hawker gained one of the first Victoria Crosses in the air on 25th July. Flying a Bristol "Scout," he attacked two Boche planes within half an hour of each other—one over Passchendaele, and one over Houthulst Forest. Both dived

ZONNEBEKE—*continued.*

and escaped, and Captain Hawker, climbing higher, espied another enemy at 11,000 feet. He gave chase and within 100 yards opened fire, blazing into the enemy machine, which crashed in flames within our lines near Zonnebeke.

The Salient had seen the flight above it of the first winner of the Cross for conspicuous gallantry in the air—Lieut. Rhodes Moorhouse. He bombed Courtrai Station from a height of only 300 to 400 feet, and was caught by rifle and machine-gun fire, both himself and the plane being hit. He piloted his machine back to Merville, flying low for thirty-five minutes, though terribly wounded. And he made a full report before he was carried to hospital, where he died next day.

Zonnebeke, 1915

The 1/Suffolks lost 280 all ranks when on the 24th April 1915 they, with the Connaught Rangers, advanced to cover the flank of the 2nd Canadian Brigade. The attack was made under heavy artillery fire, and reached the Zonnebeke—Keerselaere Road. An appeal for help was received from the Canadians; the half-battalion moved up to reinforce them. The losses of the 1/Suffolks may be appreciated by the fact that the half-battalion was under the command of a 2nd Lieutenant of three and a half years' service, Lieut. Bradley, the senior surviving officer.

Zonnebeke (Halfway House), 1917

The enemy put down a terrific bombardment on the batteries in action near Halfway House north of Zonnebeke on the 19th August, and as there was no shelter here whatsoever, all the ammunition of " G " Battery, 280th Brigade, was set on fire. Major E. R. C. Warrens ordered the untenable position to be cleared, and on mustering the men found two were missing. The gun position had become an inferno blazing from end to end, whilst shells crashed round the towering pyres of flaming cordite that drew further destruction from the watching enemy. Sergeants H. W. Linney, W. Inskipp, and Corporal S. Fall faced the imminent danger without any hesitation, and voluntarily went back to seek the missing men, succeeding in finding one badly wounded but still breathing, whom they brought away.

When the bombardment had died down, the position showed some heaps of scrapped metal where six guns had stood. Two had disappeared utterly.

Zonnebeke. (See MENIN ROAD.)

ZOUAVE WOOD, 1915 [1]

The Germans had started their first liquid-fire attack on 30th July, and the 6/Battalion Duke of Cornwall's Light Infantry were hurried through Ypres to support the 41st Brigade. They reached Zouave and Sanctuary Woods, and had to put half a battalion in each. The ground was entirely new to them. In the afternoon of the 30th July they attacked, and Lieut. G. M. Paddison, commanding " D " Company, led them forward until he fell shot through the heart ; but his men charged onward, and succeeded in lining Zouave Wood. The Germans were in position on high ground, facing the Cornwalls, and completely commanding them at about 300 yards. Although it seemed an impossible situation, the battalion was ordered to hold on at all costs. In the early hours of next morning the Germans tried to bomb them out, and later the artillery of both sides opened rapid fire. The enemy then used liquid fire, and some men of " C " Company, who had lost all their officers and N.C.O.s, broke from about 30 yards of front, and began to fall back. Sergeant Silver, who had charge of a machine gun just in rear, shouted to them : " If you don't get back to your line, I'll open fire on you. The 6th Cornwalls are d—— well going to stick it." At midnight the gallant little band were relieved, and handed over the line intact.

Zouave Wood, North of, 1917

On the morning of the 26th August the 280th Brigade R.F.A., in position near Hooge, was called upon to fire a barrage programme in support of an infantry attack. The guns started firing, when very soon a shell burst close behind one of " A " Battery's guns. Every man but one was killed or badly wounded. This man, Gunner Harding, suffered shock and concussion, but he helped the battery medical orderly to carry two desperately wounded men to such cover as there was. He then cleared the mechanism of the gun of the ghastly remains of a man who had been blown to pieces, and took his place again at the gun. There was no one available, owing to other casualties, to join Gunner Harding, and he carried out the remainder of the barrage programme with complete efficiency and perfect accuracy, serving his gun unaided and maintaining the regulated rate of fire through another forty-five minutes of continuous firing.

[1] From an account by an officer of the regiment.

ZWARTELEEN AREA, 1914[1]

The 2/Battalion Grenadier Guards, having fought throughout the retreat from Mons, did not reach the vicinity of Ypres before the 20th October, and, with the exception of sending up one company to support the Cameron Highlanders, did not become seriously engaged till the 31st. But from that date onward they took part in the most desperate and continuous fighting with practically no rest night or day until they were taken out of the line.

It was just the most critical moment in the first battle of Ypres when the battalion had to bear the brunt of the enemy's attack. After a wet night, the 31st dawned with what was then considered a very heavy bombardment of our trenches and before long the 4th (Guards) Brigade was engaged in fierce fighting all down the line. The 2nd Battalion was hard pressed and with difficulty was holding its ground when Lieut.-Colonel Smith received the following message from Lord Cavan, who commanded the Brigade: " The situation is extremely critical. You are to hold your ground at all costs. Sir Douglas Haig relies on the Grenadiers to save the I Corps and possibly the Army."

Lieut.-Colonel Smith decided to dispense with all reserve and sent up to the front trenches every available man. When he reported the measures he had taken, Lord Cavan replied, " Splendid. Hang on like grim death ; you may yet save the Army." Such an inspiring message seemed to appeal personally to every man, and nowhere is an Englishman seen to better advantage than in a desperate situation. The men fought magnificently and the enemy could make no impression on that part of the line.

After this the battalion was relieved, but was quickly back, this time at Klein Zillebeke, when it was subjected to intermittent attacks and very heavy shelling for twelve consecutive days, including a particularly critical attack on the 6th, when the line on the right was broken. When the battalion went for a rest on Corps Reserve, they had a very hard time, for in those days resting consisted in being sent up hurriedly to any part of the line that required strengthening, and when the 1st (Guards) Brigade was being heavily attacked in front of Hooge Château, they had to advance across the open under severe shrapnel fire and came in for some stiff fighting. Almost every night they were sent up to some part of the line. When the Germans made their last serious effort to force their way through to Ypres,

---

[1] From regimental account by Lieut.-Col. Sir Frederick Ponsonby.

they attacked in great force, and the fact that the battalion on
that day fired 24,000 rounds of small-arms ammunition gives
some idea of how fierce the fighting must have been.

The 2nd Battalion had repulsed twelve determined attacks in
three weeks, which it must be admitted was a fine record ; but
the casualties amongst all ranks were exceptionally heavy ;
amongst the officers the battalion lost 14, 8 killed and 6 wounded.

When the war of stagnation began and duty in the Ypres area
became a monotonous life of mud and squalor, both the 1st and
2nd Battalions of the Grenadier Guards took their turn in the
line at one time or another ; but beyond the usual shelling,
bombing, and sniping, no outstanding incident occurred.

Zwarteleen, 1914

On the 6th Nov. the line held by the French south of Zillebeke
had been pierced in three places, and their troops had fallen back
to the outskirts of Zillebeke, leaving a gap through which the
Germans poured in great numbers. The Irish Guards were outflanked and one company destroyed. Next the right company of
the 2/Grenadiers was pounded by the guns and almost every man
was killed or wounded by shell fire during the day. We had a
hundred men to fill the ominous gap ; our right flank was secured
by two companies of the Royal Sussex and one of the Oxford
Light Infantry. The Germans, unable to roll up the British
line, passed on, sweeping through the gap to Zwarteleen and
reaching almost to Verbrandenmolen, only 3,000 yards from
Ypres. The 7th Cavalry Brigade at Zillebeke (nicknamed the
Fire Brigade, from its swift response to many S.O.S.) was called
on to stop the Germans and avert a fatal disaster. Brigadier-
General Kavanagh galloped his brigade across the line of the
French retreat. Then he pulled up and dismounted the 1st and
2nd Life Guards, and, with one squadron of the Blues on horseback to cover his right and the rest in support, advanced at the
double upon Zwarteleen, now held by the enemy, clearing the
village and woods at the bayonet point and regaining the old
trenches of the Irish Guards. This was a charge that a highly
placed officer described as one of the finest things that he saw.
Colonel Gordon Wilson, with a borrowed rifle, led the Blues, his
laugh cheering them on to the assault. He was shot through
the head and died instantly in front of the regiment he had so
largely made. On his left the 2nd Life Guards advanced to the
side of a raised road to meet the swarming Germans. Major

ZWARTELEEN—*continued.*

Hugh Dawnay, that splendid and greatly-loved officer, headed his squadrons by 50 yards, and from the position by the road exultantly greeted an officer, who came up, with the cry, " This is seeing life "—*and he was given long life, even for ever and ever.* Almost immediately he was shot down.

Meanwhile two companies of French infantry and some troops of cavalry rallied from their reserve under General Moussy, who led them, sword in hand, on the right of the Household Cavalry. They were checked by the enemy, and carried back two of Kavanagh's squadrons who were moving to enfilade the German advance, but rallied on the western outskirts of Zwarteleen.

The great gap had been filled, and the open way to Ypres barred by the King's bodyguard.

Zwarteleen (Armagh Wood), 1914

On the 7th November at a critical moment after the misfortune of the French south of the Canal, the 22nd Brigade advanced to attack through the Wood in a heavy mist. The 2/Queen's led the attack in two lines supported by the 1/Staffords. The firing of a gun was to be the signal for all troops near to attack, but was unheard in the din of battle, and only the 1/Gloucesters received the order and joined in. The remnant of the 1/Staffords was led by Captain F. Vallentin. There was no officer of higher rank. He had been wounded and lay in hospital at Ypres ; and when he heard of the desperate position of his regiment he insisted on rejoining. He was again wounded, leading his men. They had the utmost confidence in him, gained by many acts of great bravery, and they now followed him with such verve that they carried the front-line trench and captured three machine guns. They were then assailed by heavy shell and machine-gun fire, their captain was killed, and the troops held on with open flanks all day. Captain Vallentin was awarded a posthumous V.C.

Zwarteleen, 1917

A V.C. was remarkably gained near Zwarteleen in 1917. The North Staffordshire Regiment were excavating a trench when they unearthed a grenade that started to burn. Sergeant John Carmichael ran to the spot, shouting to his men to get clear. He dare not try to throw the bomb out for fear of injuring the men working on top, so he placed his steel helmet over it, and

ZWARTELEEN—*continued.*

himself stood on the crown. The grenade exploded, blowing the sergeant out of the trench. He escaped alive and very badly wounded when he had without hesitation offered his life.

THE UNKNOWN DEAD [1]

He died alone in the dark, the horrible dark,
And no man knew where he lay—
His body was shattered and flung by the monstrous death
Where the shell-fiends slay !
Hurled to the winds by the mine, the terror unknown
That sudden leaps from below !
Left in the No-man's-land in the fiery hell
Where none may go.
He passed where a crash of stone, and a blazing town
Were his unwatched funeral pyre—
He fell in the flaming wreck of his broken wings
In a shroud of fire.
The infinite waters hide his burial-place
And the great waves speak no name—
He went from the Sea and the Land on unnumbered fields
Unknown to fame.

With the trumpets' peal, with the roll of the muffled drums,
Our homage we fitly bring.
We carry him home, and the Nation forms his guard,
His nearest—the King.
He lies with his peers, in the country's sanctuary,
Where makers of Britain trod,
And will hold our pride in faith till Réveillé sounds
At the call of God.

[1] First published, *Illustrated London News*, on the day of burial of the Unknown Warrior.

ENVOI

Ypres is near to you. Fighters there not ten years ago ; pilgrims to-day.

The battle-ground has been seen in the distortive values of personal experience and emotion. As time gives a truer perspective, YPRES emerges, and we begin to perceive how sublime a thing has been builded in our day. A thing incorporeal, but of such significance that it became in the building a symbol of victory. As such Ypres was assailed—and defended. As such the name will stand in history : symbol of victory through indomitable tenacity.

From the opening scene when the astonishing value of the little, the finest trained of armies, encompassed the city, the epic marches unfalteringly onwards in the line of an unbroken tradition. The flower of civilian manhood falls in, and the record is unchanged. Strong manhood is bled white : boys not yet full-grown fill up the ranks. And, in the last year of war as in the first, the tremendous crash of well-nigh intolerable odds is met, the defence is unbroken—Ypres is held.

Four years of endurance in the ways of utmost trial.

This book, tracing the outline and offering some fragments of the story, is dedicated to those who, out of that which is most terrible and hideous, have raised nearer Calvary, nearer Heaven, the ideal of beauty.

APPENDIX I

LIST OF NAMES GIVEN TO THE BATTLES AROUND YPRES BY THE BATTLE NOMENCLATURE COMMITTEE

1914

Battle of Messines : 12th October—2nd November.
Battle of Armentières : 13th October—2nd November.
The Battles of Ypres, 1914 : 19th October—22nd November.
 Battle of Langemarck : 21st—24th October.
 Battle of Gheluvelt : 29th—31st October.
 Battle of Nonne Bosschen : 11th November.

1915

The Battles of Ypres, 1915 : 22nd April—25th May.
 Battle of Gravenstafel : 22nd—23rd April.
 Battle of St. Julien : 24th April—4th May.
 Battle of Frezenberg : 8th—13th May.
 Battle of Bellewaarde : 24th—25th May.

1917

Battle of Messines, 1917, 7th—14th June.
The Battles of Ypres, 1917 : 31st July—10th November.
 I. Battle of Pilckem : 31st July—2nd August.
 II. Battle of Langemarck : 16th—18th August.
 III. Battle of the Menin Road : 20th—25th September.
 IV. Battle of Polygon Wood : 26th September—3rd October.
 V. Battle of Broodseinde : 4th October.
 VI. Battle of Poelcappelle : 9th October.
 VII. First Passchendaele : 12th October.
 VIII. Second Passchendaele : 26th October—10th November.

1918

The Battles of the Lys : 9th—29th April.
 I. Battle of Estaires : 9th—11th April.
 II. Battle of Messines, 1918 : 10th—11th April.
 III. Battle of Hazebrouck : 12th—15th April.
 IV. Battle of Bailleul : 13th—15th April.
 V. First Kemmel : 17th—19th April.
 VI. Battle of Bethune : 18th April.
 VII. Second Kemmel : 25th—26th April.
 VIII. Battle of the Scherpenberg : 29th April.
The Final Advance in Flanders :
 Battle of Ypres, 1918 : 28th September—2nd October.
 Battle of Courtrai : 14th—19th October.

APPENDIX II

BIBLIOGRAPHY

Suggested further reading comprising historical accounts and personal letters, reminiscences etc.

HISTORICAL ACCOUNTS

Regimental histories of virtually every regiment in the British Army during the First World War touch on the Ypres Salient battles. Some are very detailed, with maps and photographs, and generally the standard of presentation and material used is good. Divisional histories can also be useful. The Official History of the Great War dealing with France and Flanders (Sir J. E. Edmonds et al, HMSO 1922–1947, 26 volumes) is detailed, well mapped and generally reliable. Also useful for following operations is Conan Doyle's six volume "The British Campaign in France and Flanders 1914–1918" (London: Hodder and Stoughton, 1916–1920). Other useful publications include:

Brice (B.) with Sir William Pulteney THE IMMORTAL SALIENT: AN HISTORICAL RECORD AND COMPLETE GUIDE FOR PILGRIMS TO YPRES. x + 89pp., 6 plates, 2 maps. London: Murray. 1925. Forerunner of THE BATTLE BOOK OF YPRES, and a useful companion to it. Originally conceived as a guide book for visitors to the battlefield area, but exceeds the information usually found in such a book.

Carew (T.) WIPERS: THE FIRST BATTLE OF YPRES. viii + 230pp., 12 plates. London: Hamilton. 1974. A vivid account based mainly on accounts from the lower ranks.

Clark (A.) THE DONKEYS. 216pp., 11 plates, 5 maps. London: Hutchinson. 1961. An acclaimed examination of the year 1915: Neuve Chapelle, Second Battle of Ypres, Aubers Ridge and Loos.

Farrar-Hockley (A.) DEATH OF AN ARMY: THE FIRST BATTLE OF YPRES 1914. xii + 195pp., 8 plates, maps. London: Barker. 1967. Explains how the successful defence of Ypres ruined the Germans; after it they had no chance of rapid victory.

Liddell Hart (B. H.) THE REAL WAR 1914–1918. 539pp., 25 maps. London: Faber. 1930 (and in many subsequent editions under the title HISTORY OF THE FIRST WORLD WAR). Year by year, battle by battle account of operations; acclaimed as the best of its type.

MacDonald (L.) THEY CALLED IT PASSCHENDAELE: THE STORY OF THE THIRD BATTLE OF YPRES AND THE MEN WHO FOUGHT IN IT. xv + 253pp., 16 plates, maps. London: Joseph. 1978. Vivid and absorbing account compiled from interviews with hundreds of veterans.

267

Michelin Guide YPRES AND THE BATTLES FOR YPRES 1914–1918. 144pp., illustrated throughout. London: Michelin Tyre Company. 1919. Informative and well illustrated.

Terraine (J.) THE ROAD TO PASSCHENDAELE: THE FLANDERS OFFENSIVE OF 1917, A STUDY IN INEVITABILITY. xiv + 365pp., 4 maps. London: Cooper. 1977. Thorough and clear study.

Wolff (L.) IN FLANDERS FIELDS: THE 1917 CAMPAIGN. xxiv + 310pp, 12 plates, 7 maps. London: Longmans, Green & Co. 1959. Good account of Arras, Messines and 'Third Ypres'.

PERSONAL ACCOUNTS

Memoirs, diaries and letters of First World War servicemen are abundant. Fortunately for those people who wish to read and learn about the war, for these true life accounts give a full and real picture of what life was like at the front, in trenches or resting, in action and in day to day routine. To read such accounts is to add flesh to the historical narratives in an absorbing and enlightening way. The titles that follow are a small selection from among the many that relate men's experiences of the Ypres Salient.

Blunden (E.) UNDERTONES OF WAR. xv + 317pp. London: Cobden Sanderson. 1928. Classic memoir by the poet turned infantry officer.

Butler (Lt.Col. P. R.) A GALLOPER AT YPRES, AND SOME SUBSEQUENT ADVENTURES. 276pp., frontis. London: Fisher Unwin. 1920. With the 7th Division at the First and Second battles of Ypres

Campbell (P. J) IN THE CANNON'S MOUTH. (x) + 146pp, map. London: Hamish Hamilton. 1979. 'Third Ypres' 1917 with a Royal Field Artillery battery.

Clapham (H. S.) MUD AND KHAKI: THE MEMORIES OF AN INCOMPLETE SOLDIER. 224pp., 16 plates. London: Hutchinson. nd. With the H.A.C. in 1915, mainly around Ypres.

Gladden (N.) YPRES 1917: A PERSONAL ACCOUNT. 192pp., map. London: Kimber. 1977. Experiences with the Northumberland Fusiliers.

Gordon (H). THE UNRETURNING ARMY: A FIELD GUNNER IN FLANDERS 1917–18. x + 133pp., London: Dent. 1967.

Lambert (A.) OVER THE TOP: A P.B.I. IN THE H.A.C. 224pp. London: Long. 1930. Very personal record of a 34-year-old 1917 conscript in Flanders and Italy. The author states in the foreword that "Every effort has been made to disguise disgust at men and systems that were insults to intelligence ... every possible incidence of bravery and cheerfulness has been recorded." Good descriptions of the Salient as Lambert saw it in 1917.

Norman (T). Ed. ARMAGEDDON ROAD: A VC'S DIARY 1914–1916, BILLY CONGREVE. 223pp., 16 plates, maps. London: Kimber. 1982. Diary of a dedicated and much decorated staff officer with

a good grasp and eye for military detail, who served mainly in
the Ypres area.

Quigley (H). PASSCHENDAELE AND THE SOMME: A DIARY OF
1917. xi + 191pp. London: Methuen. 1928. Unvarnished account
of service and opinions while with 12th Royal Scots.

'A Rifleman' (Aubrey Smith MM) FOUR YEARS ON THE WESTERN
FRONT: BEING THE EXPERIENCES OF A RANKER IN
THE LONDON RIFLE BRIGADE. xvi + 409pp, maps. London:
Odhams. 1922. Vivid and interesting account, including the Second
Battle of Ypres.

Talbot Kelly (R. B.) A SUBALTERN'S ODYSSEY: A MEMOIR OF
THE GREAT WAR 1915–1917. Artillery officer's service including
Ypres in 1915 and 1917.

Taylor (A.) Ed. FROM YPRES TO CAMBRAI: THE 1914–1919 DIARY
OF INFANTRYMAN FRANK HAWKINGS. xiv + 144pp., 16
plates. Morley: Elmfield Press. 1973. With the Queen Victoria's
Rifles at Ypres 1914 and 1915.

Tennant (N.) A SATURDAY NIGHT SOLDIER'S WAR 1913–1918.
(iv) + 123pp., illus, Waddesdon: Kylin Press. 1983. Territorial gunner's experiences including Ypres battles of 1915 and 1917.

Tucker (J. F.) JOHNNY GET YOUR GUN: A PERSONAL NARRA-
TIVE OF THE SOMME, YPRES AND ARRAS. 207pp., 8 plates.
London: Kimber. 1978. Three years in France with the 13th London
Regiment.

Vaughan (E. C) SOME DESPERATE GLORY: THE DIARY OF A
YOUNG OFFICER 1917. xv + 232pp, map. London: Warne.,
1981. Gripping diary of Warwickshire Regiment subaltern
January–August 1917.

INDEX OF FORMATIONS AND UNITS